CONFEDERATE CAVALRY WEST OF THE RIVER

A cavalryman from the Trans-Mississippi complete with six-shooter, carbine, huge wheel spurs, and black felt hat. *Drawing by David Price.*

CONFEDERATE CAVALRY WEST OF THE RIVER

by Stephen B. Oates

AUSTIN · UNIVERSITY OF TEXAS PRESS

Second paperback printing, 1994

Requests for permission to reproduce material from this work should be sent
to Permissions, University of Texas Press, Box 7819, Austin, TX 78713-7819.

∞ The paper used in this publication meets the minimum requirements
of American National Standard for Information Sciences—Permanence of
Paper for Printed Library Materials, ANSI Z39.48–1984.

Library of Congress Catalog Card No. 61–10044

ISBN 0-292-71152-2 pbk.

For my closest friends:

Steve and Florence Oates

Tony and Michael Oates

PREFACE

The paragraphs which follow actually defy classification. They have a title only as a matter of convention. The first few are the traditional statement in which the writer and his book embarrass themselves by expressing gratitude to a number of sympathetic individuals. The rest are . . . well, frankly, a few opinions.

The most sympathetic individuals have been my intimate friends. Miss Frances Berry helped me discover a latent passion for writing, a passion which is now an obsession. Donald E. Robertson, a novelist who read the work as it progressed, implored me to write with imagination and taste and color, treating the English language with the respect it is due. To Mr. and Mrs. Donald K. Pickens I am deeply indebted for their encouragement and understanding (Donald Pickens' unwavering devotion to historical scholarship has been difficult to match; in fact, I've quit trying, as have a number of his associates). I must thank Lynn H. Nelson, Charles C. Alexander, and Charles Erickson who at coffee sessions listened politely to my glowing recitations on Trans-Mississippi cavalry. Their willingness to discuss with me this vitally important subject helped solve old problems, helped find some new ones, too. I am most grateful to Marvin N. Elder, Jr., whose statement years ago that I had the guts and determination to be a successful writer was for a time the only assurance I had.

Betty Alexander proofread and typed most of the manuscript, and I am indebted to Dr. Llerena Friend, Leon Mitchell, and Dwight Henderson for their aid in locating sources. Frances Parker made the maps for the book and David Price drew the Trans-Mississippi Cavalryman. I should especially like to thank Ezra J. Warner who supplied the pictures of cavalry brigadiers from the Trans-Mississippi.

The historian's task is scientific as well as artistic. Using the "scientific method" he gathers and organizes data, then strives to present it in attractive literary form. I want to thank Professor Frank E. Vandiver of William Marsh Rice University and Professor David D. Van Tassel of the University of Texas for making me more appreciative of artistic historical writing. I am most indebted to Professor Barnes F. Lathrop of the University of Texas who studied the manuscript and stressed the scientific phase of my work. His high standards, astute criticisms, and painstaking assistance impelled me to discipline myself in the principles of professional history: meticulous research, accuracy, and precision. Finally, I want to thank the University of Texas history department for what it has taught me, directly or indirectly, these past three years.

Now for opinion. This book is a revised form of my graduate thesis, one of those academic studies generally considered to be of interest to no one—general reader, scholar, or student. This is a popular misconception. A thesis does not have to be dull; there is no special requirement that it be so scholarly, abstract, and unappealing that even the student's graduate committee cannot wade through it. Many theses now collecting dust in libraries are extremely readable, besides being excellent contributions to historical knowledge. Such works are certainly more worthy of publication than many of the second-rate histories now flooding the bookstores.

There are two major reasons why more graduate studies do not appear in print: 1) publishers treat them as taboo; 2) graduate departments fail to emphasize sufficiently the artistic element in historical writing. Only time, better theses, and more open-minded publishers will overcome the first problem. The second problem will take care of itself if supervising professors allow the student to strive for originality, develop his own style of writing, present his material interestingly as well as informatively, and aim for publication.

Stephen B. Oates

Austin, Texas

CONTENTS

ILLUSTRATIONS

MAPS

TABLES

INTRODUCTION

Confederate cavalrymen in the Trans-Mississippi west never belonged to a high-style corps like Jeb Stuart's or Philip Sheridan's. They were not long on flashy drills and parades; they were mostly cowboys and farmers who could rope and fire a revolver at a gallop and who knew very little about military tactics and cared less about military discipline. They were hard-boiled troops who had to do a great deal with very little. For supplies and equipment they relied heavily upon capture from the Yankees, or seizure from peaceful citizens. But they were a brave and patriotic body of men—a part of that great army which became a legend for valor and endurance that won battles against heavy odds.

Trans-Mississippi horsemen could not brag much about their leaders, for there were no really outstanding ones, at least none comparable to Stuart, Bedford Forrest, or Joseph Wheeler. In Joseph Orville Shelby and John Sappington Marmaduke the cavalry had intrepid and tireless leaders, but neither of them possessed that natural instinct for cavalry command that made Forrest something of a military genius. Others, such as John A. Wharton, Ben McCulloch, Tom Green, and William G. Vincent, gained local fame, but never displayed any great ability or originality in the handling of large bodies of horsemen. Nevertheless, Trans-Mississippi cavalrymen did many noteworthy things during the war, and they did them out of courage and determination to save a cause which they considered just.

Accustomed to a long and intimate companionship with the horse, with the six-shooter and musket, the men of Trans-Mississippi, especially the Texans, were excellent potential cavalrymen. "They had," recalled Major General Richard Taylor, "every quality but discipline." From the mustering-in ceremony to the end of the war, they disliked the strict enforcement of orders, the gap between officers and men, the spit and polish that characterized professional cavalry of Europe. They were rowdy and individualistic, and paid little attention to rank.

In an attempt to discipline the men, officers and government officials early set up camps of instruction throughout the region. But formal drills and parades never appealed much to the raw troops. They preferred to demonstrate their daring feats of horsemanship by riding at a gallop down the streets of nearby towns, jumping off and back on their mounts, and picking small objects off the ground. Breaking wild horses in the town square was also a popular sport. One newspaperman in Van Buren, Arkansas, having watched a group of cavalrymen whoop and shout, drink and celebrate, ride horses into saloons and out, wrote that "a more decided burlesque on military parade could not be had . . . and we trust it will be at least a year, before another *occasion* occurs for preparation 'to defend our rights and liberties against northern aggression.' "

The cavalrymen may have enjoyed the "fun and frolic" to be had at recruiting and training centers, but when it came time to fight they were "like devils" who bore fatigue "like camels." "Talk of subjugating the South," mused a Texas trooper, "Why, with the cavalry around, it would take ten years to conquer Texas alone."

Like their counterparts east of the River, Trans-Mississippi cavalrymen were a little egotistical about their fighting abilities, or maybe just confident that they could win the war in their theater with or without the help of the other arms of the service, particularly the inglorious and unromantic infantry. Cavalrymen and infantrymen were always heckling and ridiculing each other, and when they met, horsemen might laugh and point and shout, "wagon dogs," "web-feet," "mud sloggers," only to be told: "There goes the buttermilk cavalry." "A hundred dollars reward for just one dead cavalryman." "All those fellows do is to find Yankees for us to kill."

This jesting was not altogether in fun, for infantrymen seriously thought the cavalry to be a greatly overrated arm. With their pompous air and prancing steeds, horsemen were little more than show-offs; when there was to be a man's fight, it must be left to the infantry.

Cavalry, according to the Texas Adjutant General, was an obsolete type of force anyway.

Cavalry in the Civil War was, on the contrary, anything but obsolete. Though the claim that Confederate cavalrymen were the best the world had ever seen is open to dispute, it is certainly true that they constituted the best mounted force ever assembled in the United States. The war reached the midway point before the Union cavalry could stand up to the Confederates in the East; in the Trans-Mississippi, Federal horsemen never stood up to the Southerners. Throughout the war Confederate cavalry west of the River performed well in almost any capacity: as train guards, as scouts and reconnoitering patrols, as screens for the main army, as raiding forces, and even as infantry. In the battles at Pea Ridge and Prairie Grove, Arkansas, cavalrymen fought on foot and were every bit as good at it as the regular infantry. A Yankee at Pea Ridge, who was impressed with the ability of Confederate horsemen to fight both mounted and dismounted, recorded that "they fought the day like devils incarnate, and as if resolved on victory or death."

The most remarkable feats of the Trans-Mississippi cavalrymen were four major raids deep into Federal Missouri. Roaming about in territory thought to be safely inside Union lines, Confederate riders cut communications, blew up bridges, burned supply depots, tore up railroads, and in general spread terror and created havoc from Cape Girardeau to Westport. Moreover, the four expeditions helped prevent Union armies from capturing all of Arkansas, and perhaps Texas, by forcing the Yankee command to commit large numbers of troops to police duty throughout the southern half of Missouri. The strategic cavalry raid was a new element in warfare and required able leaders and strong men. To make it through such an operation, said the adjutant of the Fifth Missouri Cavalry, one had to be of "iron frame, lithe of limb and eager as a bloodhound," with "a brain of fire and muscles of steel, and glorified courage."

In telling the story of cavalry in the Trans-Mississippi west, this study seeks to illuminate but one aspect of a little-known theater of the Civil War. The work does not claim to be definitive, for it makes no attempt to recount the experiences of every outfit from the region (one hundred and fourteen regiments and forty-seven battalions) or to cover all the isolated and frequently insignificant cavalry actions in

Louisiana and Texas. In short, it is neither a compilation of regimental histories nor a chronicle of military events. It is a story, told in narrative form, that treats the cavalry as an autonomous arm of the service, with artillery support and supply service. It strives to present a realistic picture of day-to-day soldiering, of living in the field, of humor as well as suffering in camps, of exacting and vigorous scouts and expeditions, and of the high excitement of battle. As it joins the growing list of Civil War histories, this book readily agrees that the war "now takes longer to read about than it took to fight" but adds with a wink that at least its pages explore relatively virgin territory.

CONFEDERATE CAVALRY WEST OF THE RIVER

RECRUITING
THE VOLUNTEERS, 1861

On the night of February 15, 1861, nearly two months before Fort Sumter and the opening of the Civil War, a thousand Texas volunteers secretly assembled at Sea Willow Creek, a few miles north of San Antonio. They had been called to arms by Ben McCulloch, colonel of cavalry in the newly formed Army of Texas, for the purpose of capturing the historic Alamo, then a storehouse for arms and military supplies under the command of General David E. Twiggs, United States Army.

The excited soldiers had gathered in small groups beneath the trees, and the noise of the meeting was compounded of men's voices, squeaking saddles, and the high-pitched whinny of horses. Mist from the creek curled through the bivouac. Soon there was a drizzle of cold rain. At midnight McCulloch rode into camp and quickly outlined to the men his plan of attack. They were to surround the Alamo and wait for the command to open fire.[1] This was typical of the way McCulloch fought. His plans and preparations were clear and simple, his manner confident.

McCulloch had won fame by the storming of the Obispado during the Mexican War and for his daring and heroic feats as a Texas Ranger. A "thin, spare man, of great muscle and activity," a tireless fighter and an excellent cavalryman, he enjoyed the admiration and

[1] J. K. P. Blackburn, "Reminiscences of the Terry Rangers," *Southwestern Historical Quarterly*, XXII (July, 1918), 38.

3

respect of citizens and soldiers alike.[2] "The name of Ben McCulloch," wrote the editor of one Arkansas paper, "wherever it is known, is a guarantee of itself."[3] The affair about to commence at San Antonio would more firmly establish the name of Ben McCulloch (Portrait on Plate 1).

The rain stopped presently, and through the long, quiet hours of early morning, the Texans sat beside campfires, cleaning their weapons and waiting for what they expected would be a good fight. The biting February wind caused them much discomfort. Some had coats, others were in shirt sleeves, and a few were wrapped in saddle blankets and old shawls. With the first rays of the sun came the order to move, and the eager troops filed quietly into town. They crept through the morning shadows of the buildings and took positions on the roofs of stores encircling the Alamo.[4] Inside the fortress, the Federals watched the stealthy movements of the blurred figures. The commander in charge, thinking the situation hopeless, surrendered the stockade to McCulloch without the firing of a shot.[5]

As the United States flag was lowered from above the old Alamo, the Texans whooped and shouted and, waving their weapons above their heads, ran to the Grand Plaza, where they celebrated the first victory of Southern cavalry in the Trans-Mississippi.

When agents of the state took charge of the Alamo on February 19, 1861, the services of the volunteers were no longer needed and they disbanded to return to their homes.[6] Many of them, including their distinguished commander, would join the Confederate Army in the months that followed.

---

[2] Quotation from Bellville (Texas) *Countryman*, September 18, 1861. For McCulloch's activities before the war see Victor M. Rose, *The Life and Services of Gen. Ben McCulloch*, pp. 40–121; and Jack Winton Gunn, "Life of Ben McCulloch," pp. 1–80.

[3] Van Buren (Arkansas) *Press*, June 5, 1861.

[4] Caroline B. Darrow, "Recollections of the Twigs Surrender," in *Battles and Leaders of the Civil War*, I, 34–35; Blackburn, "Terry Rangers," *Southwestern Historical Quarterly*, XXII, 38–39.

[5] D. E. Twiggs to C. L. Thomas, February 19, 1861, United States War Department, *The War of the Rebellion: A Compilation of the Official Records of the Union and Confederate Armies*, ser. I, vol. I, 504. Hereafter cited *Official Records*.

[6] Blackburn, "Terry Rangers," *Southwestern Historical Quarterly*, XXII, 39; Oran M. Roberts, "Texas," *Confederate Military History*, XI, 25.

Shortly after the capture of the Alamo, the Texas Committee of Public Safety[7] authorized Colonel Henry E. McCulloch (Portrait on Plate 1), brother of Ben McCulloch, and John S. "Rip" Ford (Portrait on Plate 11) to raise two regiments of volunteer cavalry for the Army of Texas. Their instructions were to capture Federal property and munitions for the state. Henry McCulloch gathered his volunteers in the Austin-San Antonio area. On February 20, after the men were fully mounted, they rode into northern Texas to capture Camp Colorado, Fort Chadbourne, Camp Cooper, and Fort Belknap. Colonel McCulloch then obtained a commission in the Confederate Army and set about raising additional companies for his cavalry regiment. On April 15, 1861, ten full companies from Bexar, Travis, Gonzales, and contiguous counties organized as the First McCulloch Texas Mounted Rifles, the first cavalry outfit from Texas to enter the Confederate service.[8]

While Henry E. McCulloch recruited in the San Antonio area, Rip Ford set up headquarters in Houston and appealed to loyal "Texians" to join his regiment. By February 18 he had 500 eager volunteers in six companies.[9] At dawn the next day, the troops marched to Galveston, boarded the steamer *General Rusk* and the schooner *Shark* and sailed down the coast to the island Brazos de Santiago, a United States stronghold several miles above Brownsville. Hoping for a fight, the Texans stormed ashore on February 21 to find only twelve defenders who struck their colors immediately and surrendered the island without bloodshed. The victorious Southerners then converged on the parade grounds to shout and wave their rifles as the Lone Star Flag was run up the flagpole to the boom of a fifteen-gun salute.[10]

[7] This committee was set up by the Texas Secession Convention to prepare the state for war. It raised a state army to fight the Federals and to ensure the safety of Texas citizens until the Confederate Army should become effective in Texas. Charles W. Ramsdell, "The Texas State Military Board, 1862–1865," *Southwestern Historical Quarterly*, XXVII, 253–260.

[8] Edward Clark to Jefferson Davis, April 4, 1861, *Official Records*, ser. I, vol. I, 621; Dudley G. Wooten, ed., *A Comprehensive History of Texas*, II, 573–574. James B. Barry, *A Texas Ranger and Frontiersman: The Days of Buck Barry in Texas, 1845–1906*, pp. 127–129.

[9] John S. Ford, Memoirs, V, 997.

[10] Ford to J. C. Robertson, February 22, 1861, *Official Records*, ser. I, vol. LIII, 651–652; James Thompson to G. D. Bailey, February 22, 1861, *ibid.*, ser. I, vol. I, 537–538.

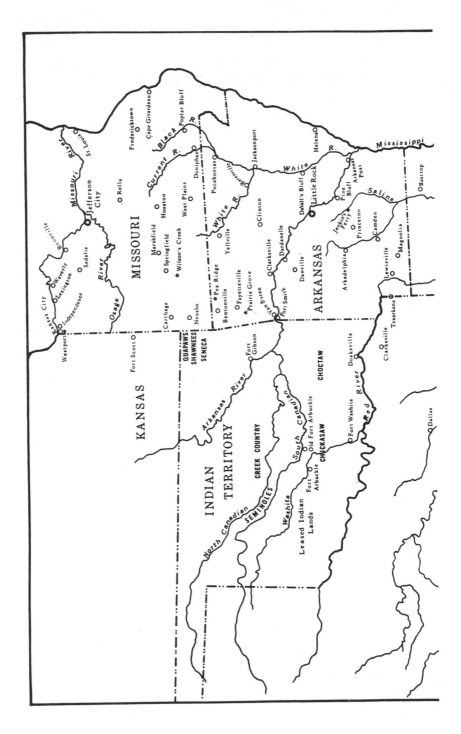

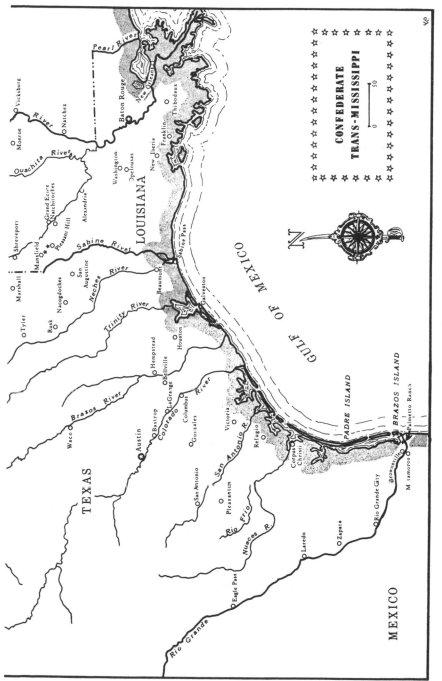

FIGURE 1

On February 22 Ford left Lieutenant Colonel Hugh McLeod in command of the island and went to the mainland to negotiate with the United States force that held Fort Brown just below Brownsville. After some difficulty, the colonel reached an understanding with the Union commander, who agreed to surrender to the Texans all the United States forts from Brownsville to El Paso.[11] Texan troops then marched northwest along the Rio Grande to occupy Fort McIntosh, Camp Wood, Fort Inge, Fort Clark, Fort Lancaster, Camp Stockton, Fort Davis, and Fort Bliss. On May 23 Ford's outfit, now numbering 1,200 men, was sworn into Confederate service by order of the governor and was designated the Second Texas Cavalry.[12]

Rip Ford was enthusiastic over the achievement of his Texan volunteers. Wearing huge wheel spurs and high black hats ornamented with the beloved Lone Star and armed with six-shooters and bowie knives, they were fearless horsemen. Texas should feel proud of them.[13]

Ford's and Henry E. McCulloch's regiments formed the nucleus of the Confederate cavalry in the Trans-Mississippi. During the rest of the year 1861 the War Department commissioned over twenty colonels to raise cavalry regiments in the region and to add them to this initial cavalry force. Most of these outfits were retained for service in the Trans-Mississippi, but some were transferred east of the River. In the absence of any over-all regional command throughout 1861, these units received their operational assignments from the War Department. The story of the recruiting of these volunteer cavalrymen in 1861 is one abounding with lively events, humor, and even tragedy.

The first need for additional cavalry in Texas came about through the appearance of serious trouble on the northern border late in February. After the convention at Austin announced, on March 1, that Texas was no longer a state in the Union, Federal troops patrol-

[11] For the documents relating to the surrender of Federal forts on the Rio Grande see *ibid.*, ser. I, vol. LIII, 618–666. Terse accounts may be found in the Galveston (Texas) *Civilian*, March 11, 1861, and the *Texas Almanac, 1861*, pp. 17–18.

[12] General Orders No. 8, May 24, 1861, *Official Records*, ser. I, vol. I, 574–575; Wooten, *Comprehensive History of Texas*, II, 520.

[13] Ford, Memoirs, V, 1000; Ford to Robertson, February 25, 1861, *Official Records*, ser. I, vol. LIII, 655; Thomas North, *Five Years in Texas: or, What You Did Not Hear during the War from January 1861 to January 1866*, p. 104.

ling the area from Fort Mason to the Red River fled to Kansas. The settlers ranching and farming in the area were thus left to the mercy of small bands of savage Comanches, who soon began attacking isolated homesteads, burning fields, destroying buildings, and killing and scalping women and children. To raise troops to protect them, the state military board placed calls for volunteers in the newspapers and sent recruiters into various counties. Volunteers were to arm, equip, and mount themselves, and to bring enough provisions for six days.[14]

Among the recruiters chosen by the governor to raise companies for frontier service was A. W. Crawford, sheriff of Harrison County. Receiving the order on April 1, Crawford immediately set up headquarters in Marshall and rode around the area appealing for the citizens to take up arms.[15] By April 10 the company was full, numbering 103 men. On muster day, April 19, wrote one member of the unit, "at an early hour the hitherto quiet of Marshall is disturbed by the 'Neigh of the war horse,' and the assembling of the Cavalry," as bodies of rowdy recruits rode in from Panola, Upshur, and Marion counties. The men were well mounted and equipped for service, except for carbines and pistols, which were to be obtained later from Austin.

The process of organizing the company took up the whole day. Horses were checked for fitness. The county judge swore each man into state service in the courthouse. And this done, the soldiers named their company the "W. P. Lane Rangers," in honor of a distinguished citizen of Marshall, Major W. P. Lane, veteran of the Texas Revolution and the Mexican War. After elections were held, which made Sam Richardson captain,[16] the Rangers sat rather restlessly through a parting sermon, delivered by the Reverend W. C. Dunlap of

[14] San Antonio (Texas) *Herald*, March 2, 1861; Belton (Texas) *Democrat*, March 8, 1861; Texas Governor, March 16—November 7, 1861 (Edward Clark), *Governor's Message: Executive Office, Austin, March 29, 1861*, p. 5.

[15] This description of the raising of Crawford's company, later the W. P. Lane Rangers, is based upon William W. Heartsill, *Fourteen Hundred and Ninety-One Days in the Confederate Army: or Camp Life, Day by Day, of the W. P. Lane Rangers from April 19, 1861 to May 20, 1865*, pp. 2–5.

[16] The common practice during the first part of the war was to allow the men to elect the corporals and commissioned officers up to the rank of colonel. Brigadier generals and higher officers were appointed by the War Department.

Marshall. Then laughing and shouting, they ran to the nearest bars to celebrate. They returned to camp much later, many of them "Half seas' over" from a little too much celebrating.

At dawn the next morning, the men broke camp and rode into Marshall. "Their spirited steeds," recorded W. W. Heartsill, made "the streets . . . ring with their proud, defiant tread." Townspeople turned out by the hundreds to cheer and yell at the soldiers. At about eight o'clock, a group of ladies congregated on the courthouse lawn and prepared to present a flag to the company. The troops moved to an empty field on the outskirts of town, fell in at parade formation, and then, riding four abreast, trotted into Marshall. At the public square they formed in a long, straight line in front of the circle of ladies and town officials. One of Marshall's fair young women then presented the flag to Captain Richardson and made a short speech praising the heroic soldiers and lauding the Confederate cause.

After the "trying time," or "crying time"—the parting from relatives and friends—the company mounted, formed in columns, and proceeded to the college, where the men were presented with a "happy surprise"—a table "groaning beneath the load" of good things to eat, prepared by the ladies as "a parting remembrance." Having gorged themselves, the soldiers regrouped, and midst shouts and whoops from the onlookers, rode out of town toward the west.[17]

At Waco the company was given a military salute and escorted through the town by two companies of the Lone Star Guards.[18] On May 8 the force reached San Antonio and then proceeded west to Earl Van Dorn's cavalry camp on Leon Creek. There, on May 23, the Rangers were sworn into Confederate service by order of the governor. Shortly afterwards the outfit became Company F of Colonel John S. Ford's Second Texas Cavalry. For the next year the Rangers served on the frontier, protecting settlers from the wild Comanches and performing general patrol duty.[19]

A second crack cavalry outfit for frontier service came from the seventh and eighth military districts around Grayson County.[20] Early in May, 1861, William C. Young, who had been a United States

[17] Heartsill, *Fourteen Hundred and Ninety-One Days*, pp. 2–5, 9.
[18] Clarksville (Texas) *Standard*, May 11, 1861.
[19] Heartsill, *Fourteen Hundred and Ninety-One Days*, pp. 14, 15–49.
[20] Special Orders No. 18, July 25, 1861, *Official Records*, ser. I, vol. IV, 95.

10

Marshall before the war, received authority from the governor to recruit volunteer horsemen. Young travelled through Grayson, Fannin, Hunt, and Collin counties seeking men. By mid-May he had ten full companies which organized as the Eleventh Texas Cavalry. The outfit crossed the Red River to capture Fort Arbuckle, Fort Washita, and Fort Cobb and afterwards rode through the Indian Territory negotiating with the Comanches, Kiowas, and Chickasaws.[21] Later, in April, 1862, the regiment was transferred east of the Mississippi, where it became part of Joseph Wheeler's celebrated cavalry corps.[22]

Like the Eleventh Texas and the W. P. Lane Rangers, all other state organizations had by mid-May been transferred to Confederate service.[23] In order to secure unity of command Governor Edward Clark had dissolved the state service and ordered all state organizations to be placed under the command of General Earl Van Dorn, a West Point graduate and nephew of Andrew Jackson, who had been appointed commander of the District of Texas. For the rest of the war, all regular cavalry regiments were raised for the Confederate Army to serve for three years or for the war.[24] Recruiting was restricted to those officers holding commissions in the Confederate service, and the procedure used to raise troops was based on regulations prescribed by the War Department.[25]

On May 13 the War Department ordered Ben McCulloch, now a brigadier general commanding the Indian Territory, to raise the first Confederate army in the Trans-Mississippi.[26] From his headquarters at Fort Smith, Arkansas, McCulloch wrote recruiting officers in the region to complete the formation of their outfits as soon as possible

[21] Roberts, "Texas," *Confederate Military History*, XI, 47; Francis W. Johnson, *A History of Texas and Texans*, IV, 1688.

[22] Wooten, *Comprehensive History of Texas*, II, 630.

[23] X. B. De Bray to L. P. Walker, August 28, 1861, *Official Records*, ser. I, vol. IV, 98–100.

[24] Texas Adjutant General, *Report, November, 1861*, p. 1; Texas Governor, March 16—November 7, 1861 (Edward Clark), *Governor's Message to the Senators and Representatives of the Ninth Legislature of the State of Texas, November 1, 1861*, p. 1. Hereafter cited (Texas) *Governor's Message, November 1, 1861.*

[25] Confederate States War Department, *Regulations for the Army of the Confederate States and for the Quartermaster's and Pay Departments, 1861*, pp. 183–184.

[26] S. Cooper to Ben McCulloch, May 13, 1861, *Official Records*, ser. I, vol. III, 575–576.

and to march to Fort Smith.[27] One of the major objectives of the force, McCulloch told them, was to check Federal advances in Missouri and perhaps even an invasion of Kansas. By August 4 McCulloch's command had been joined by the First Arkansas Cavalry under Colonel DeRosey Carroll; the First Arkansas Mounted Rifles, Colonel James McIntosh; the Third Arkansas Infantry, Colonel John R. Gratiot; the Fourth Arkansas Infantry, Colonel J. D. Walker; the Fifth Arkansas Infantry, Colonel Tom P. Dockery; the Third Texas Cavalry (South Kansas-Texas Regiment), Colonel Elkanah Greer; the Third Louisiana Infantry, Colonel Louis Hébert; and Captains W. E. Woodruff's and J. G. Reid's Arkansas artillery batteries.[28]

Colonel DeRosey Carroll's Arkansas state cavalry was the first of McCulloch's mounted regiments to be raised. The colonel had started recruiting men back in April, shortly after state militia companies had made a surprise raid on the Federal stockade at Fort Smith. Carroll's enrolling officers, working in Crawford and adjacent counties, had orders to rendezvous at Camp Walker after their companies were formed.

The recruiting captain for Crawford County, Charles A. Carroll,[29] had arrived in Van Buren on or about April 24 and had immediately placed a notice in the Van Buren *Press* calling for volunteers to join his new company. "Turn out," he urged; "let the fires of seventy-six be rekindled—let us baptise the graves of our fathers in blood!"[30] Newspapers in the area and community leaders encouraged volunteering, and Carroll himself travelled through Lee's Creek Township, Oliver's Store, Sim Coes, and Mountain Township seeking men.[31] On May 6, the day that Arkansas formally left the Union, the last man

---

[27] Rose, *Gen. Ben McCulloch*, p. 132.

[28] General Orders No. 24, August 4, 1861, *Official Records*, ser. I, vol. III, 102–103; Ben McCulloch to S. Cooper, August 12, 1861, *ibid.*, pp. 104–107; John M. Harrell, "Arkansas," *Confederate Military History*, X, 133–136.

[29] The Van Buren (Arkansas) *Press*, April 24, 1861, erroneously calls this man John A. Carroll. In the summer of 1861 DeRosey Carroll's state regiment broke up, but many of the companies formed a Confederate regiment under the command of Charles A. Carroll, who had been captain of Company A of the old state outfit. Later, in September, 1862, Charles A. Carroll was promoted to colonel in charge of the Arkansas Cavalry Brigade.

[30] *Ibid.*

[31] *Ibid.*, May 1, 1861.

12

necessary to make a full company (90 men) signed his name to Carroll's roll. Twelve days later the unit assembled at Camp Vine Prairie, just outside Van Buren. The troops conducted an election of officers and chose Carroll their captain by unanimous vote.[32]

After a week of drilling, the company broke camp and rode into Van Buren. The men paraded noisily around the courthouse square, executed a flashy military halt in front of a group of town officials, and then dismounted to stand "under arms" while Captain Carroll thanked the ladies of the town committee for food and clothing contributed to his outfit. On the lawns in front of the courthouse were wives, mothers, and sisters of several of the soldiers, many of them crying softly.

When all the speeches were finished, the troops mounted, the first sergeant shouted out the order to march, and the unit wheeled about and rode out of Van Buren, heading for DeRosey Carroll's cavalry camp at Camp Walker. An observer at the ceremony in Van Buren later wrote that he was "assured that soldiers who leave for the battlefield with such blessings as the cavalry company received on Saturday, will make the bloodiest ranks in the conflict with the enemy."[33] And perhaps the memory of this ceremony did encourage the men to fight bravely in the bitter campaigns that followed.

At Camp Walker, Carroll's outfit became Company A of the First Arkansas Cavalry Regiment. The other seven companies of the regiment came mainly from Franklin, Johnson, and contiguous counties. On May 29 the troops held regimental elections, and chose DeRosey Carroll their colonel.[34] Late in June, N. Bart Pearce, brigadier general of Arkansas in command of the western frontier, gathered Carroll's regiment, Gratiot's and Dockery's infantry regiments, and Reid's and Woodruff's batteries and marched to Fort Smith. There he placed his entire command of state troops at the disposal of General McCulloch.[35] At length, on July 15, the Arkansas Military Board

[32] *Ibid.*, May 8, 22, 1861.
[33] *Ibid.*, May 22, 1861.
[34] *Ibid.*, May 22, 29, 1861.
[35] Ben McCulloch to L. P. Walker, June 14, 1861, *Official Records*, ser. I, vol. III, 595; H. M. Rector to Walker, June 21, 1861, *ibid.*; McCulloch to Walker, June 29, 1861, *ibid.*, p. 600; Rose, *Gen. Ben McCulloch*, p. 134; and David Y. Thomas, *Arkansas in War and Reconstruction 1861–1874*, p. 108.

ordered the transfer of these state volunteers to the Confederate service.[36]

While companies were recruited for DeRosey Carroll's regiment, Colonel Thomas J. Churchill (Portrait on Plate 1), having received a Confederate commission, began in May to raise a cavalry regiment in counties around Fort Smith. He had some difficulty in obtaining volunteers at first because of the indefinite period of enlistment—for the war.[37] On May 22, however, the War Department authorized him to receive troops for twelve-months service,[38] and by June 17 he had a full regiment (768 men), which he named the First Arkansas Mounted Rifles. After holding elections, in which Churchill became colonel, the regiment joined McCulloch's command at Fort Smith.[39]

In July Captain James McIntosh organized and equipped the Second Arkansas Mounted Rifles, made up of ten companies (662 men) from various counties in northwestern Arkansas. An election was held, which resulted in McIntosh being made colonel, and then the regiment was sworn into Confederate service for the war.[40] Late in

[36] *Official Records*, ser. I, vol. III, 609–610. After Arkansas seceded in May, a board consisting of Governor H. M. Rector and two advisors was entrusted with full military powers. It immediately began to organize the Army of Arkansas. The existence of a state army meant a dual military organization in Arkansas, where the Confederate Army was already operating. After two months of competition among recruiters for state service and for Confederate service, with resultant confusion, wasted manpower, and complete chaos in some areas, the state, in hopes of securing unity of command in Arkansas, decided to transfer all state units to the Confederate Army, the troops themselves choosing by vote whether to accept the change or be mustered out of service. In pursuance of this order, Lieutenant Colonel Solon Borland's Arkansas cavalry battalion (568 men) and Lieutenant Colonel Charles W. Phifer's battalion (181 men) were transferred to the command of General William J. Hardee, who was stationed at Pitman's Ferry in northeastern Arkansas. Since Carroll's cavalry had been transferred, all mounted outfits operating in the state were now in the Confederate Army. H. M. Rector to L. P. Walker, September 30, 1861, *ibid.*, p. 710; N. B. Pearce to Walker, October 10, 1861, *ibid.*, pp. 715–716; and Thomas, *Arkansas in War and Reconstruction*, pp. 87, 92–93, 95–96.

[37] Ben McCulloch to L. P. Walker, May 20, 1861, *Official Records*, ser. I, vol. III, 581.

[38] Walker to McCulloch, May 20, 22, 1861, *ibid.*, pp. 581, 583.

[39] Fort Smith (Arkansas) *Daily Times and Herald*, June 17, 1861; Robert H. Dacus, *Reminiscences of Company "H," First Arkansas Mounted Rifles*, p. 1; Fay Hempstead, *A Pictorial History of Arkansas from Earliest Times to the Year 1890*, pp. 373–375.

[40] *Ibid.*, p. 369.

July the outfit rode into Fort Smith, bringing McCulloch's effective strength to about 3,000 men, some 2,000 of them horsemen.

While officers were raising troopers in Arkansas for McCulloch's army, Colonel Elkanah Greer and Captain J. A. Harris of Marshall, Texas, issued calls for volunteers from Dallas and surrounding counties and named Dallas as their rendezvous point.[41] The request for troops was answered promptly by many home guard companies.

Captain Frank M. Taylor of the "Lone Star Defenders," a home guard cavalry company at Rusk, Texas, received Greer's call for men on June 9. The next day, Taylor assembled his men in front of the Thompson Hotel and made preparations for the ride to Dallas. The activities of the troops aroused the inhabitants of the town, and they gathered around the hotel to watch the departing ceremonies. "Men, women, and children," recalled one trooper, "were on the streets, in tears, to bid us farewell. Even rough, hard-faced men whose appearance would leave one to believe they hadn't shed a tear since boyhood, boo-hoo'd and were unable to speak the word 'good-by.' " The day of departure, decided the soldier, "was the saddest of the war for many of us." After a "formal and very tender" farewell address from dignified old General J. L. Hogg, father of James S. Hogg, later governor of Texas, the men sorrowfully mounted their ponies and, riding out of town, sang in unison

> The Lone Star Defenders, a gallant little band,
> On the tenth of June left their native land. . . .[42]

Dallas was the scene of much activity as companies of whooping volunteers rode in to join Greer's regiment. Soon ten companies, including Taylor's unit, had reported to Greer, and on the afternoon of June 13 were organized into the Third Texas Cavalry Regiment.[43] The process of swearing the men into Confederate service was simple. "We were subjected to no physical examination or other foolishness,"

[41] Victor M. Rose, *Ross' Texas Brigade*, p. 16.

[42] Samuel B. Barron, *The Lone Star Defenders: A Chronicle of the Third Texas Cavalry, Ross' Brigade*, pp. 17–18.

[43] Rose, *Ross' Texas Brigade*, p. 16; Dallas (Texas) *Herald*, June 19, July 3, 1861. The outfit was occasionally called the South Kansas-Texas Regiment probably because at the time of organization there was a vague hope of making an expedition into Kansas. The regiment later became a part of Ross' celebrated Texas Brigade which fought east of the Mississippi.

15

recalled Lieutenant Samuel Barron, "but every fellow was taken for better or for worse, and no questions were asked, except the formal, 'Do you solemnly swear,' etc."[44] The men then held elections, choosing Greer their colonel, Walter P. Lane, lieutenant colonel, and G. W. Chilton, major.[45] On July 8 the men of the Third Texas, having been delayed for three weeks until arms were sent from San Antonio, broke camp and rode out of town two abreast by companies. Each company proudly flew its own flag, which contained its alphabetical designation and some name which connoted bravery, fierceness, and patriotism to Texas. For example, Company A was the "Texas Hunters," Company C, the "Lone Star Defenders," and Company G, the "Dead Shot Rangers."[46] With ten silk flags fluttering in the wind above their heads, the troops rode through towns and villages on the road to Fort Smith in great "military style and military pomp."[47]

At Fort Smith the regiment found that McCulloch had marched into Missouri to reinforce Sterling Price's state army, which was fighting desperately to hold southwestern Missouri for the Confederacy. Following McCulloch, the Third Texas, on August 4, reached the Confederate encampment on Crane Creek, some twenty miles southwest of Springfield.[48]

Two days later General Price turned over his Missouri State Guards to McCulloch, bringing the total force under his command to 6,000 cavalry, partly armed with shotguns, rifles, and muskets, 5,300 infantry, and fifteen pieces of artillery.[49] Opposing McCulloch in Missouri was a well-drilled, fully armed Federal army, numbering about 8,000 men, under Major General Nathaniel Lyon, then encamped at Springfield.[50]

McCulloch, deciding to engage the Federals without delay, ordered a general advance on the night of August 9. At about 1:00 A.M. the

[44] Barron, *Lone Star Defenders*, p. 23.

[45] Rose, *Ross' Texas Brigade*, p. 16; Walter P. Lane, *The Adventures and Recollections of General Walter P. Lane . . .*, p. 83.

[46] Rose, *Ross' Texas Brigade*, p. 18; Dallas (Texas) *Herald*, June 19, 1861.

[47] Barron, *Lone Star Defenders*, p. 20.

[48] Ben McCulloch to L. P. Walker, July 30, 1861, *Official Records*, ser. I, vol. III, 622–623; Sterling Price to C. F. Jackson, August 11, 1861, *ibid.*, p. 99; and Rose, *Gen. Ben McCulloch*, p. 135.

[49] McCulloch to S. Cooper, August 12, 1861, *Official Records*, ser. I, vol. III, 104; Price to Jackson, August 11, 1861, *ibid.*, pp. 98–99.

[50] J. M. Schofield's report, August 20, 1861, *ibid.*, p. 59.

Confederates, having marched over muddy roads in blowing rain, drew up in line by regiments along Wilson's Creek, a few miles below Springfield. On the left were Price's Missourians, with the brigades of Generals W. Y. Slack, John B. Clark, James H. McBride, M. M. Parsons, and James S. Rains, and William E. Woodruff's Arkansas artillery. In the center were Hébert's infantry and McIntosh's regiment of cavalry, dismounted. Completing the line on the right flank were Churchill's and Greer's cavalry, dismounted.[51]

Meanwhile, Lyon had split his force into two columns, one under himself, the other under General Franz Sigel. Simultaneous with McCulloch's advance, the two Federal columns marched to Wilson's Creek, Lyon taking a position opposite Price, while Sigel slipped around McCulloch's right flank and into his rear.[52] At 5:30 A.M., following a terrific artillery barrage, the Yankees took the offensive, with Lyon attacking Price and Sigel driving into Greer's and Churchhill's flanks. McCulloch, seeing his right wing buckling, moved McIntosh's and Hébert's regiments to cover the flank and rear of Greer's cavalry. The fighting was hot in this quarter, each side trying to outmaneuver the other. Finally, in a furious charge, McCulloch's yipping troops smashed Sigel's column, forcing it to retreat back to Springfield. McCulloch then joined Price. The combined Confederate forces completely routed Lyon's army, Lyon himself being killed in the fighting.[53]

The Confederate victory at Wilson's Creek was short-lived. McCulloch, whose army was drastically short of arms and supplies, fell back to Arkansas, where he remained for the rest of 1861. Price's haggard army, refusing to give up its home state, continued the war in southwestern Missouri until February, 1862, when exhausted and starving, it too withdrew to Arkansas.

Back in May, while enrolling officers recruited cavalry in Texas and Arkansas, McCulloch and Albert Pike, Commissioner of Indian Affairs for the Confederate government, took steps to enlist Indian cavalry in the Confederate Army.

[51] McCulloch to Walker, August 12, 1861, *ibid.*, p. 105.
[52] Schofield's report, August 20, 1861, *ibid.*, pp. 60–61.
[53] McCulloch to Walker, August 20, 1861, *ibid.*, pp. 105–107. Yankee casualties were 223 killed, 721 wounded, and 291 captured and missing. Confederate losses were 265 killed, 800 wounded, and 30 captured and missing.

The powerful Cherokee Nation, whose chieftain John Ross envisioned an independent Indian confederation, had issued in May a proclamation stating their neutrality in the current war.[54] This action angered Pike and McCulloch, and they set to work to force the Cherokees over to the side of the Confederacy. From July 10 to August 4, 1861, Pike negotiated treaties of alliance with the Creeks, Seminoles, Comanches, Chickasaws and Choctaws, the Wichitas, the Osages in the Cherokee Nation, the Senecas, the Quapaws, and the Shawnees.[55] McCulloch proceeded to surround the Cherokees with Confederate troops, white and Indian, so as to "force the conviction on the Cherokees that they have but one course to pursue—that is, to join the Confederacy."[56]

The general had recruited the first Indian cavalry unit for this purpose from the Choctaws and Chickasaws. On June 10 a Choctaw National Council convening at Doaksville authorized Chief Hudson to gather seven companies of mounted men, to be designated the First Regiment, Choctaw and Chickasaw Mounted Rifles.[57] The regiment, formed by the end of July under D. H. Cooper and numbering 1,085 men,[58] was assigned to Ben McCulloch, who promptly stationed it on the border of Cherokee country.

In August, at the time the Cherokees were assembled at a meeting in Tahlequah, McCulloch authorized squat, fiery, old Stand Watie (Portrait on Plate 2), a pro-Southern Cherokee recently commissioned a colonel in the Confederate Army, to raise a body of cavalry to protect the northern border of the Cherokee Nation "from the inroads of the jayhawkers of Kansas." Watie had strict instructions not to interfere with Cherokee neutrality,[59] but he was vehemently

[54] Proclamation to the Cherokee People, May 17, 1861, *ibid.*, ser. I, vol. XIII, 489–490.

[55] An excellent discussion of Pike's dealings in the Indian Territory may be found in Walter Lee Brown, "Albert Pike, 1809–1891," pp. 540–600. The treaties Pike negotiated with Indian tribes are in *Official Records*, ser. IV, vol. I, 445–466, 513–527, 542–554, 636–666, 669–687.

[56] Ben McCulloch to L. P. Walker, June 27, 1861, *ibid.*, ser. I, vol. III, 595–596, 600.

[57] Proclamation of Chief Hudson, June 14, 1861, *ibid.*, pp. 593–594.

[58] Abstract from Monthly Report of McCulloch's Brigade, Provisional Forces, C. S. Army, August 31, 1861, *ibid.*, p. 690.

[59] Ben McCulloch to John Ross, September 1, 1861, *ibid.*, p. 691; McCulloch to John Drew, September 1, 1861, *ibid.*; and McCulloch to L. P. Walker, September 2, 1861, *ibid.*, p. 692.

opposed to Ross' policy and succeeded in inducing adventurous young Cherokees to sneak across into Arkansas and join his unit.[60]

Arkansas citizens had earlier asked Watie to urge his nation to "join us in our efforts for mutual defense." On May 18 A. M. Wilson and J. W. Washbourne of Fayetteville had informed him that a number of "good guns" had been granted to the state for distribution to the Cherokees "in the defense of their and our frontier." In a sly P.S. the two men noted that the "notorious" "abolitionist," "robber," "murderer," and "rascal," Jim Lane, protecting the Federal agent for the Cherokees with a body of Union troops, was ignorant of Watie's pro-Confederate sentiments. Therefore, Watie should organize his Cherokees "silently," so they could the "more easily ambush and surprise him [Lane] & take *booty*."[61]

By the end of August, Watie had gathered together a battalion of 300 Indians. Taking up a position in the Cherokee neutral lands in Kansas, he awaited further instructions from McCulloch, who by that time was back at Fort Smith after his short campaign in Missouri.[62]

With many of his Indians already in the Confederate Army and contiguous tribes allied with the South, John Ross became convinced that his best course was to side with the Confederacy, and a treaty to this effect was negotiated in October.[63]

Afterwards, the Cherokee Nation not only contributed several additional companies to Watie's battalion, raising it to a full regiment of 800 men (First Cherokee Mounted Rifles), but also organized the Second Cherokee Mounted Rifles, 1,000 strong, under the leadership of John Drew.[64] By this time four additional Indian outfits had been raised in the other Nations. These were the First Creek Cavalry Regiment (900 men), Colonel D. N. McIntosh; the First Creek Cavalry

---

[60] Edward Everett Dale and Gaston Litton, eds., *Cherokee Cavaliers: Forty Years of Cherokee History as Told in the Correspondence of the Ridge-Watie-Boudinot Family*, pp. 100–101; Mabel W. Anderson, *Life of General Stand Watie: The Only Indian Brigadier General of the Confederate Army and the Last General to Surrender*, p. 14.

[61] Dale and Litton, *Cherokee Cavaliers*, pp. 106–107.

[62] Ben McCulloch to L. P. Walker, September 2, 1861, *Official Records*, ser. I, vol. III, 692.

[63] *Ibid.*, ser. IV, vol. I, 669–687.

[64] Ben McCulloch to John Drew, September 1, 1861, *ibid.*, ser. I, vol. III, 690; Annie H. Abel, *The American Indian as Slaveholder and Secessionist*; Volume I of *The Slaveholding Indians*, pp. 240–253.

Battalion (400 men), Lieutenant Colonel Chilly McIntosh; Creek Cavalry Company (75 men), Captain J. McSmith; the First Seminole Battalion, Lieutenant Colonel John Jumper; and the Second Regiment, Choctaw and Chickasaw Mounted Rifles, Colonel Tandy Walker. The War Department placed all these outfits under Albert Pike, recently appointed brigadier general to command the Indian troops raised under his treaties. Colonel D. H. Cooper was the field commander of this Indian brigade, which numbered 5,500 effectives.[65]

In July the Confederate War Department agreed to a sweeping cavalry campaign across New Mexico and Arizona, which had been proposed by General Henry Hopkins Sibley (Portrait on Plate 3), a debonair aristocrat who was conspicuous for wearing long, thin sideburns which drooped down below a flashy handlebar mustache.[66] Sibley arrived in Texas in the middle of August with orders to raise twenty companies of cavalry and a battery of howitzers with which to invade New Mexico and Arizona.[67] Having reported to General P. O. Hébert, who had replaced General Van Dorn as commander of Texas,[68] Sibley established his headquarters at San Antonio. There he hand-picked several enrolling captains and sent them into the surrounding counties to raise companies. Volunteers for these units were to furnish their own horses, rifles, and revolvers.[69]

Sibley's enrolling officer for the Hempstead-Bellville area, Captain Jerome B. McCown, began recruiting in September. First he placed notices in the Bellville *Countryman* stating that he was receiving volunteers for a cavalry company. Then he made camp on Clear Creek, just below Hempstead, where he began entering in his register the names of those enlisting. The *Countryman* assured potential vol-

[65] Pike to J. P. Benjamin, November 27, 1861, *Official Records*, ser. I, vol. VIII, 697; Abel, *American Indian as Slaveholder and Secessionist*, pp. 252–253.
[66] Captain George H. Pettis, U.S.V., "The Confederate Invasion of New Mexico and Arizona," in *Battles and Leaders of the Civil War*, II, 109; Martin H. Hall, "The Formation of Sibley's Brigade and the March to New Mexico," *Southwestern Historical Quarterly*, LXI (January, 1958), 384.
[67] S. Cooper to H. H. Sibley, July 8, 1861, *Official Records*, ser. I, vol. IV, 93; L. P. Walker to Edward Clark, July 8, 1861, *ibid.*, p. 93.
[68] Special Orders No. 123, August 14, 1861, *ibid.*, p. 98.
[69] Texas Adjutant General, *Report, November, 1861*, p. 4.

unteers that McCown "is a whole-souled fellow, and will divide his bottom dollar with a soldier."[70] By September 11 the company was full. Late that afternoon the "Jackson Cavalry" lined up by squads in front of the courthouse in Bellville, listened to long addresses from leading citizens of the community, and then set out for San Antonio to join Sibley's brigade.[71]

The streets of San Antonio were filled with the clamor of marching soldiers and the clatter of horse-drawn artillery as batteries and other cavalry outfits arrived and made ready for the New Mexico adventure. Three fully mounted regiments were organized in San Antonio and were known as "The Army of New Mexico." These regiments were the Fourth Texas Volunteer Cavalry, Colonel James Reily; the Fifth Texas Volunteer Cavalry, Colonel Tom Green; and the Seventh Texas Volunteer Cavalry, Colonel William Steele. To these would be added at El Paso Lieutenant Colonel John R. Baylor's Second Texas Mounted Rifles, bringing Sibley's total force to about 3,700 men. Several factors weighed powerfully against the success of this expedition—the strength of Federal forces in New Mexico, a shortage of ammunition and supplies, and the lack of specific information on road conditions. On February 21, 1862, the expeditionary force fought a Yankee army at Valverde, on the Rio Grande, a few miles above Fort Craig, New Mexico. Confederate columns then pushed northward and on March 26 fought a second Yankee force at Glorieta Pass, at the southern extremity of the Sangre de Cristo Range some twenty miles southeast of Santa Fe. Afterwards, Sibley's exhausted and starving horsemen began a desperate retreat down the Rio Grande, reaching Texas in the late spring of 1862, their ranks thinned by some 1,700 casualties on the campaign. Thus ended the Confederate dream of gaining all the country from the Rio Grande to the Pacific Ocean.[72]

Several of the crack cavalry outfits raised in the Trans-Mississippi during 1861 were immediately transferred to the larger seats of war

[70] Bellville (Texas) *Countryman*, September 4, 1861.
[71] *Ibid.*, September 11, 1861.
[72] The best account of the invasion is Martin H. Hall, *Sibley's New Mexico Campaign*. See also Ray C. Colton, *The Civil War in the Western Territories*, pp. 13–99; and Robert Lee Kerby, *The Confederate Invasion of New Mexico and Arizona*.

in Kentucky and Virginia.[73] One of these was Colonel William F. Slemons' Second Arkansas Cavalry Regiment, raised in July and transferred to Columbus, Kentucky, probably in August.[74] Two others were Terry's Texas Rangers, which would become one of the most celebrated of Texas cavalry regiments, and Scott's First Louisiana Cavalry Regiment, the first mounted outfit raised for the Confederate Army in that state.

Benjamin F. Terry, a wealthy sugar planter from Fort Bend County, Texas, and Thomas S. Lubbock of Houston had travelled to Virginia to volunteer in the Confederate Army shortly after Fort Sumter. The two men later served on the staff of General Pierre Gustave Toutant Beauregard at the battle of First Manassas (Bull Run), after which they secured permission from the War Department to recruit a regiment of cavalry in Texas for service in Virginia.[75]

[73] Throughout the year 1861, requests for troops from Texas, Louisiana, and Arkansas to be sent east of the Mississippi specified infantry. In April, 1861, the War Department had asked for 8,000 infantry from Texas and 8,000 from Louisiana, and in September requested 10,000 from Arkansas. Thus, most of the cavalry raised in 1861 remained in the Trans-Mississippi until ordered later in the war to cross east of the River. L. P. Walker to Edward Clark, April 8, 16, 1861, *Official Records*, ser. III, vol. V, 692; Walker to T. O. Moore, April 8, 16, 1861, *ibid.*; and A. S. Johnston to H. M. Rector, September 22, 1861, *ibid.*, ser. I, vol. IV, 422.

[74] Harrell, "Arkansas," *Confederate Military History*, X, 294. The regiment served east of the Mississippi until 1864, when it came back to Arkansas and served in Cabell's, Gano's, and Dockery's brigades, and in Fagan's division of Price's cavalry corps.

[75] Mrs. Kate Scurry Terrell, "Terry's Texas Rangers," in *Comprehensive History of Texas*, II, 682. The best single history of Terry's Texas Rangers is Leonidas B. Giles, *Terry's Texas Rangers*, which is largely reminiscent. Giles, who was a member of Company D, relates the story of the men of the regiment —"their campaigns, their marches, battles, hardships"—throughout the war. Another good account, but less interesting, is Blackburn. "Terry Rangers," *Southwestern Historical Quarterly*, XXII, 38–78, 143–179. Valuable information of the regiment after it left the Trans-Mississippi in November, 1861, may be found in the John W. Hill Letters, 1861–1865, and in the Robert Franklin Bunting Papers. Both of these collections are located in the Archives Collection of the Library of the University of Texas. The Bunting Papers include the Diary of Frank Bunting, 1861–1863, and the Letters of Robert Franklin Bunting, November 9, 1861, to 1865. The letters are preserved as a typescript copy of Bunting's war correspondence to the Houston *Daily Telegraph* and the San Antonio *Herald*. Bunting was chaplain for the Rangers. A good, terse account of the celebrated regiment is Lester N. Fitzhugh, *Terry's Texas Rangers, 8th Texas Cavalry, C.S.A.: An Address . . . before the Houston Civil War Round Table*, March 21, 1958.

Returning to Texas by rail and horseback, Terry and Lubbock established the muster center for the regiment at Houston. Then they sent ten recruiting captains into the southern part of the state. Each officer was instructed to raise a company of 100 horsemen, each volunteer to furnish his own weapon (preferably a double-barreled shotgun), a pair of six-shooters, bridle, saddle, spurs, lariat, and mount.[76]

Terry's enrolling officer for Bastrop and contiguous counties was Stephen C. Ferrell. Arriving there sometime in August, he issued an urgent call for troops and was surprised at the quick and enthusiastic response. Everyone was eager to support the Confederate cause. "War, war, war," wrote one correspondent, "is the daily conversation of every lady and gentleman that I meet."[77] Men of draft age were equally exuberant. "I was fearful," remarked one volunteer, "that the war would be over before I saw a live Yankee. So Charley McGhee and I went fifty miles from home to join" Ferrell's company being organized between Bastrop and LaGrange.[78]

Within a week, Ferrell's muster roll was full. He posted throughout Bastrop, Hays, Travis, and Burleson counties notices designating Bastrop as the organization center for the company. On the eve of the muster day, bodies of green, rowdy volunteers converged on Bastrop. They drank and celebrated well into the night. The next morning the people of the town gathered at the square to see the men conduct elections and to witness the departing ceremonies. Mingling with the troops were women, elderly men, and children who "with tears in their eyes" clasped the soldiers' hands and blessed them for their heroism and patriotism. When this "painful ordeal" was over, the company rode out of Bastrop "on what we believed was a few month's venture." The next day they entered Terry's makeshift camp at an old warehouse on the outskirts of Houston.

Within a few days all ten companies had arrived in Houston. Captain John A. Wharton (Portrait on Plate 7) brought a company from Brazoria and Matagorda counties; Captain James G. Walker one from Harris and Montgomery counties; and Captain Louis N. Strobel a company from Fayette County. Three companies were from the area

---

[76] Blackburn, "Terry Rangers," *Southwestern Historical Quarterly,* XXII, 41.
[77] Bellville (Texas) *Countryman,* August 21, 1861.
[78] D. H. Combs to L. B. Giles, January 5 [year not shown], in Giles, *Terry's Texas Rangers,* p. 7.

around Gonzales, the other four mainly from McLennan, Bexar, Goliad, and Fort Bend counties.[79] On September 9, less than thirty days after Terry and Lubbock had returned to Texas, the regiment, numbering 1,170 men, was mustered into Confederate service.[80]

For the mustering-in ceremony, all ten companies lined up on three sides of a large, open square. Lieutenant J. Sparks, who had resigned from the United States Army and was on his way to Richmond to volunteer in the Confederate Army, administered the oath of allegiance. Sparks stood in the center of the square, and in a powerful voice which drowned out the dull commotion of whispering and shuffling, he asked, "Do you men wish to be sworn into service for twelve months or for three years or for during the war?" A moment of silence followed. Then the men shouted enthusiastically "For the War!" "For the War!" After the ceremony, the troops marched back to camp where they prepared for a long, grueling march to Virginia.[81]

The personnel of the Rangers "was of the very highest." Sons of prominent families, college graduates, merchants, bankers, lawyers, cowboys, expert with lariats and six-shooters, and farmers all served as privates. They were, according to one Ranger, "all young, in their teens and early twenties." No one paid much attention to rank. "The supreme desire," said L. B. Giles of Company D, "was to get into the war in a crack cavalry regiment."[82] And the Rangers were indeed a crack regiment, as they proved later in battle.

While the Rangers waited for the order to move, Strobel's company "kept the town in a continued bustle with their daring feats of horsemanship." To "show what they could do," the men formed in squads and rode at a maddening gallop down the streets, jumping off and on their mounts and picking pieces of cloth and sticks off the ground. To the exasperation of peace-loving civilians, some of the men would break wild horses in the middle of town. With all this showmanship, a newspaperman decided the Rangers were about the toughest outfit in the Confederate Army. Hardened from encounters with "the

[79] Giles, *Terry's Texas Rangers,* pp. 13–15.

[80] Jno. Claiborne, comp., Muster Rolls of Terry's Texas Rangers, Reunion in Galveston, February 20, 1882, in the Archives Collection of the Library of the University of Texas.

[81] Blackburn, "Terry Rangers," *Southwestern Historical Quarterly,* XXII, 42.

[82] Giles, *Terry's Texas Rangers,* pp. 13–14.

stealthy panther and more savage Mexican hog, in our forests," they would be the "pride of Texas" and would make "the enemy beware" when they "get on their track."[83]

On September 10, 1861, the Rangers rode to Beaumont, left their horses, and then marched on foot to New Orleans, whence they sailed up the Mississippi to Bowling Green, Kentucky, to join General Albert Sidney Johnston's command. The election of officers, held after the unit reached Bowling Green, made Terry colonel.[84] The Rangers served the rest of the war east of the Mississippi, leaving two thirds of their numbers on some of the bloodiest battlefields of the war.

Like Terry's regiment, Colonel John S. Scott's Louisiana cavalry outfit was raised for the specific purpose of serving in either Virginia or Kentucky. As a reward for valuable services on the Peninsula and a brilliant understanding of cavalry command, President Davis had, by an order of July 15, 1861, authorized Scott to recruit a regiment for himself. Arriving in New Orleans on July 21, Scott promptly selected 10 enrolling officers to go into country parishes to raise companies of cavalry.[85]

One of the enrolling officers was a Lieutenant Hasley of New Orleans. Sometime in August, Hasley established his enrolling center at the St. Charles Hotel, but he recruited most of the company from parishes north of the city and called it the "Pointe Coupee Cavalry." On September 27 a notice in the New Orleans *Daily Crescent* asked for fifteen men from New Orleans to fill out the company. The *Crescent* described this as a "rare chance." Only the "best class of men" was being received. The men of New Orleans responded rapidly, and within a few days Hasley's company was full. It organized at New Orleans and then rode for Scott's camp, pitched near Baton Rouge.[86]

The First Louisiana Cavalry, composed of 750 men in ten companies, was mustered into Confederate service in November, 1861. In the elections for regimental officers, held shortly thereafter, Scott was chosen colonel and J. O. Nixon, editor and proprietor of the New

[83] Printed from Houston (Texas) *Telegraph*, Bellville (Texas) *Countryman*, September 18, 1861.
[84] Giles, *Terry's Texas Rangers*, pp. 13–14; Blackburn, "Terry Rangers," *Southwestern Historical Quarterly*, XXII, 42.
[85] New Orleans (Louisiana) *Daily Crescent*, November 18, 1861.
[86] *Ibid.*, September 28, 1861.

Orleans *Daily Crescent,* lieutenant colonel. The regiment then went into camp inside Baton Rouge for several weeks of drill and training in the principles of cavalry warfare.[87]

Scott's regiment had been raised without expense to the government. The cost, said to have been $50,000, was met by subscriptions from private parties in the country parishes whence over 90 per cent of the volunteers had come.[88]

Before the First left Baton Rouge, a section of light artillery, consisting of 25 men, two mountain howitzers, and one rifled four-pounder, was assigned to it from Watson's Battalion. Towards the last of November, the regiment sailed on river boats up the Mississippi to Bowling Green, Kentucky. The outfit never returned to the Trans-Mississippi theater of war.

By the end of December, 1861, the Trans-Mississippi had raised, mounted, and equipped a large number of cavalry units for Confederate service. Texas had placed sixteen regiments, three battalions, and three independent companies in the field (17,338 men);[89] Arkansas, five regiments and five battalions (5,145 men); the Indian Territory, five regiments, two battalions, and one independent company (5,460 men); and Louisiana, one regiment (750 men). See Table I.

With the exception of Louisiana this was a good showing in comparison to the number of infantry raised in 1861. In Texas only seven regiments and four battalions of infantry had been raised by December—about 7,100 men.[90] This gave the cavalry from the state a numerical superiority of approximately 2.4 to 1. Arkansas had produced eight regiments and one battalion of infantry, 5,887 men[91]—a numerical ratio of 1.2 to 1 in favor of the infantry. In Louisiana the

---

[87] Plaquemine (Louisiana) *Gazette,* November 2, 1861; New Orleans (Louisiana) *Daily Crescent,* November 4, 16, 1861.

[88] *Ibid.,* October 11, 1861.

[89] Governor Clark of Texas estimated that by November 1, 1861, the state had raised over 20,000 men, cavalry and infantry (mostly horsemen), for the Confederacy. (Texas) *Governor's Message, November 1, 1861,* p. 10.

[90] Wooten, *Comprehensive History of Texas,* II, 572–630; Roberts, "Texas," *Confederate Military History,* XI, 45–58; Texas Adjutant General, *Report, November, 1861,* pp. 1–3; Lester N. Fitzhugh, comp., *Texas Batteries, Battalions, Regiments, Commanders and Field Officers Confederate States Army, 1861–1865,* pp. 23, 25–28.

[91] Articles of Transfer of Arkansas Volunteers to the Confederate Service,

infantry was far out in front with twenty regiments and five battalions, 22,733 men,[92] in contrast to the single cavalry regiment of 750 men —an infantry supremacy of slightly more than 30 to 1. No infantry units were raised in the Indian Territory. In total figures the cavalry from the Trans-Mississippi numbered about 28,693, the infantry some 35,720—a slim advantage of 1.25 to 1 for the infantry.

The definite preference for cavalry service among the Texans provided a constant source of exasperation for Governor Clark. Back in April he had received from the War Department a request for 8,000 infantrymen from Texas to fight in Confederate armies east of the Mississippi. To meet the request, Clark obtained commissions for prominent citizens and detailed them into counties throughout the state. The officers soon found that Texans, well-known for their peerless horsemanship, would have little to do with the unromantic infantry service. Every man wanted to join the cavalry and make a lasting impression on young ladies and relatives by riding off to war on a powerful horse as an improvised band played "The Girl I Left Behind Me" or "The Yellow Rose of Texas." The preference soon became a "passion for mounted service" as men flatly refused to join any service that required walking. In desperation, the governor directed that camps of instruction be set up throughout the state to instruct raw recruits in the art of infantry service. These camps attempted to show the men that the infantry actually was every bit as glorious as the cavalry. But most of the Texans were not fooled by Clark's efforts, or by similar efforts on the part of succeeding governors, Francis R. Lubbock and Pendleton Murrah. Until conscription laws forced them into the infantry, Texans rushed to enlist as gallant cavalrymen.[93]

July 15, 1861, *Official Records*, ser. I, vol. III, 609–610; Ben McCulloch to L. P. Walker, July 18, 1861, *ibid*., pp. 611–612; Abstract of Monthly Troop Returns, August and October, 1861, *ibid*., pp. 690, 730; Hempstead, *Pictorial History of Arkansas*, pp. 363–427.

[92] Statement of Organized Confederate Units, September, 1861, *Official Records*, ser. IV, vol. I, 628; McCulloch to Walker, July 18, 1861, *ibid*., ser. I, vol. III, 611–612; Louisiana Adjutant General, *Annual Report, 1891*, pp. 12–34; Andrew B. Booth, comp., *Records of Louisiana Confederate Soldiers and Louisiana Confederate Commands.*

[93] (Texas) *Governor's Message, November 1, 1861*, pp. 7–10; Texas Adjutant General, *Report, November, 1861*, p. 1; Roberts, "Texas," *Confederate Military History*, XI, 56–57.

The results of recruiting volunteers in 1861 were for the cavalry excellent numerically, but the outfits retained in the Trans-Mississippi were hardly an effective fighting force. In the absence of an over-all regional command during 1861, there was no Trans-Mississippi army as such, and consequently no real organization of the cavalry. Mounted units were scattered from the Mississippi to New Mexico, and from the Rio Grande to Lexington, Missouri.

TABLE I

Confederate Cavalry Units Raised in the Trans-Mississippi during 1861

TEXAS[a]

Unit	Commander	Troops	Station
1st Reg. (Mted. Rifles)	H. E. McCulloch	1,000	Texas
1st Reg. (Arizona Brigade)	W. P. Hardeman	800 (est.)	New Mexico
2nd Reg.	J. S. Ford	1,200	Texas
2nd Reg. (Mted. Rifles)	J. R. Baylor	700	New Mexico
3rd Reg.	Joseph Phillips	796	Texas
3rd Reg. (South Kansas-Texas Reg.)	Elkanah Greer	1,200	Arkansas
4th Reg.	James Reily	1,000	New Mexico
5th Reg.	Tom Green	1,000	New Mexico
6th Reg.	B. W. Stone	1,150	Arkansas
7th Reg.	William Steele	1,000	New Mexico
9th Reg.	W. B. Sims	1,050	Indian Territory
10th Reg.	M. F. Locke	900 (est.)	Texas
11th Reg.	W. C. Young	855	Arkansas
12th Reg.	W. H. Parsons	940 (est.)	Arkansas
18th Reg.	N. H. Darnell	900 (est.)	Texas
Terry's Reg. (also referred to as 8th Tex.)	B. F. Terry	1,170	Kentucky
De Bray's Bn.	X. B. De Bray	700	Texas
Whitfield's Bn.	J. W. Whitfield	339	Arkansas
6th Bn.	R. S. Gould	400 (est.)	Arkansas
Burnett's Company	J. R. Burnett	84	Arkansas
Hill's Company	Hill	77	Arkansas
Turner's Company	Turner	77	Arkansas
		17,338	

LOUISIANA

Unit	Commander	Troops	Station
1st Reg.	J. S. Scott	750	Kentucky
		750	

[a] Texas data compiled from Abstracts of Monthly Troop Returns, August 31, and October, 1861, *Official Records*, ser. I, vol. III, 690, 730; Abstract of Monthly Troop Returns, December 31, 1861, *ibid.*, ser. I, vol. VIII, 718–719; Statement of Organized Confederate Units, September, 1861, *ibid.*, ser. IV, vol. I, 630; Wooten, *Comprehensive History of Texas*, II, 572–630; Dallas (Texas) *Herald*, July 31, October 30, November 6, 1861; Roberts, "Texas," *Confederate Military History*, XI, 45–58; Rose, *Gen. Ben McCulloch*, pp. 129–134; Rose, *Ross' Texas Brigade*, pp. 132–135;

ARKANSAS[b]

Unit	Commander	Troops	Station
1st Reg.[c]	C. A. Carroll	700 (est.)	Arkansas
1st Reg. (Mted. Rifles)	T. J. Churchill	768	Arkansas
2nd Reg.	W. F. Slemons	800 (est.)	Kentucky
2nd Reg. (Mted. Rifles)	James McIntosh	662	Arkansas
5th Reg.	R. C. Newton	700	Arkansas
Borland's Bn.	Solon Borland	568	Arkansas
Brooks' Bn.	W. H. Brooks	316	Arkansas
Scott's Squadron	J. R. H. Scott	181	Arkansas
Wheat's Bn.	P. H. Wheat	200 (est.)	Arkansas
Witherspoon's Bn.	B. N. Witherspoon	250 (est.)	Arkansas
		5,145	

INDIAN TERRITORY[d]

Unit	Commander	Troops	Station
1st Reg., Choct. & Chick.	D. H. Cooper	1,085	Indian Territory
2nd Reg., Choct. & Chick.	Tandy Walker	800	Indian Territory
1st Reg., Cherokee Mted. Rifles	Stand Watie	1,000	Indian Territory
2nd Reg., Cherokee Mted. Rifles	John Drew	800	Indian Territory
1st Reg., Creek Cav.	D. N. McIntosh	900	Indian Territory
1st Bn., Creek Cav.	Chilly McIntosh	400	Indian Territory
McSmith's Creek Company	J. McSmith	75	Indian Territory
1st Bn., Seminole Cav.	John Jumper	400	Indian Territory
		5,460	

Total Number of Cavalry Raised in 1861 — 28,693

Harrell, "Arkansas," *Confederate Military History*, X, 70; U.S. War Department, *List of Field Officers, Regiments and Battalions in the Confederate Army, 1861–1865*, pp. 71–78; and other sources cited in the text. For a list of these outfits see Fitzhugh, *Texas Batteries, Battalions, Regiments, Commanders and Field Officers Confederate States Army*, pp. 4–5, 11–17.

[b] Arkansas data compiled from Abstracts of Monthly Troop Returns, August 31, and October, 1861, *Official Records*, ser. I, vol. III, 690, 730; Abstract of Monthly Troop Returns, December 13, 1861, *ibid.*, ser. IV, vol. I, 788–789; Abstract of Monthly Troop Returns, December 31, 1861, *ibid.*, ser. I, vol. III, 718–719; Statement of Organized Confederate Units, September, 1861, *ibid.*, ser. IV, vol. I, 627; Harrell, "Arkansas," *Confederate Military History*, X, 70; Hempstead, *Pictorial History of Arkansas*, pp. 363–427; Colonel V. Y. Cook, "List of General and Field Officers, Arkansas Troops, C.S.A., and State Troops," *Publications of the Arkansas Historical Association*, I (1906), 411–421; and other sources cited in the text.

[c] DeRosey Carroll's First Arkansas Cavalry broke up in the summer of 1861. Company A of this regiment under Charles A. Carroll formed the basis of a new regiment, composed of many of DeRosey Carroll's old companies and a few new ones. Charles A. Carroll's outfit took the designation of the First Arkansas Cavalry.

[d] Albert Pike to J. P. Benjamin, November 27, 1861, *Official Records*, ser. I, vol. VIII, 697; Abel, *American Indian as a Slaveholder and Secessionist*, pp. 240–253; and Harrell, "Arkansas," *Confederate Military History*, X, 70, 98, 198.

THE ORGANIZATION
OF THE CAVALRY, 1862

In December, 1861, only eleven regiments and five battalions out of the twenty-four regiments and ten battalions of cavalry serving west of the Mississippi were in brigade organization and under the command of cavalry generals. General Sibley had a brigade in New Mexico; Colonel D. H. Cooper, one in the Indian Territory; and Colonel James McIntosh, a brigade in McCulloch's army, stationed at Fort Smith, Arkansas. The rest of the mounted outfits were scattered over the region, serving in some parts as scouts and couriers for infantry brigades and in others as home guard or frontier patrols or as escorts for supply trains. Their orders came from infantry brigadiers who were little versed in the art of cavalry warfare. In back of this arrangement was the crippling old theory that a mounted outfit was more or less a staff unit, like the signalers, and that a cavalry commander ranked as a member of the brigade general's staff rather than as a leader of combat troops. The essence of the problem of organization was whether cavalry was to be regarded as a collection of train guards and scouts for the infantry, or as a compact fighting unit. Contrary to popular opinion in 1861, and as experience would later prove, cavalry with its rapid mobility was a powerful offensive weapon when organized at least in brigades, each composed of four to six regiments, but preferably in divisions, each one consisting of two or more brigades. Cavalry formed in either of these arrangements was in large enough units to fight effectively and to be self-sustaining and independent of the need for infantry support.[1]

[1] First Lieutenant S. R. Gleaves, United States Cavalry, made a study of

30

Confederate commanders in the Trans-Mississippi had not as yet been confronted with a situation calling for a rapid striking force, that is, for cavalry organized in compact fighting units. However, the Indian Territory was soon to see a crisis which would require quick action on the part of two of the three cavalry brigades now in operation and which would show the need for more mounted brigades.

As the winter of 1861 set in, a bloody uprising flamed up in Creek country and threatened to engulf the entire Indian Territory. The old Creek chieftain Hopoetholoyahola, violently opposed to Confederate alliances with the Five Nations, had gathered 2,000 of his warriors in October and gone on the warpath, crushing D. H. Cooper's Confederate Indian cavalry in running battles at Round Mounds (November 19)[2] and Bird Creek (December 9).[3] With Cooper's crippled force retreating to Fort Gibson, the chieftain led his Indians

---

cavalry organization and tactics during the Civil War. He concluded that experience gained during the war proved that cavalry operated best when formed in divisions. "The Strategic Use of Cavalry," *Journal of the U.S. Cavalry Association*, XVIII (July, 1907), 9–25. Captain Alonzo Gray, United States Cavalry, agrees with Gleaves in his *Cavalry Tactics as Illustrated by the War of the Rebellion . . .* , pt. I, 6, 7, 175. Major General James H. Wilson of the Federal Army wrote after the war that he believed cavalry operated more efficiently when organized on a corps basis (a corps was made up of two or more divisions), properly commanded and properly cared for. With such an organization, he noted, the strength of cavalry was not frittered away by unnecessary detachments or unprofitable work. "The Cavalry of the Army of the Potomac," in *Civil and Mexican Wars, 1861, 1846*; Volume XIII of *Publications of the Military Historical Society of Massachusetts*, pp. 85, 87. J. P. Dyer, in his study, "Some Aspects of Cavalry Operations in the Army of Tennessee," *Journal of Southern History*, VIII (May, 1942), 210–225, pointed out that cavalry in this army functioned very effectively in division organization. Major General Richard Taylor, Confederate hero in Louisiana during the war, wrote in his book, *Destruction and Reconstruction: Personal Experiences of the Late War*, p. 65, that it was natural for cavalry officers to desire large commands, but they "were too much indulged in this desire." In many instances brigades and divisions numbered no more than an average regiment. Nevertheless, he continued, cavalry organized in brigades and divisions rendered excellent service. Army regulations for 1861 also advised commanders to form their cavalry into brigades, divisions, or corps. Confederate States War Department, *Regulations for the Army of the Confederate States, and for the Quartermaster's and Pay Departments, 1861*, pp. 103–104.

[2] D. H. Cooper's report, January 20, 1862, *Official Records*, ser. I, vol. VIII, 8.
[3] *Ibid.*; Cooper to James McIntosh, December 11, 1861, *ibid.*, p. 709.

in a northwesterly direction to Shoal Creek, where he encamped to plan further conquests.[4]

Thoroughly beaten and weakened from desertions to the enemy, Cooper was forced to request reinforcements from Colonel James McIntosh (Portrait on Plate 1), temporary commander of Confederate forces at Van Buren, Arkansas.[5] McIntosh agreed to help, and picking 1,600 of his best horsemen, all veterans of Wilson's Creek, he rode to join Cooper at Fort Gibson. There the two men planned a trap for Hopoetholoyahola. McIntosh would approach the Union Indians from the front by moving up the Verdigris with parts of the Third, Sixth, and Eleventh Texas Cavalry and the Second Arkansas Mounted Rifles. Cooper, reinforced with John W. Whitfield's Texas battalion, would ride up the north side of the Arkansas and get in the Indians' rear. McIntosh picked up Hopoetholoyahola's trail on December 25, following it back into the Big Bend of the Arkansas River. The next day, his scouts were fired upon by enemy snipers while fording Shoal Creek, a tributary of the Verdigris.

Deciding to engage immediately without waiting for Cooper to join him, McIntosh dismounted his veterans and formed a line some 300 yards away from the Indians, who were posted on top of a ridge overlooking Shoal Creek. After firing several volleys, the Confederates charged across an open field, splashed through the creek, and wormed their way up the rocky slope of the ridge, only to be pinned down near the top by murderous fire from the Indians. For two hours they were unable to move. Then in a furious assault a group of Texans under Lieutenant Colonel Walter P. Lane swept over the top and the battle of Chustenahlah was won. The Creeks fled toward Federal Kansas.

Exhausted from battle, the soldiers walked slowly back to Shoal Creek and pitched camp. They left nine bodies on the ridge, and brought away forty men seriously wounded. At sundown Colonel

---

[4] Wiley Britton, *The Civil War on the Border*, I, 171.

[5] General McCulloch had gone to Richmond to explain to the War Department why he had refused to help Price hold southern Missouri after Wilson's Creek. McIntosh, the ranking colonel in McCulloch's Division, had received the command and along with it the power to deploy troops at his discretion. McIntosh to Sterling Price, December 14, 1861, *Official Records*, ser. I, vol. XIII, 712–713; McIntosh to Cooper, December 7, 1861, *ibid.*, p. 703.

Stand Watie and his 300 Cherokees rode into the bivouac and planned an exciting chase after the fugitives the next day. McIntosh returned to Fort Smith on the following morning, leaving to Watie and Cooper the sport of tracking down the remnants of Hopoetholoyahola's force.[6]

While Watie rode north for Kansas, capturing stragglers and cornering Alligator, one of Hopoetholoyahola's Seminole officers, Cooper and his Indians travelled northwest. The latter force, following fresh tracks in the snow and searching clumps of trees and shrubbery, captured and killed small bands of refugees hidden in makeshift shelters.[7] At Fort Leavenworth a Federal agent wired Washington that "Hopoetholoyahola . . . needs help badly . . . hurry up Lane."[8] By January 5, 1862, all Federal resistance had been stamped out in the Creek nation. Plainly the First Cavalry Brigade, McCulloch's division, and the Indian Cavalry Brigade had succeeded in suppressing the Creek uprising and keeping the Indian Territory in the Confederacy.

This victory proved that a force capable of rapid action was a definite asset to an army. It attested that cavalry brigades were large enough and strong enough to track down and defeat the enemy. An army of cavalry brigades such as these would give Confederate forces in the Trans-Mississippi tremendous striking power. The generals in the region were slow, however, to grasp the significance of the achievement of Cooper's and McIntosh's brigades. While the number of cavalry regiments rose sharply, the process of merging regiments into brigades would not begin seriously until October, 1862. Many changes in command would take place and several mounted outfits would even be converted to infantry before Confederate generals in the region fully realized the potential power existing in a cavalry properly organized.

[6] James McIntosh's report, January 1, 1862, *ibid.*, pp. 22–25; Britton, *Civil War on the Border*, I, 171–174; and Walter P. Lane, *The Adventures and Recollections of General Walter P. Lane . . .* , pp. 87–88.

[7] Britton, *Civil War on the Border*, I, 173–174; Annie H. Abel, *The American Indian as Slaveholder and Secessionist*; Volume I of *The Slaveholding Indians*, pp. 259–262.

[8] Quoted in Annie H. Abel, *The American Indian as a Participant in the Civil War*; Volume II of *The Slaveholding Indians*, p. 76.

On January 10, 1862, the War Department placed the Trans-Mississippi under the over-all command of Major General Earl Van Dorn[9] (Portrait on Plate 4), a West Pointer with Mexican War service and an excellent record as a cavalry colonel in Texas. Under Van Dorn the process of organizing and recruiting cavalry proceeded for the first time under the guidance of a regional command. The General ordered all leaves of absence in cavalry and infantry commands to be canceled and took steps to persuade six- and twelve-months-volunteer cavalrymen, whose terms were near expiration, to re-enlist for two years.[10] He ordered battalion commanders to recruit their units to regimental size and authorized enrolling officers to raise new mounted outfits to reinforce meager Confederate forces in Arkansas. Then he set about helping Sterling Price persuade soldiers in the Missouri State Guards to transfer to Confederate service.

The enlargement of battalions into regiments was effected either by merging existing battalions or by further recruiting. Late in January, Solon Borland's Arkansas battalion, bivouacked near Fort Smith, became the Third Arkansas Cavalry with the addition of three companies of Williamson's battalion of infantry. The new regiment then joined Field General McCulloch's division, operating in northwestern Arkansas.[11] In February Lieutenant Colonel Xavier B. De Bray (Portrait on Plate 7) expanded his Texas cavalry battalion, encamped at Galveston, by recruiting three new companies in Montgomery, Grimes, and adjacent counties.[12] On March 16, 1862, De Bray, a native of France and graduate of the famous European military academy at St. Cyr,[13] was elected colonel of the regiment, styled

[9] Special Orders No. 8, January 10, 1862, *Official Records*, ser. I, vol. VIII, 734.

[10] On January 30 McIntosh appointed special recruiting officers in each regiment of his command (Third, Sixth, and Eleventh Texas Cavalry and Second Arkansas Mounted Rifles) to persuade all six- and twelve-months men to re-enlist. A $50 bounty and a thirty-day furlough were given each soldier who decided to stay. Van Buren (Arkansas) *Press*, January 30, 1862; Dallas (Texas) *Herald*, February 5, 1862.

[11] Colonel V. Y. Cook, "List of General and Field Officers, Arkansas Troops, C.S.A., and State Troops," *Publications of the Arkansas Historical Association*, I (1906), 413.

[12] Xavier B. De Bray, *A Sketch of the History of De Bray's Twenty-Sixth Regiment of Texas Cavalry*, p. 4. De Bray's sketch may also be found in *Southern Historical Society Papers*, XIII (1885), 153–165.

[13] Ella Lonn, *Foreigners in the Confederacy*, pp. 136–137.

the Twenty-Sixth Texas Cavalry. For the rest of the year the outfit performed general patrol duty along the Texas coast.[14]

From February, 1862, onward, recruiting of new regiments followed regulations set forth by an act of Congress approved January 27, 1862. Only field officers or captains holding commissions from the War Department were to raise bodies of cavalry. The pay of officers so engaged would not commence until their units were organized and mustered-in for three years or the war. In each department the general in charge would select the command in which the new troops were to serve. To encourage volunteering, enrolling officers had orders to offer each man a $50 bounty for his signature.[15]

In practice the new regulations did not change the procedure of recruiting the volunteers. For example, in raising the Thirty-First Texas Cavalry, Colonel T. C. Hawpe, authorized by the War Department to recruit a regiment of Texas Cavalry, set up headquarters at Dallas on or about February 1 and issued calls for volunteers. He then sent enrolling officers into Dallas and surrounding counties. Hawpe had a bright idea to prompt volunteering. He put a warning in the Dallas *Herald* hinting broadly at invasion of the Texas coast. "Who will defend Texas?" he asked. "Texas, and Texans alone. Fellow citizens, flock as soldiers to our country's standard, and we will make our enemies bite the dust!"[16] The men of Dallas responded, and on May 15 Hawpe's regiment, numbering 1,000 strong, organized in Dallas as the Thirty-First Texas Cavalry. After the men held elections, choosing Hawpe their colonel, part of the outfit left for Little Rock, the remainder following in June.[17]

While colonels recruited volunteers for Van Dorn's command, Price's Missouri State Guards, now encamped near Fort Smith after having given up their home state to superior Federal forces, began to transfer to Confederate service under the Congressional Act of January 27, 1862. According to this act, volunteers were to decide by vote whether to be transferred or be retained in the state service. Those making the change were to agree to serve for three years. By March

[14] De Bray, *Twenty-Sixth Texas Cavalry*, pp. 4–5.
[15] James M. Matthews, ed., *The Statutes at Large of the Provisional Government of the Confederate States of America . . .*, p. 254.
[16] Dallas (Texas) *Herald*, February 5, 1862.
[17] *Ibid.*, May 17, June 7 and 14, 1862; Dudley G. Wooten, ed., *A Comprehensive History of Texas*, II, 639.

1, 1862, the Missouri mounted regiments that had joined the Confederate Army were the First Missouri Cavalry, Colonel Elijah Gates; the Second Missouri Cavalry, Colonel Robert McCulloch, Jr.; and the Third Missouri Cavalry, Colonel D. Todd Samuel. All three outfits became a part of the First Missouri Confederate Brigade, Van Dorn's Second Corps, Army of the West. Price himself received a Major General's commission and joined Van Dorn's command.[18]

With Price's army thrown out of Missouri, Major General John Pope, commander of Union forces in Kansas and Missouri, ordered his armies to advance across the Arkansas line and crush Confederate resistance. After Price and Ben McCulloch, Van Dorn's field generals, went Major General Samuel R. Curtis, an able but then underrated Union officer. Curtis had an army of 10,000 strong. On March 6 the two forces met near Pea Ridge, Arkansas, at the southern extremity of the Ozarks. Van Dorn, having almost a two-to-one superiority, thought it safe to split his army and make a combined attack from front and rear. But the tactical execution of the plan miscarried. While the left wing under Price and Van Dorn was successful, the right wing crumbled under the terrific hammering of combined infanty and artillery assaults. McCulloch and McIntosh, ranking officers of the First Division, were killed and the men were soon in complete rout. The next day, surrounded on both flanks, Van Dorn withdrew his beaten army from the battlefield. While Curtis moved his victorious forces eastward along the southern Missouri border, the Confederates trudged slowly back to Fayetteville. There, a few days later, Van Dorn received orders to move his forces east to reinforce Major General A. S. Johnston in Mississippi. The following month witnessed a general removal of troops from the Trans-Mississippi. McIntosh's old brigade, now commanded by Colonel Elkanah Greer, left for Mississippi late in April, and the region thus lost its best cavalry outfit. The sixteen regiments, one battalion, and three companies of cavalry crossing the Mississippi are listed in Table II.[19]

---

[18] C. F. Jackson to Jefferson Davis, December 30, 1861, *Official Records*, ser. I, vol. VIII, 724–725; Sterling Price to J. P. Benjamin, January 17, 1862, *ibid.*, p. 736; Price's address to soldiers of the Missouri State Guards, April 8, 1862, *ibid.*, p. 824; R. S. Bevier, *History of the First and Second Missouri Confederate Brigades, 1861–1865*, pp. 76–81.

[19] Special Orders No. 52, April 15, 1862, *Official Records*, ser. I, vol. VIII,

TABLE II

Confederate Cavalry Units Crossing the Mississippi in the Spring of 1862

Unit	Commander	Effectives
Texas:		
3rd Reg. (Greer's Brig.)	W. P. Lane	707
6th Reg. (Greer's Brig.)	B. W. Stone	803
9th Reg.	W. B. Sims	657
10th Reg.	M. F. Locke	565
11th Reg. (Greer's Brig.)	J. J. Diamond	599
14th Reg.	M. T. Johnson	1,024
16th Reg.	William Fitzhugh	1,000
17th Reg.	G. F. Moore	1,000
27th Reg.	J. W. Whitfield	1,007
32nd Reg.	R. P. Crump	472
		7,834
Arkansas:		
1st Reg.	T. J. Churchill	636
2nd Reg. (Greer's Brig.)	B. T. Embry	499
3rd Reg.	Solon Borland	399
Brooks' Bn.	W. H. Brooks	450
		1,984
Missouri:		
1st Reg.	Elijah Gates	536
2nd Reg.	Robert McCulloch, Jr.	600
3rd Reg.	D. T. Samuel	444
Hill's Company	Hill	51
Murphy's Company	Murphy	100
Reves' Company	Timothy Reves	52
		1,783
Total Cavalry Crossing the River		11,601

With 22,000 cavalry and infantry moved across the River by mid-May, the Trans-Mississippi was virtually stripped of defenders. General John S. Roane, who had been left in command, had at his disposal 3,453 Indian and Texas cavalry under Pike in the Indian Territory, and perhaps 1,000 scattered infantry and cavalry in Arkansas—a pitifully small force with which to contend with Curtis'

818; Abstract from Troop Returns of Trans-Mississippi District, April 16, 1862, *ibid.*, ser. I, vol. XIII, 818; Organization of the Army of the West, at Corinth, Mississippi, May 4, 1862, *ibid.*, ser. I, vol. X, pt. II, 489–490; Statement of Missouri Troops in the Army of the West, May 5, 1862, *ibid.*, p. 495; John N. Edwards, *Shelby and His Men: or, The War in the West*, p. 64; John Henry Brown, *History of Texas from 1685 to 1892*, II, 415; and John M. Harrell, "Arkansas," *Confederate Military History*, X, 96.

powerful divisions.[20] This exigency produced much discontent among the people of Arkansas. The Arkansas delegation in Congress complained bitterly to Davis, warning that the state would be easy prey for Missouri Federals.[21] Governor Rector stated that if the Trans-Mississippi states were to be abandoned they would recall their troops for defense.[22]

In answer, General P. G. T. Beauregard, now the ranking Confederate commander in the West, sent Major General Thomas C. Hindman (Portrait on Plate 6) into the region on May 26 with orders to raise an army. Having full authority to conscript troops under the Congressional Act of April 6, 1862,[23] Hindman divided the Trans-Mississippi into districts, detailed enrolling officers into each to draft men of military age who would not volunteer, and began to organize an army "to drive out the enemy or to perish in the attempt."[24] Hindman, a tireless worker, a first-class soldier, and an excellent administrator, would succeed in repelling the enemy.

Under the guiding hand of Hindman the dangerous practice of recruiting volunteer horsemen by expeditions into Federal Missouri began in the summer of 1862. One such expedition, commanded by Vard Cockrell and Joseph Orville Shelby, merits particular attention, for it was to result in the formation of the most famous cavalry brigade that fought in the Trans-Mississippi.

Jo Shelby (Portrait on Plate 9), born in Lexington, Kentucky, in 1831, had attended Transylvania College for three years and then moved out to Missouri. On the eve of the war he operated a rope factory at Waverly. Shelby was a stubborn and adventurous man, a born leader, and strongly proslavery in his beliefs. When he learned of the

---

[20] Albert Pike to [?], May 4, 1862, *Official Records*, ser. I, vol. XIII, 819–823; Abstract from Troop Returns of the Department of the Indian Territory, May, 1862, *ibid.*, p. 831; D. H. Maury to Roane, April 11, May 11, 1862, *ibid.*, pp. 813, 827.

[21] (April 15, 1862), *ibid.*, pp. 814–816.

[22] David Y. Thomas, *Arkansas in War and Reconstruction, 1861–1874*, pp. 139–147.

[23] Special Orders No. 59, May 26, 1862, *Official Records*, ser. I, vol. IX, 713. By the same order the Trans-Mississippi was made a full military department, comprising Missouri, Arkansas, Louisiana (west of the Mississippi), Texas, and the Indian Territory.

[24] An Address by Hindman to the Soldiers and Citizens of the District, May 31, 1862, *ibid.*, ser. I, vol. XIII, 830; Hindman to S. Cooper, June 19, 1863, *ibid.*, pp. 30–33.

battle of Fort Sumter he organized and equipped at his own expense a company of horsemen.[25] They joined the Missouri State Guard and gave invaluable service as cavalry scouts throughout the ill-fated Missouri campaign of 1861. A month after the battle at Pea Ridge, he and his company followed Van Dorn and Price across the River. In mid-April, his term in the Guards about to expire, Shelby requested permission to recruit a regiment of Confederate cavalry. He received approval from the War Department, and with his devoted company immediately left for Arkansas. After a long and hazardous trip, he arrived at Little Rock, whence he moved to join Cockrell near Van Buren, Arkansas.[26]

At Frog Bayou, on July 15, Cockrell and Shelby planned an expedition into Missouri, departing late that evening. After a week of strenuous riding their raiding column reached Grand Rapids, Missouri, and there split, Shelby heading for Dover while Cockrell turned west toward Independence. At Dover Shelby and his hardened troopers were received as liberators. Young girls "scattered flowers upon the road and flags among the soldiers," women wept "tears of intense joy," and fathers offered their "half grown sons" for service in Shelby's outfit.[27] The company encountered a similar response at Waverly in Lafayette County, the home of Shelby and his men, and the recruiting center for the new regiment. "From every portion of the surrounding countryside troops came pouring in for enlistment,"[28] so rapidly that in four days a thousand raw recruits were ready for the perilous ride back to Confederate Arkansas.[29]

While Shelby recruited at Waverly, Cockrell and his 800 horsemen, reinforced by two regiments under Upton Hays and John T. Coffee, stirred up a hornet's nest in Jackson County. At sunrise on August 16 they galloped with pistols blazing down the streets of Lone Jack to swamp 740 Federals under Major E. S. Foster, bivouacked at one end of town. Bloody hand-to-hand combat followed in the streets and

[25] Howard L. Conrad, ed., *Encyclopedia of the History of Missouri*, V, 577; Bennett H. Young, *Confederate Wizards of the Saddle* . . . , pp. 195–198; and Edwards, *Shelby and His Men*, pp. 28, 30.

[26] Edwards, *Shelby and His Men*, pp. 56–69.

[27] *Ibid.*, pp. 69, 72.

[28] *Ibid.*, p. 73; Shelby to John S. Marmaduke, October 27, 1862, *Official Records*, ser. I, vol. XIII, 979–980.

[29] Shelby to Marmaduke, October 27, 1862, *ibid.*, p. 980.

from house to house. Having cornered a small band of Federal sharp-shooters in the hotel, merciless Confederates set fire to the building, roasting the occupants alive. Major Foster's troops, thinking the yipping Confederates to be Quantrill's terrible guerrillas, fought fran-tically, but by afternoon were in complete rout. The next day 2,000 Federal cavalry under General Blunt reached Lone Jack and set out in hot pursuit of Cockrell's force, now racing for Arkansas.[30]

Two days later (August 18), Shelby's troopers, miles away at Waverly, stole out of town under cover of darkness, slipped past Federal patrols searching for them, and followed Cockrell. The ordeal that transpired was one of acute suffering. "The cohesive power of danger," recalled Major John N. Edwards, Shelby's adjutant,

is probably stronger than any other, and in all that long line of undisci-plined horsemen . . . not one faltered, not one missed answer in the constant roll calls. Rest and refuge were almost gained. Crazy and blinded from eight days and nights of uninterrupted watching, the command staggered in [sic] a camp on the little stream of Coon Creek, in Jasper county, to snatch a few hours' sleep before nightfall and before the march was resumed, for Captain Shelby had wisely determined to leave nothing to chance that might be accomplished by energy. To those unacquainted with the effects produced by loss of sleep, the sensations would be novel and almost incredible. About the third night an indescribable feeling settles down upon the brain. Every sound is distinct and painfully acute. The air seems filled with exquisite music; cities and towns rise up on every hand, crowned with spires and radiant with ten thousand beacons. Long lines of armed men are on every side, while the sound of bugles and harsh words of command are incessantly repeated. Often, upon almost boundless prairies, destitute of tree or bush, the tormented dozer turns suddenly from some fancied oak, or mechanically lowers his head to avoid the sweeping of pendent branches. Beyond the third night stolid stupor generally prevails, and an almost total insensibility to pain. . . . On the march men . . . dropped from the saddle unawakened by the fall, while on more than a dozen occasions his [Shelby's] rear guard pricked the lagging sleepers with sabers until the blood spouted, without changing a muscle of their blotched, bloated faces.[31]

[30] E. S. Foster to James Totten, May 1, 1863, *ibid.*, pp. 238–239; J. G. Blunt's report, August 20, 1862, *ibid.*, pp. 235–236, 238; Britton, *Civil War on the Border*, I, 335–342; and Jay Monaghan, *Civil War on the Western Border, 1854–1865*, pp. 255–256.

[31] Edwards, *Shelby and His Men*, p. 75.

The rest stop at Coon Creek was cut short. Shelby's scouts galloped into camp to report that Federal cavalry was approaching from the north.[32] The Confederates doused fires, grabbed rifles, and ran into the trees just ahead of the enemy that swarmed into the clearing. For several minutes a heated skirmish flared, with hissing bullets and clouds of blue powder smoke. The Confederates fired desperately at the enemy from behind rocks and trees. Soon the Yankees, having tried unsuccessfully to get in the Confederates' rear and suffering relatively heavy casualties, retired from Coon Creek. Shelby's men raced for their horses and rode to Elm Springs, Arkansas, then moved to McKissick's Springs, from there to Pineville, and finally to a cavalry camp on Elkhorn Creek, where Hays' and Coffee's Missouri regiments were bivouacked. On September 9, 1862, General Hindman arrived at camp and organized the three regiments into a brigade of over 2,000 men under the command of Colonel Shelby.[33] Thus was born the immortal "Iron Brigade" which would bring terror and destruction to Federal Missouri.

Other recruiting expeditions had produced results comparable to Shelby's. By September, 1862, five regiments, in addition to those in Shelby's brigade, had been raised for Hindman's army. These were the First Missouri Cavalry, Colonel Joseph C. Porter; the Third Missouri Cavalry, Colonel Colton Greene; the Fourth Missouri Cavalry, Colonel John Q. Burbridge; the Tenth Missouri Cavalry, Colonel Emmett McDonald; and Clark's Missouri Cavalry, Colonel H. E. Clark.[34]

Besides encouraging recruiting adventures in Missouri, General Hindman sanctioned the formation of appreciable numbers of partisan rangers.[35] These mounted bands of "irregulars"—the mildest Federal term for them was "guerrillas"—were meant to function behind

[32] Part of the Sixth Kansas. Britton, *Civil War on the Border*, I, 342.

[33] Shelby to Marmaduke, October 27, 1862, *Official Records*, ser. I, vol. XIII, 979.

[34] T. C. Hindman to S. Cooper, June 19, 1863, *ibid.*, pp. 43, 45; United States War Department, *List of Field Officers, Regiments and Battalions in the Confederate Army, 1861–1865*, pp. 42–47; and Organization of the Army of the Trans-Mississippi, December 12, 1862, *Official Records*, ser. I, vol. XXII, pt. I, 904.

[35] General Orders No. 17, June 17, 1862, *ibid.*, ser. I, vol. XIII, 835. The formation of partisan rangers had been authorized by the War Department on April 28, 1862. General Orders No. 30, *ibid.*, ser. IV, vol. I, 1094–1095.

enemy lines for the purpose of forcing the enemy to commit large forces to police duty.[36] Among the "lawless" guerrilla bands that fought as Confederates during the Civil War, the most legendary, perhaps, is the one of William Clarke Quantrill. Vicious, cunning, showing no quarter in battle, this notorious band "literally wrote . . . [its] name in blood across the western border" during 1862 and 1863.[37] Included in its ranks were men who would later become infamous as outlaws on the western frontier—Bud and Jim Younger, Dick Yager, and the two James boys, Jesse and Frank.

The leader of the band, William C. Quantrill, was born either in Canal Dover, Ohio, on July 31, 1837,[38] or Hagerstown, Maryland, on July 20, 1836.[39] As a young man he taught school for two years in the Canal vicinity[40] and then moved to Kansas in 1857. At Christmas, 1861, he formed a 10-man guerrilla band to avenge the bloody outrages committed by Federal irregulars under Jim Montgomery, Doc Jennison, and Jim Lane.[41] As the terrible guerrilla war raged across the borderland during the following year, Quantrill's band steadily increased, until it had by mid-August some 150 members, most of them mere youngsters craving revenge against the Yankee partisans or seeking "sheer excitement."[42] On August 14 the band, having crushed a Federal force twice its size at Independence, sought shelter from the enemy at the Morgan Walker farm. There it organized as a partisan ranger company, being sworn into Confederate service by Colonel G. W. Thompson. The men elected Quantrill to the Cap-

[36] See Ethelbert C. Barksdale, "Semi-Regular and Irregular Warfare in the Civil War," for an analysis of the purposes and results of partisan warfare during the war. See also Captain Kit Dalton, *Under the Black Flag: A Guerilla Captain under Quantrell and a Border Outlaw for Seventeen Years*, pp. 15–17, for the justification of guerrilla activity and for the philosophy of the partisan.

[37] Richard S. Brownlee, *Gray Ghosts of the Confederacy: Guerilla Warfare in the West, 1861–1865*, p. 53; Albert E. Castel, *A Frontier State at War: Kansas, 1861–1865*, pp. 102–106.

[38] William E. Connelley, *Quantrill and the Border Wars*, p. 42. It should be noted that the famous guerrilla was referred to as both Quantrell and Quantrill. Connelley wrote to condemn the man.

[39] John N. Edwards, *Noted Guerrillas*, p. 32.

[40] Allen Johnson and Dumas Malone, eds., *Dictionary of American Biography*, XV, 294.

[41] Connelley, *Quantrill*, pp. 200–201.

[42] John McCorkle, *Three Years with Quantrill: A True Story*, p. 35; Brownlee, *Gray Ghosts*, pp. 61, 62.

taincy.[43] Then Thompson gave Quantrill a captain's commission, under authority granted him by General Hindman.[44]

In the two months that followed the partisan company spread terror across the border, raiding Olathe, Kansas (September 6) and attacking numerous Federal garrisons in southwestern Missouri (October 6–16).[45] Having made Federal Kansas and Missouri "the scene of the most revolting hostilities,"[46] the triumphant band repaired in mid-November to Arkansas, where it joined Colonel Shelby's Iron Brigade.[47]

Though branded by the North as murderers and thieves, the desperate partisan cavalrymen led by Quantrill and other men such as George Todd, Bill Anderson, and John Thraikill, played a conspicuous part in the effort to carry the war into Missouri. General Hindman complimented the men for their work. In a departmental report which dealt considerably with partisan warfare, he said:

With the view to revive the hopes of loyal men in Missouri and to get troops from that State I gave authority to various persons to raise companies and regiments there and to operate as guerrillas. They soon became exceedingly active and rendered important services, destroying wagon trains and transports, tearing up railways, breaking telegraph lines, capturing towns, and thus compelling the enemy to keep there a large force that might have been employed elsewhere.[48]

While Confederates gathered volunteers in Missouri, cavalry officers in Hindman's command had also been at work recruiting in the other Trans-Mississippi states. The outfits raised in Texas by mid-September are listed in Table III.[49]

---

[43] McCorkle, *Three Years With Quantrill*, p. 23; John P. Burch, *Charles W. Quantrell: A True History of His Guerrilla Warfare on the Missouri and Kansas Border during the Civil War of 1861–1865*, pp. 77–95.

[44] T. C. Hindman to T. H. Holmes, November 3, 1862, *Official Records*, ser. I, vol. XIII, 48.

[45] Connelley, *Quantrill*, pp. 274–275; Brownlee, *Gray Ghosts*, p. 103.

[46] J. M. Schofield's report, December 10, 1863, *Official Records*, ser. I, vol. XXII, pt. I, 15.

[47] Connelley, *Quantrill*, p. 277.

[48] Hindman to S. Cooper, June 19, 1863, *Official Records*, ser. I, vol. XIII, 33.

[49] This chart was put together from numerous sources and works. Wooten, in his monumental *Comprehensive History of Texas*, II, 630, 631, 633, 636–637, 639–641, 642, 643, 644–645, gives the commanders, the approximate date of organization, and sometimes the organizational strength of each of the outfits

TABLE III

Confederate Cavalry Units Raised in Texas by Mid-September, 1862

Unit	Commander	Troops	Station
1st Partisan Ranger	W. P. Lane	1,000	Louisiana
13th Reg.	J. H. Burnett	900 (est.)	Arkansas
15th Reg.	G. W. Sweet	1,000	Tennessee
19th Reg.	N. M. Burford	850 (est.)	Arkansas
20th Reg.	T. C. Bass	850 (est.)	Arkansas
21st Reg.	G. W. Carter	800 (est.)	Arkansas
22nd Reg.	R. H. Taylor	873	Indian Territory
24th Reg.	F. C. Wilkes	900 (est.)	Arkansas
25th Reg.	C. C. Gillespie	900 (est.)	Arkansas
28th Reg.	Horace Randal	1,000	Arkansas
30th Reg.	E. J. Gurley	800 (est.)	Indian Territory
34th Reg.	A. M. Alexander	806	Indian Territory
35th Reg.	R. R. Brown	927	Texas
36th Reg.	P. C. Woods	823	Texas
46th Reg. (Frontier Reg.)	J. M. Norris	1,240	Texas
Waul's Legion (6 companies cav.)	T. N. Waul	1,100	Arkansas
3rd Bn.	W. O. Yager	404	Texas
8th Bn.	J. T. Taylor	407	Texas
11th Bn.	A. W. Spaight	400	Texas
13th Bn.	Ed Waller	450	Louisiana
Gano's Bn.	R. M. Gano	500	Kentucky
Total		16,930	

listed above. Albert Pike to [?], May 4, 1862, *Official Records*, ser. I, vol. XIII, 819–823, indicates that the Twenty-Second, Thirtieth, and Thirty-Fourth Texas Cavalry were stationed in the Indian Territory. The Organization of the Army of the Trans-Mississippi Department, December 13, 1862, *ibid.*, ser. I, vol. XXII, pt. I, 903, shows that these units were still there in the winter. The aggregate and effective strengths of the three regiments are in the Abstract from Troop Returns for the Department of the Indian Territory, May, 1862, *ibid.*, ser. I, vol. XIII, 831. P. O. Hébert's letter to H. H. Sibley, August 18, 1862, *ibid.*, ser. I, vol. IX, 729–730, reveals that the Thirtieth and Thirty-Sixth Regiments, the Third Battalion, the Eighth Battalion, the Thirteenth Battalion, and a number of independent companies were formed for Hindman's command by August 18, 1862. This letter also gives the station of these units. Special Orders No. 39, September 28, 1862, *ibid.*, ser. I, vol. XIII, 884, lists the Thirteenth, Fifteenth, Nineteenth, Twenty-Second, Twenty-Fourth, Twenty-Fifth, and Twenty-Eighth Texas Regiments, and Gould's Battalion as having been raised for Hindman's army. Abstracts from Troop Returns from the First District of Texas, October and November, 1862, *ibid.*, ser. I, vol. XV, 851, 870–871, show the strengths of the Thirty-Sixth Regiment, the Third and Eighth Battalions, and several companies, all stationed in Texas. Hindman's report to S. Cooper, June 19, 1863, *ibid.*, ser. I, vol. XIII, 43, mentions the number of Texas cavalry regiments formed in the summer of 1862. Walter P. Lane in his *Adventures and Recollections*, pp. 104–105, describes the formation of the First

In addition to these outfits there were sixteen independent cavalry companies, two battalions, and one unattached regiment, a total of 2,677 effectives, stationed at various points in Texas for home guard purposes.[50]

In comparison to Texas, Louisiana had produced little in the way of cavalry—three regiments, two battalions, and several independent companies by late October, 1862. On September 15 Colonel William G. Vincent mustered ten companies, a total of 908 men, into service as the Second Louisiana Cavalry.[51] Colonel Vincent was a little man who had a large nose and wore spectacles. He looked more like a clerk than a cavalry commander.[52] He was a good fighter, however, and he was a valuable addition to Richard Taylor's Army of Western Louisiana. The next month, Colonel James H. Wingfield organized the First

---

Regiment, Texas Partisan Rangers, in the summer of 1862. The arrival of Waller's Thirteenth Battalion in Louisiana (probably in the early fall of 1862) was mentioned in Taylor's *Destruction and Reconstruction*, p. 130. Brown, *History of Texas*, II, 417, has a terse essay on the formation of the Thirteenth and Twentieth Regiments. The Dallas (Texas) *Herald*, June 21, 1862, mentions the Nineteenth Regiment as having bivouacked near Dallas in June to obtain arms. The outfit was then en route to Arkansas. Since De Bray's Twenty-Sixth Cavalry and Hawpe's Thirty-First Cavalry were discussed earlier in the chapter, they were not listed above. During the fall of 1862, De Bray's unit was stationed near Galveston and Hawpe's in northwestern Arkansas.

[50] These were Captains Durant's and Andrew's companies (70 men each) at Virginia Point; Captain Bowles' company (70 men) near Galveston; Captain Daley's partisan company (70 men) at Fredericksburg; Captain Rhode's company (70 men), Captain Santos Benavides' company (76 men), Captain Refugio Benavides' company (79 men), and Captain James Duff's two partisan companies (142 men all told), all in the San Antonio vicinity; Captain J. A. Ware's company (83 men) at Corpus Christi; Captain J. T. Brackenridge's company (79 men) at Lavaca; Captain A. Navarro's company (80 men) at Atascosa; Captain Simmes' Bayou Cavalry (60 men) near Houston; Morgan's Point Cavalry (76 men); Harrisburg Cavalry (708 men) at Harrisburg; cavalry company at Beaumont (150 men); four cavalry companies at Matagorda (294 men); and Lieutenant Colonel Hardeman's Arizona Cavalry (500 men) at Columbus. Hébert to Sibley, August 18, 1862, *Official Records*, ser. I, vol. XI, 731; H. O. Bee's Subdistrict of the Rio Grande, State of Forces, November 1, 1862, *ibid.*, ser. I, vol. XV, 851; and Abstract from Troop Returns of the First District of Texas (including a breakdown of the forces in X. B. De Bray's Houston Subdistrict), November, 1862, *ibid.*, pp. 883–884.

[51] Andrew B. Booth, comp., *Records of Louisiana Confederate Soldiers and Louisiana Confederate Commands*, III, bk. II, 938; Louisiana Adjutant General, *Annual Report, 1891*, p. 35.

[52] George C. Harding, *Miscellaneous Writings*, p. 321.

Louisiana Partisan Rangers by adding three companies from east Louisiana to the seven companies in his battalion of partisan rangers. The aggregate of the regiment at organization was 852 men.[53] The Third Louisiana Cavalry, born late in October from a mysterious and unfortunate chain of events in the Delhi vicinity (later known as the Delhi Fiasco), was composed of several partisan companies and a former battalion under Lieutenant Colonel Samuel L. Chambliss. The Third numbered 810 troops. Colonel J. Frank Pargoud was the commander. Because of the fiasco under which it came into being, the regiment broke up on January 16, 1863, and Chambliss' battalion was restored to its original organization.[54] The rest of the outfits formed by late October comprised Major W. H. Bayliss' Battalion of Partisan Rangers, organized in July, 1862, in eastern Louisiana; Miles Legion Cavalry Contingent, Captain John W. Jones; the Second Cavalry Company, Captain J. Duncan Stuart; the Third Company, New River Rangers, Captain Joseph Gonzales; Nutt's Company, Captain L. M. Nutt, attached to Garland's Texas Infantry Brigade in Arkansas; and Denson's Company, Captain W. B. Denson, also attached to Garland's Brigade.[55]

In Arkansas three regiments and two battalions of cavalry had by September, 1862, been raised for Hindman's army. Near Devall's Bluff, Colonel Thomas J. Morgan had mustered a cavalry battalion sometime in June and joined Hindman at Little Rock. The next month three more companies had been raised by Morgan's recruiters and

---

[53] Louisiana Adjutant General, *Annual Report, 1891*, pp. 36–37.

[54] The affair at Delhi is a bit confusing. It appears that Brigadier General Albert G. Blanchard, commander of Confederate forces in the Delhi area, had early in November forced Chambliss' battalion to become a part of a regiment commanded by Pargoud. This had aroused much discontent among Chambliss' men. (Edward Sparrow to James A. Seddon, January 19, 1863, *Official Records*, ser. I, vol. XI, 952–953.) Colonel Pargoud, recommended to Taylor as a worthy and valuable officer, had so poorly executed his orders to deploy his troops to stop Federal incursions in the Dallas-Delhi vicinity that Taylor on January 16, 1863, relieved him of his command. Chambliss' battalion was then restored to its original organization. "The whole affair," Taylor lamented later, "was disgraceful to the service in the extreme." He placed most of the blame for the "fiasco" on the incompetent General Blanchard. Richard Taylor to James Seddon, February 19, 1863, *ibid.*, pp. 983–984; and W. L. Riddick to J. F. Pargoud, November 25, 1862, *ibid.*, p. 954.

[55] Louisiana Adjutant General, *Annual Report, 1891*, pp. 37–40.

attached to the outfit, making it a full regiment (designated the Second Arkansas, successor to Newton's Fifth Arkansas, its term of enlistment having expired).[56] On September 1, Colonel James C. Monroe's Arkansas Cavalry Regiment, numbering about 1,000, was formed by the merger of Wheat's and Johnston's battalions near Arkansas Post.[57] Other Arkansas cavalry raised for Hindman's command were Crawford's Regiment, Colonel W. A. Crawford; Wright's Battalion, Lieutenant Colonel J. C. Wright; and Chrisman's Battalion, Major F. M. Chrisman.[58]

The tremendous surge of volunteers for cavalry service in the summer and fall of 1862 was due largely to strict enforcement of the draft laws.[59] Thousands of men of draft age, regarding conscription as an utter disgrace, flocked to enlisting centers. Most of these men, especially the Texans, requested cavalry service. This preference resulted in a lack of sufficient numbers of infantry, a situation which forced the high command to convert much of the Texas cavalry into infantry. Late in August, 1862, Robert S. Gould's Texas Battalion, raised in early summer in Leon and surrounding counties, was dismounted at Houston, the horses being sent home.[60] On September 28, the battalion was merged with Colonel N. H. Darnell's Eighteenth Texas and Colonel R. H. Taylor's Twenty-Second, all dismounted, to form an infantry brigade under Brigadier General Allison Nelson (later to be commanded by Colonel James Deshler). This brigade was stationed in northwestern Arkansas. Also on September 28, the departmental command ordered Colonel Horace Randal to dismount his Twenty-Eighth Texas Cavalry and to form an infantry brigade

[56] Cook, "List of General and Field Officers, Arkansas Troops, C.S.A., and State Troops," *Publications of the Arkansas Historical Association,* I, 421.

[57] Fay Hempstead, *A Pictorial History of Arkansas from Earliest Times to the Year 1890,* p. 363.

[58] T. C. Hindman to S. Cooper, June 19, June 29, 1863, *Official Records,* ser. I, vol. XIII, 43–45; Cook, "List of General and Field Officers, Arkansas Troops, C.S.A., and State Troops," *Publications of the Arkansas Historical Association,* I, 412–422.

[59] For a survey of the application of the draft laws in the region, see Margaret N. Goodlet, "The Enforcement of the Confederate Conscription Acts in the Trans-Mississippi Department."

[60] William D. Wood, comp., *A Partial Roster of the Officers and Men Raised in Leon County, Texas, for the Service of the Confederate States . . . ,* pp. 8–9.

consisting of his regiment and three infantry regiments. The brigade was to operate in northwestern Arkansas. The same was true of Colonel F. C. Wilkes' Twenty-Fourth Texas Cavalry and Colonel C. C. Gillespie's Twenty-Fifth Texas Cavalry which were dismounted by the departmental commander and attached to Garland's infantry brigade. Two other regiments converted to infantry were Colonel J. H. Burnett's Thirteenth Texas, assigned to Young's infantry brigade, and Colonel William Fitzhugh's Sixteenth Texas, recently returned from Mississippi, which was placed in T. B. Flourney's infantry brigade.[61]

The troopers did not take the dismounting lightly. They had bought their horses expecting active cavalry service, and here the army was, telling them to get down off their own property and fight on foot as infantry. They griped and moaned, threatened to desert if they were not remounted, and wrote home about the awful way the army was treating them. Being converted to lowly "mud sloggers," or "web-feet," was about the worst thing that could be done to good cavalrymen. But their entreaties were to no avail, and for the rest of the war they fought on foot, calling themselves "dismounted cavalry" rather than infantry.[62]

By the end of October, 1862, General Hindman had a field army of 6,600 horsemen (including dismounted cavalry) and 6,500 infantry.[63] Clearly the efficiency and swiftness with which this impressive force had been raised were due to the superb generalship of Tom Hindman. But this fine officer had not lasted long as commander of the Trans-Mississippi Department. His ambitious plans for carrying the war into Missouri and thus open a third front in the Confederacy, his strict enforcement of the draft, his zealous promotion of guerrilla warfare, and his use of martial law had apparently been too much for Confederate authorities in Richmond. On July 26 he had been replaced with deaf old Theophilus H. "Granny" Holmes (Portrait on Plate 5), who "limped over from Richmond, possessory orders in his

[61] General Orders No. 39, September 28, 1862, *Official Records*, ser. I, vol. XIII, 884; Abstract from Troop Returns, District of Arkansas, December 12, 1862, *ibid.*, ser. I, vol. XXII, pt. I, 904.

[62] Letter to Captain Edmund P. Turner, September 30, 1863, *Official Records*, ser. I, vol. XXVI, pt. II, 278–279.

[63] Thomas, *Arkansas in War and Reconstruction*, pp. 153–154.

pocket, and a lieutenant general's stars upon his collar."[64] Hindman was demoted to Ben McCulloch's old position as field commander of Confederate armies in Arkansas with stern orders from Holmes not to take the offensive.[65]

Under this new command, the process of organizing into brigades the cavalry raised under General Hindman began in the fall of 1862. Most of this organizing was encouraged by Hindman, who meant to have his cavalry fight in compact units under cavalry brigadiers. He was responsible for the formation of Shelby's famous brigade. He urged Holmes to form more cavalry brigades, and the departmental commander responded. Early in September, Colonel William H. Parsons' Twelfth Texas Cavalry, Colonel George Washington Carter's Twenty-First Texas Cavalry, and Lieutenant Colonel Chrisman's battalion (four companies) were organized at Cotton Plant, Arkansas, into Parsons' Texas Brigade, numbering 1,110 effectives.[66] The brigade served in General Henry E. McCulloch's division in Arkansas[67] until ordered to General Richard Taylor's army in Louisiana early in 1863.

Near Fort Smith, on about September 15, Charles A. Carroll's First Arkansas Cavalry, Colonel James C. Monroe's Arkansas Cavalry, Colonel William A. Crawford's Arkansas Cavalry, and probably Lieutenant Colonel John C. Wright's Arkansas Battalion were merged into the Arkansas Cavalry Brigade, Colonel Carroll becoming commander.[68] Troop returns for September 17, 1862, show that the brigade had 3,828 men present for duty.[69]

At about the same time, Bradfute's Texas Brigade came into being with the merger of Colonel Thomas C. Bass' Twentieth Texas Cavalry, Colonel T. C. Hawpe's Thirty-First Texas Cavalry, Colonel A. M.

[64] Edwards, *Shelby and His Men*, p. 109; Special Orders No. 164, July 16, 1862, *Official Records*, ser. I, vol. XIII, 855.

[65] General Orders No. 39, September 28, 1862, *ibid.*, p. 884; T. C. Hindman to T. H. Holmes, November 3, 1862, *ibid.*, p. 48.

[66] General Orders No. 39, September 28, 1862, *ibid.*, p. 884; Abstract from Troop Returns, District of Arkansas, September 17, 1862, *ibid.*, p. 881.

[67] Special Orders No. 42, September 30, 1862, *ibid.*, p. 978.

[68] T. C. Hindman to S. Cooper, June 19, 1862, *ibid.*, p. 884; C. A. Carroll to E. G. Williams, November 29, 1862, *ibid.*, ser. I, vol. XXII, pt. I, 53; Organization of the Army of the Trans-Mississippi, December 12, 1862, *ibid.*, p. 903.

[69] *Ibid.*, ser. I, vol. XIII, 881.

Alexander's Thirty-Fourth Texas Cavalry, and Lieutenant Colonel G. S. Guess' Thirty-First Texas Battalion. Colonel W. R. Bradfute commanded the brigade.[70]

The Departmental Command formed two more brigades in October. Colonel M. J. White's Missouri Brigade, composed of the Third Missouri Cavalry under Colonel Colton Greene and the Fourth Missouri Cavalry under Colonel John Q. Burbridge, was probably organized early in October. The brigade became a part of Thomas J. Churchill's Second Division, Second Corps, Army of the Trans-Mississippi.[71] At Hempstead, Texas, on October 28, 1862, three of the four regiments which had made up the defunct Army of New Mexico[72] formed a new brigade. The next month Colonel Tom "Daddy" Green of the Fifth Texas became brigade commander.[73] Green was an able officer and certainly worthy of brigade command. A man of "boundless courage" and "fortitude," he had displayed a brilliant understanding of cavalry tactics during Sibley's New Mexico campaign and had gained the trust and admiration of his men.[74]

On October 28, 1862, General Hindman ordered the brigades of Bradfute and Shelby, stationed near Fayetteville, Arkansas, to organize into the first division of cavalry in the Trans-Mississippi.[75] This was a landmark in the two years of recruiting and organizing in the region. Hindman placed the division under the command of General John Sappington Marmaduke (Portrait on Plate 8), a Southern aristocrat and native of Missouri.

[70] T. C. Hindman to T. H. Holmes, November 3, 1862, *ibid.*, p. 48; Organization of the Army of the Trans-Mississippi, December 12, 1862, *ibid.*, ser. I, vol. XXII, pt. I, 904.

[71] *Ibid.*

[72] These regiments, it will be recalled, were Colonel John R. Baylor's Second Texas Mounted Rifles, Colonel James R. Reily's Fourth Texas Cavalry, Colonel Tom Green's Fifth Texas Cavalry, and Colonel William Steele's Seventh Texas Cavalry. Baylor's regiment was not a part of the new brigade.

[73] S.S. Anderson to G. M. Bryan, T. H. Holmes to Bryan, October 18, 1862, *Official Records*, ser. I, vol. XV, 833; J. H. McLeary, "History of Green's Brigade," in *Comprehensive History of Texas*, II, 695–740. The brigade was ordered to Taylor's command in Louisiana on January 20, 1863. Special Orders No. 16, *Official Records*, ser. I, vol. XV, 954.

[74] Young, *Confederate Wizards of the Saddle*, pp. 169–170; Francis R. Lubbock, *Six Decades in Texas* . . . , p. 536; Sidney South Johnson, *Texans Who Wore the Gray*, pp. 67–68.

[75] T. C. Hindman to T. H. Holmes, November 3, 1862, *Official Records*, ser. I, vol. XIII, 48.

Hindman expected Marmaduke to be a capable cavalry brigadier. A West Point graduate, he had served under A. S. Johnston in the Utah Campaign. When war broke out he had resigned from the United States Army and joined the Missouri State Guards, rising to the rank of colonel. Going from there into Confederate service, he was placed under his old chief, A. S. Johnston, whom he followed through the bitter campaigning in Kentucky and Mississippi. Good fighting had earned him a brigadier general's commission,[76] and Hindman had asked for his transfer to the Trans-Mississippi.[77]

In late October, 1862, the division of cavalry at Marmaduke's disposal amounted to 1,068 men in Shelby's brigade, weakened from sicknesses reported to be increasing "100 per day,"[78] and four skeleton regiments in Bradfute's brigade. A few days later Bradfute's regiments, which were, in Hindman's opinion, "worthless as cavalry," were dismounted to be reformed into two large infantry regiments.[79] Colonel Charles A. Carroll's Arkansas Brigade then joined the cavalry division, bringing its total strength to perhaps 5,000.

As 1862 drew to a close, most of the cavalrymen who fought the war were now in the field. Recruiting of new regiments declined after 1862 and came to a complete halt in 1864. Volunteers and the few horsemen that were drafted in 1863 were assigned to old outfits to keep them up to effective strength.[80] With five brigades and one division, the cavalry, in December, 1862, was ready to fulfill the purpose of cavalry—to campaign and raid in organizations large enough to be effective, self-sustaining, and independent of need for infantry support. To Tom Hindman goes the credit of making the cavalry useful instead of ornamental. Because of this man a new day had dawned for the cavalry. Mounted units had been taken away from infantry brigadiers. The generals must do without their couriers and escorts. Hindman had made the cavalry in the Trans-Mississippi an arm of the service.

[76] Johnson and Malone, *Dictionary of American Biography*, XXII, 290; Conrad, *Encyclopedia of the History of Missouri*, V, 199.

[77] Special Orders No. 39, September 28, 1862, *Official Records*, ser. I, vol. XIII, 884.

[78] J. O. Shelby to John S. Marmaduke, October 27, 1862, *ibid.*, p. 980.

[79] Hindman to Holmes, November 3, 1862, *ibid.*, p. 48.

[80] See Appendix A.

FOOD AND CLOTHING

Once having gathered the volunteers, unit commanders were faced with the problem of how to obtain the basic needs of food and clothing. Arms and mounts might perhaps be supplied in a more leisurely manner, but clothes and especially food must be had at once. From the outset, state governments and the Confederate War Department were unable to supply these needs, and outfits were forced to provide for themselves. Commanders attached officers to their staffs who were charged with the transporting, clothing, arming, and feeding of the troops. This arrangement extended down to the company level, with commissary, ordnance, and quartermaster sergeants handling such matters.

At rendezvous and training camps cavalry outfits were fed by contributions from citizen committees or from private sources. Company A of the First Arkansas Cavalry, encamped at Van Buren in May, 1861, and Captain J. B. McCown's Company of Sibley's Brigade, bivouacked at Bellville, Texas, during September, 1861, subsisted for weeks upon gifts of beef, ham, bacon, flour, salt, coffee, tea, peas, and other vegetables.[1]

Once cavalry units left for duty, they had more difficulty in obtaining food. Poor transportation facilities in most areas impeded receipt of commissary stores, and communities generally were reluctant to donate provisions to strange outfits. From Brownsville, Texas, in May, 1861, Colonel John S. "Rip" Ford, commander of the Second

[1] Van Buren (Arkansas) *Press*, May 22, 1861; Bellville (Texas) *Countryman*, September 11, 1861.

52

Texas Cavalry, wrote to Governor Clark that "we have used every effort in our power to procure supplies, and to all appearances we can hope for success no longer."[2] The next month Ford managed to obtain meat and flour through contracts with local merchants, but in amounts scarcely enough to feed adequately his 800 troopers.[3]

Frequently, outfits on patrol duty in the more remote areas were forced to supplement their food supply with wild game and whatever else they could obtain from the country through which they moved. While stationed on the northern Texas frontier, the Lane Rangers lived largely upon turkey, deer, antelope, and even prairie dog.[4] Down along the Rio Grande the Thirty-Second Texas Cavalry roped and butchered beeves from roving herds, giving vouchers for them to the Mexican owners.[5] In the western areas of the region, meat was preserved by "jerking" it, that is, by cutting it into long, thin slices which were strung by ropes to dry in the sun. No salt was needed.[6] Meat thus prepared would never spoil and obviously became a major portion of the cavalryman's daily ration. In Louisiana and in the eastern areas of Arkansas the horseman's meat diet consisted largely of salted meat or blue beef, and to a lesser extent mutton and pork.[7]

When flour was available the horseman, usually short of proper cooking utensils, was likely to manufacture biscuits by mixing a dough, rolling it out to "about the size and shape of a snake," coiling it around a small stick or ramrod, and then roasting it over an open fire.[8] Another method was to roll the dough up in a "wet shuck" for

[2] Texas Adjutant General, *Report, November, 1861*, p. 7.

[3] *Ibid.*, pp. 7–8; Texas Governor, March 16—November 7, 1861 (Edward Clark), *Governor's Message to the Senators and Representatives of the Ninth Legislature of the State of Texas, November 1, 1861*, p. 1.

[4] William W. Heartsill, *Fourteen Hundred and Ninety-One Days in the Confederate Army: or, Camp Life, Day by Day, of the W. P. Lane Rangers from April 19, 1861 to May 20, 1865*, pp. 37, 38, 39.

[5] H. A. Graves, *Andrew Jackson Potter: The Fighting Parson of the Texas Frontier . . .*, pp. 137–138.

[6] Heartsill, *Fourteen Hundred and Ninety-One Days*, pp. 26–27.

[7] John Q. Anderson, *A Texas Surgeon in the C.S.A.*, p. 26; General Orders No. 40, June 9, 1864, Confederate States Army, Trans-Mississippi Department, *General Orders, Headquarters, Trans-Mississippi Department, from March 6, 1863, to January 1, 1865*, pp. 32–33. Hereafter cited as *General Orders of the Trans-Mississippi Department*.

[8] Samuel B. Barron, *The Lone Star Defenders: A Chronicle of the Third Texas Cavalry, Ross' Brigade*, p. 36.

deposit in the hot embers of the fire. The product was called "hot doger."[9]

Far removed from commissary depots, cavalry out in the Indian Territory lived exclusively upon wild game or beef and flour.[10] During the winter of 1863–1864, a temporary shortage of meat induced Stand Watie's troopers to refer to their winter camp in Choctaw Country as "Camp Starvation." But in spite of the misery of a cold and stormy winter and the lack of meat, some of Watie's men maintained their sense of humor. In a letter to the Colonel's wife, the brigade adjutant wrote that

The Colonel started on a scout yesterday with a crowd of Cherokees, Creeks, Chickasaws, and white vagabounds [sic] and Border Ruffians and with reasonable luck will return after having burnt up Gibson. . . . The Cherokees were sent up here to keep the dogs off and since we came here, a few straggling Chickasaws and Creeks have got into our camp to get something to eat and the Colonel no doubt having in mind the Scripture injunction that man should eat his bread in the sweat of his face concluded that the best thing he could do with them was to take them along with him and make them sweat. . . . You will receive by Mr. Matlock, a Bedstead, Table, some chairs, a sack of coffee, some soap, candles, pepper, rice, and Desicated [sic] Mixed Vegetables. This latter article is intended to season soup with though I believe the article itself will make very good soup as the Boys say they find it composed of hindlegs of bull-frogs, Snails, Screwworms, etc.[11]

The cavalryman could justly complain of the quality of his diet much of the time, but extreme privation seldom occurred except during strenuous campaigning. Troops might then be cut off from commissary supplies and forced to subsist upon whatever they could find, good or bad, if they could find anything. For example, the men of Jo Shelby's Iron Brigade, returning from operations in Missouri

[9] Heartsill, *Fourteen Hundred and Ninety-One Days*, p. 229.

[10] William Steele to S. S. Anderson, February 15, 1864, *Official Records*, ser. I, vol. XXII, pt. I, 30.

[11] Thomas F. Anderson to Mrs. Watie, October 27, 1863, Cherokee Letters in the Phillips Collection of the Library of the University of Oklahoma, as cited in Edward Everett Dale, "The Cherokees in the Confederacy," *Journal of Southern History*, XIII (May, 1947), 181.

during which they had gone for days without food,[12] resorted to stealing hogs and beeves from loyal Confederate farmers around Batesville, Arkansas. One officer recalled an incident involving the Colonel himself.

On that raid we were half-starving, and Shelby and I rode down to the White River to water our horses. A detachment of the troops was doing the same thing just below us. Among them was Dick Gentry. He was a gallant private and a good fellow. Slung across his saddle was a sack, carefully tied and bleeding at one end. Shelby demanded what he had got there.

"Been having my clothes washed," said Gentry.

"You'd better get back to camp," said Shelby, "or your clothes will bleed to death."

Gentry was lodged in the guardhouse at Shelby's order. That night a quarter of fresh pork found its way to Shelby's headquarters. Shelby looked at it and said, "I haven't an idea where this comes from, but go round to the guardhouse, orderly, and tell 'em to turn Gentry loose. No use keeping a man shut up all his life for a little laundry."[13]

The campaigns in Louisiana and Arkansas during 1864 gave rise to numerous reports of starvation and looting. Half-crazed from hunger, the men of De Bray's Twenty-Sixth Texas Cavalry ransacked homes to get food and stole cows and hogs.[14] Troopers in Brooks' Texas Cavalry Regiment, having lived for several months on nothing but parched corn, thieved hogs and beeves from farms along the lower branch of the Arkansas River.[15]

Rather than resort to looting, some troopers during campaigns sought to trick farmers into giving them food. The Third Texas Cavalry, while marching through Madison County, Arkansas, after the battle of Pea Ridge, sent foragers to scour the country and to "beg

[12] John S. Marmaduke to R. C. Newton, February 1, 1863, *Official Records*, ser. I, vol. XII, 197–198; John N. Edwards, *Shelby and His Men: or, The War in the West*, p. 147.

[13] Interview with Jake Stonestreet, Kansas City Star, February 14, 1897, as quoted in Daniel O'Flaherty, *General Jo Shelby: Undefeated Rebel*, p. 168. A slightly different version of this incident, said to have occurred in 1864, is in Wilfred R. Hollister and Harry Norman, *Five Famous Missourians*, p. 373.

[14] Graves, *Andrew Jackson Potter*, pp. 165–166.

[15] Joe M. Scott, *Four Years' Service in the Southern Army*, pp. 63–64.

[the people] for a little food 'for sick and wounded men.' " One man recalled that

the sorrowful tales that were told in behalf of the poor sick and wounded soldiers we were hauling along in ambulances, with nothing with which to feed them, would have melted a heart of stone. The ruse was a success, as the details came in at night with divers small contributions made from scant stores for "the sick and wounded men," which were ravenously consumed by the well ones.[16]

Of course, as was said, food was not always short. When the infrequent supply trains did make it to the front, the men would receive plenty of salt or dried meat, flour or corn meal, desiccated vegetables, fresh potatoes, and molasses, soap, and candles.[17] But during the long weeks and sometimes months between such "ration days" the staples of life were beef and corn meal.

How to procure adequate clothing proved in the long run a more difficult problem than that of securing food. Compelled at the outset to admit its incompetence to provide uniforms, the Richmond government simply stated that initial clothing supply was the responsibility of the states and of the volunteers themselves.[18] But the states were equally impotent. Manufacturing of textiles or clothing was slight in the Trans-Mississippi, and large expansion under wartime conditions was next to impossible. In the absence of a well-organized and efficient quartermaster department during the first two years, private citizens and the troopers themselves furnished most of the clothing for the cavalry.[19]

Probably the largest source of clothing was the innumerable women's organizations that began to be formed almost concurrently with the raising of the first regiments. In Marshall, Texas, four committees were set up on July 31, 1861, to collect blankets, socks, shoes,

[16] Barron, *Lone Star Defenders*, p. 75.

[17] Anderson, *A Texas Surgeon in the C.S.A.*, p. 26; General Orders No. 40, June 9, 1864, *General Orders of the Trans-Mississippi Department*, pp. 32–33; Heartsill, *Fourteen Hundred and Ninety-One Days*, p. 52; and Joseph P. Blessington, *The Campaigns of Walker's Texas Division*, p. 42.

[18] An Act to Provide for the Public Defense, March 6, 1861, *Official Records*, ser. IV, vol. I, 126; L. P. Walker to H. M. Rector; Walker to Edward Clark, August 7, 1861, *ibid.*, p. 534.

[19] James Lynn Nichols, "Confederate Quartermaster Operations in the Trans-Mississippi Department," pp. 8, 20, 44–45, 123–124.

hats, and miscellaneous items to be sent to the Lane Rangers, then on their way for duty on the Texas frontier.[20] Clothing for McIntosh's, Carroll's, and Churchill's Arkansas cavalry regiments came from the citizens of northwestern Arkansas, who donated not only every piece of material they had that could be converted into clothing, but also blankets, curtains, and carpets for bedding.[21] The cavalry companies raised at Fort Smith, and even some that rendezvoused there, were supplied with uniforms made by the women living in the community.[22]

In other communities Ladies' Aid Societies were organized to make uniforms and collect accessory items which might add to the comfort of the troopers. By November, 1861, the Ladies' Aid Society of the Lancaster vicinity had collected and sent to B. W. Stone's Texas Cavalry Regiment coats, jeans, flannel and linsey shirts, winter drawers, winter vests, boots, shoes, woolen mittens, bed comforters, blankets, and other items, valued at $1,676.50.[23]

Volunteers provided much of their own attire, receiving an allowance for it when they were mustered-in.[24] Fearing that they would be inadequately supplied, men who joined the Lane Rangers at Marshall, Texas, April, 1861, brought with them an incredible array of clothing and miscellaneous items. W. W. Heartsill recalled that upon his horse "Pet" there were

myself, saddle, bridle, saddle-blanket, curry comb, horse brush, coffee pot, tin cup, 20 lbs ham, 200 biscuit, 5 lbs ground coffee, 5 lbs sugar, one large pound cake .... 6 shirts, 6 prs socks, 3 prs drawers, 2 prs pants, 2 jackets, 1 pr heavy mud boots, one Colt's revolver, one small dirk, four blankets, sixty foot of rope, with a twelve inch iron pin attached; with all these, and divers and sundry little mementoes from friends.[25]

Other troopers were similarly furnished. As they rode out of Marshall, Heartsill reflected that "an old Texas Ranger would rather think us a Caravan, crossing the desert, with a tremendious [sic] stock of mer-

[20] Ernest Berglund, Jr., *History of Marshall* [Texas], p. 19.

[21] Fay Hempstead, *Historical Review of Arkansas*, I, 218.

[22] Fort Smith (Arkansas) *Daily Times and Herald*, July 18, 1861.

[23] Dallas (Texas) *Herald*, November 10, 1861.

[24] *Official Records*, ser. IV, vol. I, 126; An Act Concerning the Transportation of Soldiers, and Allowance for Clothing of Volunteers ..., May 21, 1861, *ibid.*, p. 340.

[25] Heartsill, *Fourteen Hundred and Ninety-One Days*, p. 5.

chandise; than a regularly organized Company going out Indian hunting in the far west."[26]

Winter demands for additional clothing and blankets forced the quartermaster for General Ben McCulloch's army, encamped at Van Buren, Arkansas, to appeal for contributions from the citizens and merchants of Arkansas. A receiver assigned to each town was to package the articles donated and send them to Fort Smith.[27] Contributions being slow, the quartermaster soon appointed two agents to purchase clothing and blankets, the costs to be deducted from the soldiers' pay.[28] The quartermaster also requested contributions from Texas.[29] In Dallas and contiguous counties, citizens working in collaboration filled three wagons with clothes, transmitting them to Greer's Third Texas Cavalry of McCulloch's army.[30]

Late in 1861 Rip Ford's Second Texas Cavalry was deplorably short of clothing. Since being stationed on the Texas frontier, it had received no contributions from the people of the state. Captain H. A. Hamner, commander of one of the frontier forts, lamented that his troopers were "near literally naked, and without shoes and socks." To remedy this the ladies of Jackson County set about collecting clothes and blankets to be sent to the regiment.[31]

In January, 1862, Sibley's army in New Mexico was "thinly clad, and almost destitute of blankets." Sibley later complained that his troops had fought through the entire campaign without a dollar of help from the quartermaster department.[32] Upon returning to Texas, however, the men received large contributions of clothing from the Ladies' Southern Aid Society of San Antonio.[33]

Shortages of warm clothing for cavalrymen became still more acute during the exceptionally cold winter of 1862. The men of Shelby's Iron Brigade, encamped for the winter at Camp Marmaduke,

[26] *Ibid.*

[27] Van Buren (Arkansas) *Press*, September 18, 1861.

[28] *Ibid.*, October 9, 1861.

[29] One example of these requests is in Dallas (Texas) *Herald*, November 25, 1861.

[30] Van Buren (Arkansas) *Press*, October 31, 1861.

[31] Bellville (Texas) *Countryman*, November 13, 1861.

[32] H. H. Sibley to S. Cooper, May 4, 1862, *Official Records*, ser. I, vol. IX, 507.

[33] Lois Council Ellsworth, "San Antonio during the Civil War," p. 97.

Arkansas, were in great need of blankets, overcoats, shoes, and socks. Shelby complained to Marmaduke that "we have never drawn any clothing, shoes, salt, or anything else" from the quartermaster department. What little clothing the men had they had collected for themselves.[34] Many of the Texas and Arkansas cavalry regiments were in the same condition. Unit commanders sent special agents to home counties to request contributions.[35]

The agent for Darnell's Eighteenth Texas Cavalry, then stationed in northwestern Arkansas, returned on September 13 to Dallas, where he placed in the *Herald* an urgent request for clothes. Items specified were flannel, linsey, shoes, hats, leather, or additional clothing of "any description whatever." He would pay for clothing upon delivery.[36]

From Camp Walker, Arkansas, a soldier of Hawpe's Thirty-First Texas Cavalry wrote the Dallas *Herald* describing the suffering of the troops and urging citizens to provide clothing.

Chill winter is now at hand, and, with it, hard, heavy, severe suffering for the soldier. . . . We are far, far from home. Will our kind friends, our countrymen, the good people of Texas, help aid and assist us with clothing for the winter? One pair of good yarn socks, may prevent a soldier's feet from being frozen and save him to his country. . . . How would your hearts rejoice to know that you had saved one poor soldier from the pangs of the cripled [*sic*]?[37]

Agents from the Thirty-First Texas Cavalry, their activities authorized by the quartermaster department, were sent to Dallas and Austin to receive contributions.[38]

Similar appeals were made on behalf of Arkansas cavalry units.[39] The Third Arkansas, having lost most of its possessions in the battle of Corinth, Mississippi, sent an officer to Benton, Arkansas, to attempt to collect blankets and clothing.[40]

[34] J. O. Shelby to J. S. Marmaduke, October 27, 1862, *Official Records*, ser. I, vol. XIII, 981.
[35] Bellville (Texas) *Countryman*, October 11, 1862.
[36] Dallas (Texas) *Herald*, September 13, October 4, 1862.
[37] *Ibid.*, October 4, 1862.
[38] Austin *Texas Almanac—Extra*, November 1, 1862; Dallas (Texas) *Herald*, November 8, 1862.
[39] Little Rock (Arkansas) *Patriot*, December 25, 1862.
[40] Little Rock (Arkansas) *True Democrat*, October 29, 1862.

Cavalry out in the Indian Territory were severely short of clothing and other supplies. From Cherokee country, an officer in Stand Watie's brigade wrote his wife in September, 1863, that out of 5,000 men, 1,000 were unarmed and without shoes and a change of clothing. Watie's army, according to the officer, looked "more like Siberian exiles than soldiers." There seems to have been no disposition to blame the Confederate government, for he added that the "Confederacy certainly does not know our condition. Good Soldiers but without the means of resistance. We are neither discouraged or whipped and God forbid we ever shall be. . . . I have still got an old grey shirt and pair of pants on but they are thread bear [sic]."[41] Late in October four small wagonloads of provisions and clothing arrived; certainly not enough to bring any substantial relief to the men.[42]

While cavalry outfits attempted to clothe themselves, the quartermaster department had not been idle. Under General T. H. Holmes, commander of the Trans-Mississippi Department from July, 1862, to January, 1863, a central bureau for receiving and distributing clothing had been established, and by late 1863 was doing a fair job of supplying the troops. By February, 1864, the cavalry for the first time might be said to be properly supplied with clothing and blankets.[43]

The "uniforms" of the cavalry were, as the circumstances of their procurement might suggest, as promiscuous in color and assortment as they were insecure in fabrication. Footwear was of all shapes and types—moccasins, high-cut boots, short-top boots, and low quarter-shoes called "pumps." Socks, usually cotton or wool, were of all colors. The typical trousers were either gray woolen "Kentucky jeans" or woolen plaid jeans. Some men, such as Captain Sam Richardson of the Lane Rangers, asserted their individuality by wearing gaudy leopard skin pants. The usual shirt, called the "gray back," was made of cotton long-sleeved, with a high collar. Men often enlisted in their "Sunday" shirts. Coats were both single- and double-breasted

[41] James M. Bell to Mrs. Caroline Bell, September 2, 1863, Cherokee Letters in the Frank Phillips Collection of the Library of the University of Oklahoma, as cited in Dale, "Cherokees in the Confederacy," *Journal of Southern History*, XIII, 180.

[42] William Steele to S. S. Anderson, February 15, 1864, *Official Records*, ser. I, vol. XXII, pt. I, 34.

[43] See Nichols, "Confederate Quartermaster Operations in the Trans-Mississippi Department," pp. 28–45.

and varied widely in color and design. The hat which "topped off" the soldier's attire was likely to be either a wide-brimmed felt, colored brown or jet-black, or a gray cap, shaped like a French kepi. Sometimes bright-colored handkerchiefs were worn when hats were not available.[44]

Trimming for cavalry uniforms—yellow gilt or brass buttons and braid or lace—was scarce in the Trans-Mississippi. Occasionally, officers received such accessories from home, but most of the men had to wear their heterogeneous garbs without the regulation buttons and yellow-striped cavalry pants.[45]

[44] James Arthur Lyon Fremantle, a British traveler who was in Texas in 1863, described the dress of a Texas Cavalry company as consisting of jack boots with huge spurs, ragged black or brown trousers, flannel shirts, and black felt hats "ornamented with the 'lone star of Texas.' " *The Fremantle Diary* . . . , ed. by Walter Lord, p. 7. The details of the cavalryman's uniform were gleaned from a number of the sources cited in the pages immediately preceding. See also James A. Abney, *An Abriged Autobiography of Some of the Many Incidents and Experiences of James A. Abney, M.D., Confederate Veteran,* [no page], for an excellent description of a cavalry uniform made in entirety by the mother of a seventeen-year-old volunteer. Regulations for the dress of Confederate cavalrymen may be found in Confederate State War Department, *Uniform and Dress of the Army of the Confederate States* . . . ; and Joseph Wheeler, *A Revised System of Cavalry Tactics for Use of the Cavalry and Mounted Infantry, C.S.A.,* Introduction.

[45] Lieutenant Cade, Twenty-Eighth Texas Cavalry, wrote home to his wife late in June, 1862, explaining the scarcity of uniform trimmings and urging her to purchase and send to him buttons, braid, and yellow cloth strips with which to make stripes for his trousers. Anderson, *Texas Surgeon in the C.S.A.*, pp. 19, 23.

ARMS AND MOUNTS

I

In 1861 a proud and determined southern trooper, after learning that his outfit would receive no arms from the government, boasted that "we can lick 'em with cornstalks."[1] Though never forced to use cornstalks for weapons, the cavalry in the Trans-Mississippi would be confronted throughout the war with severe shortages of carbines and revolvers, the preferred weapons for mounted troops.

On May 17, 1861, the War Department, having only 150,000 shoulder arms, a mere 20,000 of them modern rifles,[2] informed Colonel T. C. Hindman, recruiting near Little Rock, Arkansas, that it would "dispense the arms in its possession only when it became absolutely necessary in connection with the most weighty movements."[3] In other words, during 1861 the furnishing of arms for volunteers in the Trans-Mississippi was to be left to the states.

In Texas the first two cavalry regiments, recruited in February, 1861, were furnished with weapons captured from the United States arsenal at San Antonio and from eighteen other arsenals and posts

---

[1] Quoted in Richard D. Steuart, "How Johnny Got His Gun," *Confederate Veteran Magazine*, XXXII (May, 1924), 166.

[2] Lieutenant Colonel J. W. Mallet, "Work of the Ordnance Bureau," *Southern Historical Society Papers*, XXXVII (January, 1909), 1. Mallet was superintendent of Confederate ordnance laboratories. See also Josiah Gorgas, "Extracts from My Notes Written Chiefly after the Close of the War," in *The Confederate Soldier in the Civil War 1861–1865*, ed. by Ben La Bree.

[3] *Official Records*, ser. I, vol. III, 578.

throughout the state.[4] Most of these were old .69 or .54 caliber flint-lock rifled muskets, provided with percussion locks.[5] Part of the Second Texas Cavalry acquired .52 caliber Mississippi rifles, then highly esteemed for accuracy and durability.[6]

When the supply of captured arms was gone, the Texas Committee of Public Safety urged citizens to turn over their personal arms to state ordnance officers. Early in March, 1861, it authorized Ben McCulloch to purchase "or otherwise obtain" 1,000 Morse rifles or 1,000 Colt's revolvers for the cavalry.[7] Unable to secure the rifles, McCulloch bought enough handguns to arm several newly formed regiments and some independent companies.[8]

In Arkansas the seizure of the United States arsenal at Little Rock in May, 1861, supplied the State Military Board with 10,000 stand of percussion muskets (Hall's rifles) and .50 caliber Model 1854 cavalry carbines.[9] The Board distributed about 7,500 of these arms to General N. B. Pearce's state infantry and Colonel DeRosey Carroll's Arkansas cavalry; it turned the remainder over to Ben McCulloch, who had just assumed command of the Indian Territory.[10] Having thus depleted its supply of captured arms, the Military Board employed a legislative appropriation of $100,000 in an effort to purchase private weapons.[11]

[4] The San Antonio (Texas) *Herald*, February 23, 1861, estimated that $1,209,500 worth of ordnance stores, mules, wagons, horses, tools, clothing, and commissary stores were captured with the nineteen forts.

[5] Texas Adjutant General, *Report, November, 1861*, p. 10; Claude E. Fuller and Richard D. Steuart, *Firearms of the Confederacy . . .* , pp. 30, 39, 40–41.

[6] William W. Heartsill, *Fourteen Hundred and Ninety-One Days in the Confederate Army: or, Camp Life, Day by Day, of the W. P. Lane Rangers from April 19, 1861 to May 20, 1865*, p. 35. This weapon was also known as the "Kentucky Rifle," the "Harper's Ferry Yager," and the "Windsor Rifle." Fuller and Steuart, *Firearms of the Confederacy*, pp. 37–38.

[7] Texas Governor, March 16—November 7, 1861 (Edward Clark), *Governor's Message to the Senators and Representatives of the Ninth Legislature of the State of Texas, November 1, 1861*, p. 7. The Morse rifle referred to was probably the Morse Breech Loading .50 caliber carbine. The small dimensions and light weight (6½ lbs.) of this carbine made it an excellent cavalry arm. Fuller and Steuart, *Firearms of the Confederacy*, pp. 87–88.

[8] Oran M. Roberts, "Texas," *Confederate Military History*, XI, 56.

[9] Ben McCulloch to L. P. Walker, May 20, 1861, *Official Records*, ser. I, vol. III, 579; David Y. Thomas, *Arkansas in War and Reconstruction 1861–1874*, p. 86; Fuller and Steuart, *Firearms of the Confederacy*, pp. 19, 40–41.

[10] Thomas, *Arkansas in War and Reconstruction*, p. 86.

[11] John M. Harrell, "Arkansas," *Confederate Military History*, X, 3.

Most of the 2,500 arms given McCulloch were rusty and entirely unserviceable. In desperate need of good weapons, McCulloch wrote to the Secretary of War on May 20–21 requesting the shipment to Fort Smith of sufficient numbers of carbines, pistols, and sabers for his cavalry regiments.[12] Walker replied hopelessly that the War Department had no rifles.[13] Several months later he ordered the Baton Rouge arsenal to ship rifles, muskets, and revolvers to Arkansas.[14] There is no evidence that the order was ever executed.

In June McCulloch's situation became more desperate. The huge Federal army being concentrated against Price near St. Louis quite possibly meant an invasion of Arkansas and the Indian Territory.[15] To meet this threat he had an army drastically deficient in firearms. In disgust, he wrote Walker on June 29 that "my embarrassment here has been very great. Sent here [to the Indian Territory] without force, without transportation, and without arms, I have found myself very much crippled." He added emphatically that "we are in much need of arms and ammunition."[16]

Some of McCulloch's cavalry took it upon themselves to procure arms, placing in the Fort Smith *Daily Times and Herald* requests for citizens to sell them Maynard and Sharp's carbines or other weapons.[17] Two companies of the Third Texas Cavalry purchased shotguns from private sources in Fort Smith.[18] Some of the other companies of the regiment were indifferently armed with old United States Model 1852 carbines and squirrel rifles "of a very inferior quality" that had been sent from San Antonio.[19] Requests for Texas

---

[12] *Official Records*, ser. I, vol. III, 579–581, 582.

[13] May 22, 1861, *ibid.*, p. 583.

[14] Walker to Josiah Gorgas, August 16, 1861, *ibid.*, p. 652.

[15] McCulloch to Walker, May 23, 1861, *ibid.*, p. 583.

[16] *Ibid.*, p. 600.

[17] Fort Smith (Arkansas) *Daily Times and Herald*, June 20, 1861. The .52 caliber Maynard carbine, manufactured in the North, was an exceptionally well-made arm and one of the most popular among cavalry troops. The .58 caliber Sharps, originally made in New England, were manufactured for the Confederacy by S. C. Robinson Arms Co., Richmond, Virginia. The Confederate Sharps were inferior to the famous Maynard carbine. Fuller and Steuart, *Firearms of the Confederacy*, pp. 194–195, 196; William A. Albaugh and Edward N. Simmons, *Confederate Arms*, p. 79.

[18] Victor M. Rose, *Ross' Texas Brigade*, pp. 17–18; McCulloch to Walker, July 30, 1861, *Official Records*, ser. I, vol. III, 623.

[19] Rose, *Ross' Texas Brigade*, p. 17.

authorities to supply more and better arms for the outfit were flatly refused.[20] A few of the Texas horsemen had their own Colt's revolving rifles and six-shooters brought from home. Those without firearms had huge Bowie knives, some three feet in length; according to one trooper, they were "heavy enough to cleave the skull of a mailed knight through helmet and all."[21]

After sending Walker two more pleas for weapons, McCulloch gathered his haphazardly armed troops and led them into Missouri to reinforce Sterling Price's state forces at Cassville.[22] The battle that ensued at Wilson's Creek cost the Confederates some 300 stand of what they had. For the rest of 1861 McCulloch continued to complain of the shortage of weapons, particularly for his cavalry. There were no arms anywhere suitable for mounted troops.[23]

Cavalry outfits in Price's state army were even more deficient in arms than those in McCulloch's Division. Lieutenant Colonel Vaughan's (or Baughn's) battalion, Captain Jo Shelby's company of scouts, and Captain Campbell's company were scantly armed with shotguns, squirrel rifles, and revolvers; more than half the men in Colonel Ben Brown's regiment and Lieutenant Colonel J. P. Major's battalion were completely unarmed.[24]

By late August, 1861, state ordnance reserves were completely exhausted. General A. S. Johnston, ranking Confederate officer in the West, wrote Governor H. M. Rector of Arkansas on September 22, 1861, that since arms could not be obtained from Richmond, volunteers in the Trans-Mississippi should bring their own rifles, shotguns, or other weapons.[25] This practice had already begun in Texas. Men volunteering for Sibley's Brigade during August and September had

[20] McCulloch to Walker, July 30, 1861, *Official Records*, ser. I, vol. III, 623.

[21] Rose, *Ross' Texas Brigade*, p. 18.

[22] June 20, July 5, 1861, *Official Records*, ser. I, vol. III, 600, 639.

[23] McCulloch to Walker, May 21, September 2, October 14, 1861, *ibid.*, pp. 582, 692, 718–719; McCulloch to Jefferson Davis, August 24, 1861, *ibid.*, p. 671; McCulloch to J. P. Benjamin, November 8, 1861, *ibid.*, pp. 733–734.

[24] Lieutenant Colonel R. A. Vaughan's (or Baughn's) report, July 19, 1861, *ibid.*, p. 29; Colonel R. L. Y. Peyton to J. S. Rains, July 19, 1861, *ibid.*, p. 27; R. S. Bevier, *History of the First and Second Missouri Confederate Brigades, 1861–1865*, pp. 35–36; and William Monks, *A History of Southern Missouri and Northern Arkansas*, pp. 51–53.

[25] *Official Records*, ser. I, vol. IV, 422.

brought shotguns and knives with them.[26] There were so many shot-guns among the troops in Sibley's Brigade that one soldier in Rip Ford's Second Texas Cavalry suggested that "as our Regiment is called Texas Mounted Rifles, that they be called 'Texas Mounted Shot Guns'. . . ."[27] Recruits for Terry's Texas Rangers had also provided themselves with weapons, either purchased from Houston merchants or brought from home.[28] One correspondent, observing the armament of the Rangers assembled at Houston, wrote that "every man has a six-shooter and a bowie knife in his belt as well as a rifle or a double barrel shotgun to be slung to the saddle bow."[29]

Having the troops furnish much of the arms supply had by early spring of 1862 produced such good results throughout the South that the Confederate Congress passed a law requiring each man to provide himself with musket, shotgun, rifle, or carbine. The mustering officer was to evaluate the weapon. If the owner consented to sell it, he was to be paid its ascertained value. The volunteer not wishing to sell his weapon was to receive one dollar a month for its use.[30]

The Confederate government in the summer of 1861 sent Ballard S. Dunn into the Trans-Mississippi to purchase weapons from private citizens. Dunn designated agents in the more populous cities and ran articles in several newspapers urging the people to sell their arms.[31] Private firearms brought into Confederate service were to be stamped with Confederate identification marks, and, if possible, converted to the standard .58 caliber.[32] According to General Hindman, Dunn's agents were by June, 1862, "everywhere" purchasing arms for his army.[33]

Under authority granted by the War Department or the Trans-

[26] Texas Adjutant General, *Report, November, 1861*, p. 4; Bellville (Texas) *Countryman*, September 4, 11, 1861.

[27] Camp Hudson *Times*, January 17, 1862, in Heartsill, *Fourteen Hundred and Ninety-One Days*, p. 50.

[28] Leonidas B. Giles, *Terry's Texas Rangers*, pp. 15–16; J. K. P. Blackburn, "Reminiscences of the Terry Rangers," *Southwestern Historical Quarterly*, XXII (July, October 1918), 41.

[29] Bellville (Texas) *Countryman*, September 18, 1861.

[30] *Official Records*, ser. IV, vol. I, 1096.

[31] New Orleans (Louisiana) *Daily Crescent*, September 6, 1861; Bellville (Texas) *Countryman*, September 11, 1861.

[32] Martin Rywell, *Confederate Guns and Their Current Prices*, p. 7.

[33] Hindman to S. Cooper, June 9, 1862, *Official Records*, ser. I, vol. XIII, 883.

Mississippi high command, some cavalry outfits in the summer of 1862 undertook to procure arms for themselves. Colonel N. M. Burford, whose Nineteenth Texas Cavalry was bivouacked near Dallas in June, offered to buy arms from the citizens of Dallas and Tarrant Counties. "The Colonel does not wish forcibly to take any arms," explained the editor of the Dallas *Herald*, "he therefore appeals to the people to bring in their guns." To encourage rapid response, the editor added "wouldn't it be a shame to see any soldier leaving the state to fight the battles of Texas unarmed?" Burford established a board of officers to value the arms, and the quartermaster gave receipts for them. Within a week, the soldiers had plenty of rifles, shotguns, and revolvers.[34]

Early in July, 1862, Colonel Walter P. Lane, formerly Lieutenant Colonel of Greer's Third Texas Cavalry, returned to Texas to recruit a regiment in the vicinity of Jefferson. Soon mustered-in as the First Texas Partisan Rangers,[35] his men were completely unarmed. Lane wired General T. H. Holmes at Little Rock, asking for weapons, only to be told: "Colonel, I have no arms; but a man like you, who has raised a full regiment in a month, can arm it. I send you carte blanche orders to seize, press, or buy arms wherever you can find them." Lane ordered details, each consisting of ten men, to procure arms in the counties where his companies had been organized. Within a week a number of rifles and ten-gauge shotguns were in the hands of the volunteers. After the regiment reached Thibodeauxville in the Lafourche District of Louisiana, it acquired a full supply of Federal Enfields.[36]

Many of the revolvers and carbines supplied the cavalry in the last two years of war came from privately owned establishments in Texas. A factory near Tyler, erected in May, 1862, by George Yarbrough, W. S. N. Biscoe, and J. S. Short, was producing by the fall of 1862 a well-made .54 and .57 caliber rifle variously known as the "Texas Rifle," the "Australian Rifle," and the "Enfield Rifle."[37] The Tyler

[34] Dallas (Texas) *Herald*, June 21, 1862.
[35] Walter P. Lane, *The Adventures and Recollections of General Walter P. Lane . . .* , p. 104; Dudley G. Wooten, ed., *A Comprehensive History of Texas*, II, 572.
[36] Lane, *Adventures and Recollections*, pp. 104–105.
[37] Steuart, "How Johnny Got His Gun," *Confederate Veteran Magazine*, XXXII, 167; Fuller and Steuart, *Firearms of the Confederacy*, pp. 144–145.

arsenal continued to operate in private hands until the fall of 1863, when it was purchased by the Confederate government.[38] The Tucker, Sherrod, and Co., a private firm at Lancaster, Dallas County, manufactured under the management of Colonel Crockett hundreds of revolvers for cavalry use. They were patterned after the famous United States Army and Navy Colts.[39] An excellent description of the .44 caliber "Tucker-Sherrod Colt Dragoon" appeared in the *Texas Almanac*:

SIX-SHOOTERS

We were shown the other day a beautiful specimen of a six-shooter, manufactured near Dallas by Colonel Crockett, who has a large armory now in successful operation. The pistol appears in every respect quite equal to the famous Colt's six-shooter, of which it is an exact copy, with the exception of an extra sight on the barrel which we think is a decided improvement. We learn that Colonel Crockett has now 400 of these pistols on hand, which he has manufactured within the last six months, and which he has offered to the Governor at remarkable [*sic*] low figures—not one third of what they could be sold at by retail. We hope they will not be allowed to go out of the state, as it is notorious how deficient we are in arms for home defense.[40]

The government had its own plans and made efforts to manufacture arms in the Trans-Mississippi.[41] By July, 1863, an arsenal at San Antonio was producing substantial numbers of rifles, carbines, and revolvers.[42] In addition there were armories at Baton Rouge and

[38] Fuller and Steuart, *Firearms of the Confederacy*, p. 145; Frank E. Vandiver, *Ploughshares into Swords: Josiah Gorgas and Confederate Ordnance*, p. 192.

[39] The Army Colt, caliber .44, held six shots and had an eight-inch barrel. The Navy Colt, caliber .36, also had six shots but was slightly smaller than the Army model. Confederate States War Department, *The Ordnance Manual for the Use of the Officers of the Confederate States Army, 1862*, p. 130. Hereafter cited as *Confederate Ordnance Manual, 1862*.

[40] Austin *TexasAlmanac—Extra*, February 28, 1863.

[41] President Davis in a letter to Senator R. W. Johnson of Arkansas, July 14, 1863, said that skilled workmen had been sent to the Trans-Mississippi and that he had encouraged the establishment there of "manufactories for all munitions of war." *Official Records*, ser. I, vol. LIII, 880.

[42] San Antonio (Texas) *Herald*, September 13, 27, October 11, November 1, 15, 1862; Vandiver, *Ploughshares into Swords*, pp. 191–192.

Little Rock[43] and a foundry at Shreveport.[44] By the winter of 1863–1864 private and government factories in the region were making about 800 guns a month.[45] Slow transportation and incompetent ordnance officers impeded deliveries to the troops.

Until the fall of New Orleans, most cavalry sabers and other edged weapons for the army were made by Thomas, Griswold & Co. of New Orleans. Dufilho's of New Orleans, a much smaller company, also made a few cavalry swords. In Arkansas blacksmiths were engaged to make sabers for the army on a contract basis. Most of these weapons were crude and clumsy, but the few made by master blacksmiths were well-balanced instruments, fashioned from remarkably good steel.[46]

The saber was regulation equipment for all horsemen and all line officers, foot and mounted, but in most cases was disliked by the men.[47] To the frontiersman and cowboy used to a long and intimate

[43] Mallet, "Work of the Ordnance Bureau," *Southern Historical Society Papers*, XXXVII, 8.

[44] E. K. Smith to Jefferson Davis, June 16, 1863, *Official Records*, ser. I, vol. XXII, pt. II, 871.

[45] T. C. Reynolds to Davis, September 11, 1863, *ibid.*, p. 1003.

[46] Albaugh and Simmons, *Confederate Arms*, pp. 105, 107.

[47] There seems to be some difference of opinion among students of cavalry history and tactics as to the extent the saber was used in the Civil War. For instance, Captain Alonzo Gray argued that the Confederates used sabers only for shock action or close-quarter combat. Revolvers and carbines were used in all other types of fighting. *Cavalry Tactics as Illustrated by the War of the Rebellion . . .*, pt. I, 24–25. The eminent British historian of cavalry, George T. Denison, insisted that Southerners generally had a feeling of contempt for the saber, rarely using it in action. *A History of Cavalry from the Earliest Times*, p. 360. G. F. R. Henderson agreed with Denison. *The Civil War: A Soldier's View*, pp. 32, 35, 108, 109, 125, 126, 210. Major General James H. Wilson, one of the best of the Federal cavalry commanders, said that the saber should be used as a supplementary weapon to the carbine. "The Cavalry of the Army of the Potomac," in *Civil and Mexican Wars, 1861, 1846*; Volume XIII of *Publications of the Military Historical Society of Massachusetts*, p. 85. In his Confederate cavalry manual, Major General Joseph Wheeler discussed at some length the virtue of the cavalry saber. Though not comparable to the rifle or revolver, it had advantages when fighting broke down into individual combats. *A Revised System of Cavalry Tactics for Use of the Cavalry and Mounted Infantry, C.S.A.*, pp. 58–60. Major General J. F. C. Fuller, probably the most perspicacious of all modern writers on Civil War tactics and generalship, maintains that in the Civil War, the "first of all modern wars," the rifle "reigned supreme." It "killed the bayonet" and "rendered useless the sword." *Grant & Lee: A Study in Personality and Generalship*, pp. 247, 248, 249; *The Generalship of Ulysses S. Grant*, p. 361.

companionship with the six-shooter and carbine or rifle, the saber was indeed a strange weapon. How was this awkward instrument to be used in combat? The cavalry manual instructed the soldier to carry the sword hand to the shoulder while approaching the opponent. Upon reaching the enemy, he should extend the sword hand quickly to full length and ram the blade home. The follow-through should consist of a backhanded slash made horizontally across the victim's body. But in comparison to the six-shooter, which could be fired simply by pulling the trigger, this was a complicated and cumbersome procedure. The horseman understood the revolver; he knew how to use it and enjoyed the feeling of power that it gave to him. The saber was, perhaps, all right for drills and parades, but when it was time to fight, every trooper wanted to be astride a good steed with a pair of Colt's six-shooters in his hands. When asked what was the mental effect of being mounted on a powerful horse and armed with a six-shooter, one Texas Ranger was quick to reply, "They just run together like molasses."[48]

After the troops reached the front they were obliged to rely heavily upon capture from the enemy for their ordnance stores. The conquest of Lexington, Missouri, in September, 1861, netted Price's Missouri State Guards 3,000 stand of rifles and cavalry carbines, and a few sabers.[49] Together with the arms already in the hands of the troops, these confiscated weapons gave Price's army a most heterogenous collection of types and calibers. A newspaperman, observing the cavalry filing out of Lexington shortly after the battle, wrote that

Scarcely a hundred of the Confederates were uniformed; scarcely two had guns alike—no two exhibited the same trappings. Here went one fellow in a shirt of brilliant green, on his side an immense cavalry sabre, in his belt two navy revolvers and a Bowie-knife, and slung from his shoulder a Sharp's rifle. Right by his side was another, upon whose hips dangled a light medical sword, in his hand a double-barreled shotgun,

[48] Quoted in Walter Prescott Webb, *The Great Plains*, p. 494. Colonel John S. Mosby, in claiming that he was the first cavalry commander to discard the saber as useless and to arm his men only with revolvers, apparently was ignorant of the activities of cavalrymen west of the Mississippi, especially the Texans. See Mosby, *Mosby's War Experiences and Stuart's Cavalry Campaigns.*

[49] Sterling Price to C. F. Jackson, September 21, 1861, *Official Records*, ser. I, vol. III, 188.

in his boot an immense seythe [sic], on his heel the inevitable spur—his whole appearance, from tattered boot, through which gazed audaciously his toes, to the top of his head, indicating that the plunderings of many a different locality made up his whole. Generally the soldiers were armed with shotguns or squirrel rifles; some had the old flintlock muskets; a few had Minie guns, and others, Sharp's or Maynard rifles, while all, to the poorest, had horses.[50]

The battle of Prairie Grove, Arkansas, in December, 1862, yielded Marmaduke's calvary division 400 stand of arms and large quantities of ammunition and quartermaster supplies.[51] While raiding Federal Missouri in 1863, Shelby's Iron Brigade seized Neosho, richest supply depot in the state, thus acquiring 400 Sharp's carbines and 460 new Colt's navy revolvers.[52]

Between 1862 and the end of the war, various partisan ranger units operating along the Arkansas-Missouri border captured from the enemy enormous quantities of ordnance, commissary, and quartermaster supplies,[53] usually keeping them for their own use.[54] In great need of arms for cavalry and infantry,[55] the Trans-Mississippi high command on March 3, 1863, ordered that partisan commanders turn

[50] Quoted in W. L. Webb, *Battles and Biographies of Missourians: or, The Civil War Period of Our State*, p. 104.

[51] J. O. Shelby to J. S. Marmaduke, December 11, 1863, *Official Records*, ser. I, vol. XXII, pt. I, 153.

[52] Shelby to J. L. McLean, November 16, 1863, *ibid.*, p. 678.

[53] During 1862 and 1863 southwestern Missouri was the scene of a fearful amount of pillaging and marauding. Several counties were virtually stripped by foraging parties from partisan bands, both Union and Confederate. United States Record and Pension Office, *Organization and Status of Missouri Troops, Union and Confederate, during the Civil War*, pp. 53, 57. Plundering and vandalism were even worse in northwestern Arkansas. See Thomas, *Arkansas in War and Reconstruction*, chapters XV, XVI.

[54] General Orders No. 4, March 23, 1863, Confederate States Army, Trans-Mississippi Department, *General Orders, Headquarters, Trans-Mississippi Department, from March 6, 1863, to January 1, 1865*, p. 2. Hereafter cited as *General Orders of the Trans-Mississippi Department*.

[55] On October 26, 1862, General Holmes informed the War Department that some 7,000 of the 27,000 men in his army were completely unarmed, and a "large part of the remainder have only the shot-guns and rifles of the country. You can readily see," he added, "that it is only the moral force of numbers, whose condition is carefully concealed that has kept the enemy in check." *Official Records*, ser. I, vol. XIII, 898.

over to supply officers all the weapons and equipments that they captured.[56]

While cavalry outfits endeavored to arm themselves, the Confederate Ordnance Bureau bestirred itself to assist the Trans-Mississippi Department. In the fall of 1862, Gorgas ordered 25,000 arms to be sent west of the River, 21,000 of them to go to Holmes in Arkansas, the rest to Dick Taylor in Louisiana.[57] This was not much, but it was all that could be done without severe damage to other departments. In a letter to the Confederate Adjutant General acknowledging receipt of a few thousand of these arms, Holmes wrote that "my list of unarmed men is worse than I had supposed. Ten thousand muskets, in addition to the last 3,000 sent by Captain Carrington, would not put a weapon in the hand of every man."[58]

Irate governors complained loudly of the lack of ordnance support for the Department. On November 13, 1862, Governor Francis R. Lubbock wrote President Davis that Texas had provided to that date sixty regiments of cavalry and infantry for the Confederacy, many of them still in the state without arms. How could Texas be expected to thwart a Federal invasion or to participate effectively in the war in the West if her soldiers had no weapons? Lubbock asked for old guns discarded by armies east of the River, if nothing else could be done.[59]

Cavalry in other parts of the Department were also short of good arms. Ed Waller's Texas battalion, serving in Louisiana, had only a few "worthless" flintlocks and Federal Enfields.[60] General William Steele's 3,500 horsemen, stationed around Fort Smith, were sparingly armed with shotguns, rusty Texas rifles, and muskets, most of them "scarcely serviceable."[61]

After the fall of Vicksburg, which severed the Trans-Mississippi

[56] General Orders No. 4, March 23, 1863, *General Orders of the Trans-Mississippi Department*, p. 2.

[57] J. S. Whitney to J. E. Matlock, September 7, 1862, *Official Records*, ser. I, vol. XI, 734. On October 20, 1862, the Secretary of War wrote Holmes that 5,000 arms had been lost in crossing the Mississippi, leaving some 16,000 that would actually reach him. *Ibid.*, ser. I, vol. XIII, 889–890.

[58] November 3, 1862, *ibid.*, ser. I, vol. XIII, 908.

[59] *Ibid.*, ser. I, vol. LIII, 833–834.

[60] Richard Taylor, *Destruction and Reconstruction: Personal Experiences of the Late War*, p. 130.

[61] Extract of Ordnance Report for Cooper's Cavalry Brigade, August 23, 1863, *Official Records*, ser. I, vol. XXII, pt. II, 1098.

from the rest of the Confederacy, the arms situation became even more critical. Agents from the Department went to Bermuda[62] and Europe to try to secure rifles, pistols, artillery, and ammunition.[63] In a desperate effort to preserve the limited supply on hand, the Trans-Mississippi high command issued on December 1, 1864, a general order warning the troops that the cost of any arms lost would be deducted from their pay according to the following schedule:[64]

Musket	$200
Rifle	200
Carbine	200
Pistol (Navy)	400
Pistol (Army)	500

It was hoped that these charges, which were very high in terms of army pay (about $12 a month for privates), would induce the soldier to hold on to his weapon at all costs.

The great variety of calibers of guns actually on hand resulted in difficulty in procuring the right type of ammunition, if any could be obtained at all. It was next to impossible for the few arsenals in the Trans-Mississippi to supply enough ammunition for 25,000 to 30,000 men.[65] Efforts to bring in ammunition through the blockade and from Mexico met with little success.[66] In Arkansas much of the ammunition supply derived from home manufacture.[67] Frequently, cavalry commanders asked their men to prepare their own ammunition.[68] In such cases, it was not uncommon to find trace chains, iron rods, smooth stones, and hard pebbles substituted for shot and Minie balls.[69] Cart

---

[62] Josiah Gorgas to E. Kirby Smith, July 22, 1863, *ibid.*, ser. I, vol. XVI, pt. II, 118–119.

[63] Joseph H. Parks, *General Edmund Kirby Smith, C.S.A.*, p. 352; Vandiver, *Ploughshares into Swords*, p. 98.

[64] General Orders No. 93, *General Orders of the Trans-Mississippi Department*, p. 83.

[65] T. G. Rhett to J. P. Johnson, January 19, 1864, *ibid.*, ser. I, vol. XXII, pt. II, 1140.

[66] Parks, *Kirby Smith*, pp. 352–353.

[67] Fay Hempstead, *Historical Review of Arkansas*, I, 218.

[68] P. O. Hébert to Robert E. Lee, June 18, 1862, *Official Records*, ser. I, vol. IX, 719.

[69] Bevier, *History of the First and Second Missouri Confederate Brigades*, p. 36.

ridge boxes were often unavailable, and without them, much ammunition was lost in rainy weather.[70]

The general picture, then, was one of severe deficiency of weapons and ammunition in the region throughout the four long years of war. Cavalry were compelled to rely heavily upon shotguns, percussion lock muskets, squirrel rifles, and Bowie knives. Shotguns, though they might be effective short-range weapons in the hands of skilled horsemen, were not comparable with Sharp's or Maynard carbines or Colt's revolvers for effectual fighting under any condition. Lacking sufficient and proper armament, the cavalry in the Trans-Mississippi could hardly be expected to equal the performances of its counterparts east of the River.

II

In the Trans-Mississippi, unlike the other parts of the Confederacy, the supply of horses was adequate to wartime needs.[71] The total military population (white males aged seventeen to thirty-nine, inclusive) in 1860 was 484,065, the total number of horses, 919,532, with Texas having much the highest ratio of horses to men.[72]

Though horses were evidently plentiful in the Trans-Mississippi, a poor method of procurement hindered systematic and efficient mounting of the cavalry. Under an act of the Confederate Congress approved March 6, 1861, volunteers for mounted service were to furnish their own horses and accouterments, receiving in return forty cents a day and compensation if the animal should be killed in action.[73] Horses brought into service were to be branded with the initials

[70] Lane, *Adventures and Recollections*, p. 83; Rywell, *Confederate Guns*, p. 22.

[71] Professor Charles W. Ramsdell was the first to point out that the shortage of horses in the East throughout the war was a major factor in the demise of the Confederacy. "General Robert E. Lee's Horse Supply, 1862–1865," *American Historical Review*, XXXV (July, 1930), 758–777. Two recent works, one by Clement Eaton and the other by Frank E. Vandiver, give considerable attention to the lack of horses as a chief problem of Confederate logistics. Eaton, *A History of the Southern Confederacy*, pp. 103, 104, 138, 258; and Vandiver, *Rebel Brass: The Confederate Command System*, pp. 105–107.

[72] United States Eighth Census, 1860, vol. I, *Population*, pp. 12–13, 188–189, 276–277, 472–476; vol. III, *Agriculture*, pp. 6, 66, 92, 148.

[73] *Official Records*, ser. IV, vol. I, 126, 127.

TABLE IV

The Supply of Horses in the Trans-Mississippi

State	Horses	Military Population	Horses per Man
Arkansas	140,198	65,061	2.15
Louisiana	91,762	82,523	1.11
Missouri	361,874	241,455	1.49
Texas	325,698	95,026	3.41
Total	919,532	484,065	

"C.S."[74] The government adopted this measure in the belief that the troops could obtain better horses than the government could supply and that they would take considerably better care of their own than of government property.[75] The quartermaster department had the responsibility of providing grain and "long forage"—hay and fodder.

Most volunteers in the Trans-Mississippi had little difficulty initially in furnishing mounts. Farmers and cowboys from the vast rural areas simply rode their own steeds to enlisting centers. In cases where the recruit owned no horse, cavalry units called upon citizens to meet the need. For instance, the Lone Star Guards, while riding to join Greer's Third Texas Cavalry at Dallas in 1861, found at Larissa, Texas, a young man eager to join the cavalry and become a bugler, but who seemed "to own nothing beyond his wearing apparel." Since the Guards needed a bugler, they appealed to the citizens who "had gathered . . . to see the soldiers pass, and in little more time than it takes to tell" the recruit was rigged with horse, saddle, bridle, and blankets. He proved to be "a fine bugler," and "a most gallant young fellow."[76]

When citizens did not donate horses and equipments, units sometimes attempted to purchase them. Thus in November, 1861, Captain Rector, having recruited a company of Arkansas cavalry, advertised in the Little Rock *Daily State Journal* for any horses and mule teams.[77]

Some of the cavalry outfits obtained their mounts from wild herds,

[74] Confederate States War Department, *Regulations of the Army of the Confederate States, 1862: Containing a Complete Set of Forms*, p. 68.

[75] Ramsdell, "Lee's Horse Supply," *American Historical Review*, XXXV, 758, 766.

[76] Samuel B. Barron, *The Lone Star Defenders: A Chronicle of the Third Texas Cavalry, Ross' Brigade*, p. 20.

[77] Little Rock (Arkansas) *Daily State Journal*, November 6, 1861.

which roamed the wilderness areas of the Trans-Mississippi. While marching from New Iberia to Brashear City, Louisiana, late in 1861, troops in one company of Terry's Texas Rangers, having left their horses at Beaumont, Texas, began to complain loudly of sore feet. The captain sent details into the surrounding countryside to search for horses. They returned several hours later with 100 steeds of all sizes and breeds, which they had gathered from wild herds. After constructing a makeshift pen, the men lassoed the animals, and, midst shouts and whoops, began the tedious process of "breaking" them. For the most part, the horses, ranging in age from three to eight years, were slim and spirited, good for cavalry purposes. A few of the older horses, deemed "sleezy" old nags by private J. K. P. Blackburn, were turned back to pasture. Blackburn himself secured a big claybank gelding, slow but sturdy.[78]

Shelby's Missouri horsemen, at the beginning of their summer recruiting expedition into Missouri in 1862, were mounted upon "horses and mules of every size, variety, and condition" gathered from surrounding pastures. "Saddles, sheepskins, and blankets," said Adjutant John N. Edwards, "were all used for seats; and bark bridles and rope bridles completed the heterogeneous equipments."[79] During the expedition the men obtained better mounts and accouterments. "The rich prairies," related Edwards, "had furnished their best six year olds for these heavy riders, and the captured Federals had equipped them with as fine McClellan saddles and bridles as ever gleamed upon the Potomac, or went down in the battle's van before Jeb Stewart's [sic] reckless raiders."[80]

Most of the horses brought into service from Texas, northwestern Arkansas, and the Indian Territory were of the mustang or Spanish breeds, which apparently were good cavalry horses.[81] According to Richard Irving Dodge, frontiersman, Indian fighter, army officer, and author of several books on the West, the Spanish horse, though very small, was

[78] Blackburn, "Terry Rangers," *Southwestern Historical Quarterly*, XXII, 43–45.
[79] John N. Edwards, *Shelby and His Men: or, The War in the West*, p. 69.
[80] *Ibid.*, pp. 71–72.
[81] Professor Ramsdell, on the other hand, adjudged the small mustang ill-suited for cavalry use. "Lee's Horse Supply," *American Historical Review*, XXXV, 758.

strong and extremely docile. . . . Averaging scarcely fourteen hands in height, he is rather slight in build, though always having powerful fore-quarters, good legs, short strong back, and full barrel. He has not the slightest appearance of blood, though his sharp nervous ears and bright vicious eyes indicate unusual intelligence and temper, but the amount of work he can do, and the distance he can make in a specified (long) [sic] time, put him fairly on a level with the Arabian or any other animal of creation.[82]

Major General William H. Carter, United States Army, expert on horses and their history, wrote in 1923 that "no admixture of breeds will ever produce a gamier, hardier, and more enduring animal" than the "wide-ranging" mustang.[83] These two testimonies, made by men who knew and appreciated the Spanish horse or mustang, would seem to indicate that they were good horses for cavalry purposes.

A vast majority of the horses brought into the army from Missouri, Arkansas, and Louisiana were mixed-bred American saddle horses, referred to either as "gaited saddlers" or "hunters."[84] As one might expect in a section predominantly rural, mules and work horses of the Morgan or Great Conestoga breeds were ridden to enlisting centers by farmers and homesteaders.[85] Most of these animals were later transferred to the artillery service.

Accouterments, obtained by various means, varied widely in types, styles, and assortments. Usually a full set of accouterments comprised two bridles—the regular riding bridle, equipped with a bit, and a watering bridle; a halter; a saddle, usually the Spanish horn type if furnished by the men, or the Jenifer's tree or McClellan tree types if supplied by the quartermaster bureau; one or more pairs of spurs;

[82] Colonel Richard Irving Dodge, *Our Wild Indians: Thirty-Three Years' Personal Experience Among the Red Men of the Great West*, pp. 586–587. See Sir Walter Gilbey, *Small Horses in Warfare*, pp. 32–33; L. F. Sheffy, *The Spanish Horse on the Great Plains*, pp. 6, 7, 8; and J. Frank Dobie, *The Mustangs*, p. 61.

[83] Major General William Harding Carter, U.S.A., "The Story of the Horse: the Development of Man's Companion in War, Camp, on Farm, in the Marts of Trade, and in the Field of Sports," *National Geographic Magazine*, XLIV, (November, 1923), 524.

[84] *Ibid.*, pp. 500, 512.

[85] Edwards, *Shelby and His Men*, p. 206; Walter Scott McNutt, *A History of Arkansas from the Earliest Times to the Present*, p. 147.

surcingle; saddle blanket; currycomb; horse brush; picket pin; and lariat.[86]

The campaigns at the front during 1862 and 1863 took a heavy toll of the initial supply of horses and accouterments. Operations in northern Arkansas and southern Missouri gave rise to a temporary shortage of horses in Marmaduke's cavalry division. His horses for the most part were completely worn out and unshod by continuous and vigorous service.[87] The number of horses actually killed in battle during the winter of 1862–1863 was slight. During the skirmishing in Arkansas in the fall of 1862, Colonel Charles Carroll's Arkansas Brigade, numbering 1,200 effectives, lost only eight horses.[88] In the heated engagement at Prairie Grove, Arkansas, in December, 1862, Colonel Emmett MacDonald's Missouri Brigade lost but three mounts on the battlefield.[89] These surprisingly low figures probably reflected poor Federal marksmanship, for enemy soldiers certainly aimed to kill horse as well as rider. Losses of horses in the division were due mainly to lameness from lack of horseshoes, to disease, and to exhaustion. Many animals were rendered useless by serious diseases known as "grease wheel" or "soft hoof" and "sore tongue." On one particularly arduous campaign in Missouri, at least 200 men abandoned their sick and exhausted animals to die along the roadside and continued the raid on foot, marching "many a weary mile through snow and deep mud, some barefooted."[90] Colonel Jo Shelby said that the fighting during the fall had rendered more than half his horses unfit for duty. Many were dying, "owing to the heavy labor they have been compelled to do."[91] No doubt much of the loss of horses was caused by the failure of the men to rest, water, and feed them properly. By October, 1863, the division managed to overcome its temporary shortage of animals.

Once his horse was lost, the trooper was required by law to re-

[86] *Confederate Ordnance Manual, 1862*, pp. 148–151; Heartsill, *Fourteen Hundred and Ninety-One Days*, p. 5; General Orders No. 73, September 24, 1864, *General Orders of the Trans-Mississippi Department*, p. 66; Rywell, *Confederate Guns*, p. 22.

[87] Marmaduke to R. C. Newton, January 18, 1863, *Official Records*, ser. I, vol. XXII, pt. I, 195.

[88] Carroll's report, November 29, 1862, *ibid.*, p. 55.

[89] MacDonald to F. B. Davidson, December 9, 1862, *ibid.*, p. 157.

[90] Marmaduke to R. C. Newton, February 1, 1863, *ibid.*, p. 198.

[91] Shelby to Marmaduke, October 27, 1862, *ibid.*, ser. I, vol. XIII, 979–980.

mount himself. He was reimbursed only if his horse had been killed in action, and then only in a sum equal to the value established by mustering officers. Because of low army pay and the depreciation of Confederate currency, the dismounted cavalryman might find it difficult to purchase another horse. In the event that he failed to obtain one within forty days, he was, under a departmental general order of June 10, 1864, to be transferred to one of the infantry units from his state.[92] The Trans-Mississippi high command directed district commanders to have their cavalry outfits inspected monthly to carry out this order.[93]

Remounts, and equipment if needed, might be obtained by two methods. The most common practice during the first two years was to furlough a man home so that he might provide for himself. This resulted in the extended absences of many men badly needed at the front. Undoubtedly, as was the case east of the River, many homesick soldiers, in order to obtain the wondrous furloughs, deliberately disabled their mounts. Beginning in 1864 remounts could be purchased from horse infirmaries of the department of field transportation, which was responsible also for the manufacture of cavalry saddles, bridles, and harnesses.[94] Under regulations of September, 1864, troops could buy these items from the department according to the following schedule:[95]

Skeleton saddles	$70	Bit	$2
Halter	12	Girth	5
Crupper	3	Stirrups	2
Stirrup leathers	6	Bridle reins	7
Moss blanket	4	Spurs	1.50
Halter reins	5	Curry comb	1.25
Head stall	7	Nose bag	2.50
Horse brush	2	Caps	.25
Bridle	14		

[92] *General Orders of the Trans-Mississippi Department*, p. 34.

[93] General Orders No. 29, April 26, 1864, *ibid.*, p. 22.

[94] Another responsibility of this department was the reclassification of all worn-out cavalry horses. Those not completely run-down were to be transferred to the artillery; the rest were to be used for hauling purposes. General Orders No. 41, June 10, 1864, *ibid.*, p. 34; Special Orders No. 76, March 29, 1864, in Galveston (Texas) *Tri-Weekly News*, April 8, 1864.

[95] General Orders No. 73, September 24, 1864, *General Orders of the Trans-Mississippi Department*, p. 66.

The ill-conceived law requiring the men to remount themselves had by 1863 stirred up considerable controversy among the authorities in Richmond. Secretary of War James A. Seddon opposed the measure, complaining constantly of the hardships it placed upon the horseman. He reported to President Davis on November 26, 1863, that

it is becoming daily more difficult, and it is feared will soon become impracticable, to keep mounted a sufficient number for effective service. Under the advance in price and the increasing scarcity of suitable horses few have the ability to supply themselves, while the contingencies of active and exhaustive service, often on inadequate forage, too frequently imposes the necessity. The difficulty is inhanced by the limited range of casualties for which provision is made—only those "killed in action." . . . Justice as well as the interest of the service urges the correction of these evils, and it is suggested either that the system be changed and horses be furnished by the Government to both officers and men with a disallowance of the compensation granted for the service or loss of the horse, or that provision be made to pay all officers, as well as men, the appraisal values of their horses when lost by any of the actual contingencies of service, and not through remissness or neglect.[96]

Nothing was done to follow Seddon's suggestions until February, 1865, when a bill was introduced into Congress requiring that dismounted cavalrymen be supplied with horses by the quartermaster bureau. The bill did not pass, and even if it had, it was too late to bring any noticeable relief to the situation.[97]

The difficulty in buying horses and accouterments and the impotence of the quartermaster bureau to provide forage were probably the major causes of a serious rise in the number of illegal impressments during 1863 and 1864. Under a law of Congress of March 6, 1863, unit commanders could, after obtaining authority from district or departmental commands, legally seize private properties, paying for them according to prices established by district impressment boards.[98] While the impressment measure was meant to enable the

[96] *Official Records*, ser. IV, vol. II, 1002, 1003.

[97] United States Congress, *Journals of the Congress of the Confederate States of America, 1861–1865*, IV, 498–499; VII, 400, 419, 513, 543–544; Ramsdell, "Lee's Horse Supply," *American Historical Review*, XXXV, 775.

[98] The only study of the enforcement of impressment laws in the Trans-Mississippi is Jonnie M. Megee, "The Confederate Impressment Acts in the Trans-

army to secure badly needed supplies in a lawful manner, roving cavalry units in Arkansas and Texas used it as a shield for jayhawking, robbing, and plundering. Northern Arkansas was a scene of turmoil and confusion from the summer of 1863 to the end of the war. Marauding cavalry bands led by irresponsible officers plagued peaceful farmers, seizing their horses, horse equipment, and forage. By January, 1864, illegal impressments were so widespread and complaints so numerous that the departmental commander warned district commanders that they would be held responsible for all outrages. If depredations could be traced clearly to a certain cavalry unit, it was to be dismounted immediately and its horses transferred to the artillery service.[99] To deprive a trooper of his horse was a worse punishment than the guardhouse, possibly even worse than a court martial.

The year 1864 was disquieting for citizens of Texas. Cavalry outfits on the march or temporarily stationed at forts often sent details of horsemen into surrounding areas to make enforced purchases. Frequently these bands resorted to robbery, taking guns, horses, and equipage without paying for them. For instance, in March, 1864, an outraged farmer who resided near Columbus, Texas, wrote Governor Pendleton Murrah that a mounted regiment stationed nearby had entered his farm, demanding forage and equipment. No responsible officers were present. According to the farmer, he pleaded and argued with the soldiers, explaining to them that he barely had enough for himself. They ignored him, took what they wanted by force, and rode away.[100]

Mississippi States." Price schedules for horses, food, and equipment were published in newspapers in each state. For examples see Austin *Texas State Gazette* and Houston (Texas) *Telegraph, passim,* November, 1863, to end of war. Impressment prices for horses were usually only 50 per cent of the fair market values, often only 25 per cent. Thus horses normally selling for $1,500 to $6,000 on the market would bring only $675 according to impressment schedules. B. H. Epperson to Pendleton Murrah, June 14, 1864, Letters of Governors Francis Lubbock and Pendleton Murrah, Executive Correspondence.

[99] General Orders No. 18, June 13, 1863, *General Orders of the Trans-Mississippi Department,* p. 7; General Orders No. 1, January 9, 1864, *ibid.,* p. 1; J. O. Shelby to J. B. Love, June 19, 1864, *Official Records,* ser. I, vol. XXXIV, pt. IV, 683.

[100] J. T. Harcourt to Murrah, Executive Correspondence; Megee, "Impressment Acts in the Trans-Mississippi," p. 141.

As discipline declined and pillaging grew worse, farmers and ranchers began to fear their own cavalry almost as much as the enemy. Perhaps the famous Confederate humorist, Bill Arp, expressed the feelings of the peaceful citizens of Arkansas and Texas when he remarked, "I have travelled a heap of late, and had occasion to retire into some very sequestered regions, but nary hill or holler, nary mountain gorge or inaccessible ravine have I found, but what the cavalry had been there, and *just left*. And that is the reason they can't be whipped, for they have always *just left*, and took an old horse or two with 'em." And these peculiar activities, he said, were called damning, for "they dam their eyes, they dam their ears, and they dam their guns, and their boots, and their mill-saw spurs, and they dam their horses to make 'em go faster, and they dam the fences to make 'em come down, and they dam the poor farmer to make him dry up."[101] Being referred to as "the damn cavalry" must certainly have hurt the pride and destroyed some of the chivalry of the Confederate mounted service.

By June, 1864, reports of robbing and vandalism were so numerous that the Trans-Mississippi high command ordered all impressment of horses and illegal seizures of food and accouterments to stop. Any violations of this order were to be reported immediately by inspectors and commissary generals.[102] Impressment could be done only by commissioned officers with written authority.[103] During the months that followed, the number of illegal impressments seems to have subsided considerably.

Whatever the difficulties of the individual cavalryman, there is no evidence that a general shortage of horses for cavalry purposes ever occurred. That Texas had a substantial horse supply is indicated by two plans to help the Army of Northern Virginia. On November 14, 1862, the Secretary of War proposed to strengthen Lee's cavalry by purchasing 1,000 horses in Texas and shipping them to Virginia.[104] This plan was never carried out. On July 15, 1864, General Lee,

---

[101] Charles H. Smith, *Bill Arp, So Called*, pp. 75–76, 116.

[102] General Orders No. 41, June 10, 1864, *General Orders of the Trans-Mississippi Department*, p. 34.

[103] Shelby to Love, June 19, 1864, *Official Records*, ser. I, vol. XXXIV, pt. IV, 683; Shelby to T. H. McCray, June 21, 1864, *ibid.*, p. 690.

[104] *Ibid.*, ser. I, vol. XIX, pt. II, 716.

whose cavalry was desperately in need of mounts, suggested to President Davis that horses be brought from Texas.[105] This plan also never reached fruition.

District reports in the fall of 1862 reveal that cavalry outfits in Texas had plenty of horses. In October-November, 1862, General Hamilton P. Bee, commanding the Rio Grande Subdistrict of Texas, reported that he had 1,189 horses, only five of them unserviceable, for about 1,000 cavalry.[106] Colonel Xavier B. De Bray, commanding the Houston Subdistrict of Texas, reported 2,016 mounts, all of them fit for duty, for the 2,088 horsemen in his command.[107]

The cavalry in Arkansas and the Indian Territory were also adequately supplied with horses. In October, 1863, Marmaduke's cavalry division had a surprising surplus of horses in five of the six brigades.[108]

TABLE V

Horses in Marmaduke's Cavalry Division

Brigade	No. Men	No. Horses
Marmaduke's Brigade	1,408	1,751
Shelby's Brigade	306	1,674
Cabell's Brigade	870	963
Dobbins' Brigade	449	563
Texas Brigade	333	1,110
Brooks' Brigade	1,518	1,518
Temporary Dismounted Reg.	166	217
Woods' Battalion	219	222
Total	5,269	8,018

The Major and Inspector General of the Department, in a report of his semiannual inspection of the district, October 26, 1863, informed W. R. Boggs, Chief of Staff, that while many of the cavalry outfits in the district lacked arms, equipment, and clothing, they were all sufficiently mounted.[109] The situation did not change in 1864. In midyear

[105] Robert E. Lee, *Lee's Dispatches . . . to Jefferson Davis and the War Department of the C.S.A., 1862–1865*, p. 273.

[106] Abstract from Troop Returns of the First District of Texas, October, November, 1862, *Official Records*, ser. I, vol. XV, 851, 883–884.

[107] Abstract from Troop Returns of the First District of Texas, November, 1862, *ibid.*, pp. 883–884.

[108] Abstract of Monthly Troop Returns of Marmaduke's Division of Volunteer Cavalry, October 31, 1862, *ibid.*, ser. I, vol. XXII, pt. II, 1054; Harrell, "Arkansas," *Confederate Military History*, X, 226.

[109] *Official Records*, ser. I, vol. XXII, pt. II, 1049–1052.

General Shelby stated that he could march into Missouri with 5,000 men and "mount them, arm them, equip them, and place them on a thorough footing without expense to the government."[110] This was no mere boast. By late summer he had in his command some 7,500 "well mounted," "well armed" troopers.[111] And with this impressive force Shelby would follow General Sterling Price into Missouri on the largest cavalry expedition of the war, of which more will be said later.

By way of conclusion it might be said that had the irrational law requiring horsemen to remount themselves been dropped and the government itself assumed the responsibility, there would never have been shortages of horses in Marmaduke's division and troops would not have had to resort to illegal impressment. Nevertheless, with the exception of the disquieting year of thievery and pillaging, 1863 and early 1864, it was never as hard to obtain horses for cavalrymen as it was to procure food, clothing, and arms for them.

[110] Shelby to S. S. Anderson, July 27, 1864, *ibid.*, ser. I, vol. XLI, pt. II, 1027.
[111] J. F. Belton to S. S. Anderson, August 1, 1864, *ibid.*, p. 1036.

CAMPAIGNING: CANE HILL
AND PRAIRIE GROVE

TACTICAL USE OF CAVALRY

Various students of cavalry have contended that mounted forces in the American Civil War were the best the world had ever seen.[1] However that may be, it is certainly true that fundamental changes in cavalry tactics came about during the Civil War. In Europe cavalry was in the main an auxiliary arm whose purpose was to fight with infantry in pitched battles. Characterized by professionalism, cavalry had, according to an English officer of the Napoleonic Wars, one main purpose: "to give tone to what otherwise simply would be a vulgar brawl."[2] In the United States, however, eighty-five years of Indian fighting and frontier service had given rise to a new conception of cavalry tactics. The American horseman learned to fight in running campaigns, to ride for days without food, to fire a revolver from his horse at full gallop, to fight on foot as well as on horseback, and to sleep on the ground, head on saddle and reins in hand, ready for instant action. Service at frontier posts, far removed from telegraph or railroads, had given officers invaluable experience

[1] First Lieutenant S. R. Gleaves, "The Strategic Use of Cavalry," *Cavalry Journal*, XVIII (July, 1907), 9; George T. Denison, *A History of Cavalry from the Earliest Times*, pp. 394–395; Captain Alonzo Gray, *Cavalry Tactics as Illustrated by the War of the Rebellion . . .* , p. 3; Brigadier General Theodore H. Rodenbough, U.S.A. (retired), ed., *The Cavalry*, Volume IV of *Photographic History of the Civil War*, pp. 18–26.
[2] Quoted in Major John K. Herr and Edward S. Wallace, *The Story of the United States Cavalry, 1775–1942*, p. 89.

in such fundamentals as the handling of supply trains, the conduct of long marches, the construction of military roads, and the tending of cavalry horses and draught animals.[3]

With this background, cavalry in the Civil War came to regard itself as an autonomous arm of the service. Organized after the first year of war into brigades, divisions, and even corps, supported by horse artillery and accompanied by auxiliary troops and supply service, cavalry began not only to assist the army during the campaigns, but also to make strategic raids. In performing the first function, cavalry operated tactically as an auxiliary to the main forces engaged. In its raiding capacity, cavalry fought strategically as an independent force with the object of destroying the enemy's ability to make war.

Cavalry operating tactically proved to be indispensable to the army. Its two most important duties were to reconnoiter enemy installations and movements and to screen the maneuvers of the main forces, concealing from the opponent the plan of attack. Cavalry contributed, by its interposition far out in front and by the information it sent back, to the security of the entire army. Other tactical functions of the cavalry were to ride on the flanks of the army, protecting it from surprise, and to cover the rear in a general retreat. During an engagement cavalry harassed the enemy's flanks and rear and severed his communications. Mounted troops usually avoided direct engagement with infantry, since it was next to impossible for them to stand off or to break through masses of foot soldiers. In a pitched battle, however, the army commander frequently dismounted his cavalry to fight in line as infantry. When this was done, the fourth man of each squad acted as horse holder.[4]

[3] The best single studies on the development of cavalry in America are Albert G. Brackett, *History of the United States Cavalry, from the Formation of the Federal Government to the First of June, 1863* . . . ; Herr and Wallace, *Story of the United States Cavalry*, pp. 1–150; and Rodenbough, *The Cavalry*, Volume IV of *Photographic History of the Civil War*, pp. 16–38. A comparison of war and tactics in Europe to those in America may be found in Alfred T. Mahan, *The Influence of Sea Power Upon History, 1660–1783*, Introduction, Chapter I; and Gordon B. Turner, ed., *A History of Military Affairs Since the Eighteenth Century*, pp. 1, 2, 3–179. See also Captain Lewis E. Nolan, *Cavalry: Its History and Tactics*, pp. 1–34; and Captain Arthur L. Wagner, ed., *Cavalry Studies from Two Great Wars*.

[4] Besides the works by Herr and Wallace, Gleaves, Rodenbough, Denison, Gray, and Nolan, cited in the three preceding notes, those most helpful for an

Throughout the war Confederate cavalry in the Trans-Mississippi performed these tactical functions with merit. Although the infantry was generally the backbone of military power, Confederates in the region early employed the cavalry branch of the service as an auxiliary force. Of the major operations—Wilson's Creek, Missouri (August, 1861), Pea Ridge, Arkansas (March, 1862), Prairie Grove, Arkansas (December, 1862), and the Red River expedition (1864) —the Prairie Grove campaign best illustrates the tactical role of cavalry. The account of Prairie Grove that follows has the combined purpose of demonstrating a cavalry function and of telling the story of a decisive battle that decided major issues. After the engagement Federal armies occupied all of Missouri and northwest Arkansas above the Arkansas River. Never again were the Confederates able to take the offensive. Consequently they began to use their cavalry for raiding purposes, and it was in this strategic role (to be discussed later) that Confederate cavalry in the region gave its best performance.

---

understanding of cavalry tactics in the Civil War are Colonel G. F. R. Henderson, *The Civil War: A Soldier's View*, pp. 32, 33, 35, 108–109, 124–125, 210; and P. S. Hugh Rees, *Cavalry in Action*, pp. 550–558. The Confederate and Federal cavalry manuals are also useful: Joseph Wheeler, *A Revised System of Cavalry Tactics for Use of the Cavalry and Mounted Infantry, C.S.A.*, pt. III, 22–43; Phillip St. George Cooke, *Cavalry Tactics: or, Regulations for the Instruction, Formations and Movements of the Cavalry of the United States*; and Colonel James Lucius Davis, comp., *The Troopers Manual: or, Tactics for Light Dragoons and Mounted Riflemen*, pp. 49, 128–139, 208, 217, 219. Confederate States War Department, *Regulations for the Army of the Confederate States, and for the Quartermaster's and Pay Departments, 1861*, pp. 100–105, lists a few of the general tactical functions of cavalry. See also, Major General James H. Wilson, "The Cavalry of the Army of the Potomac," in *Civil and Mexican Wars, 1861, 1846*; Volume XIII of *Publications of the Military Historical Society of Massachusetts*, pp. 85–88; Major General J. F. C. Fuller, *Grant & Lee: A Study in Personality and Generalship*, pp. 276–277; Francis T. Miller, ed., *Photographic History of the Civil War*, V, 39–70, 71–114, 115–128, 129–140, 181–203, 215–258; and John Lamb, "The Confederate Cavalry: Its Wants, Trials, and Heroism," *Southern Historical Society Papers*, XXVI (December, 1898), 359–364.

One interested in what Europe thought about cavalry tactics in the American Civil War must read Jay Luvaas, *The Military Legacy of the Civil War: The European Inheritance*, pp. 4–5, 17–18, 21, 28, 33, 46, 47, 50, 54, 55, 57–59, 65–66, 72–74, 82, 84–85, 90, 95–96, 104, 108–115, 123–126, 129–130, 136, 139–140, 147–148, 153–164, 173, 177–178, 193–197.

CANE HILL AND PRAIRIE GROVE

In the late summer of 1862 Federal forces west of the Mississippi undertook an invasion of Confederate Arkansas. An army led by General Samuel R. Curtis and General Frederick Steele moved down the White River in eastern Arkansas, capturing everything from Batesville to Helena. A second force—the "Army of the Frontier," composed of the best fighting men the Federals had in Missouri and commanded by competent and pugnacious James G. Blunt—drove into northwestern Arkansas, shoving Confederate forces back across the Boston Mountains to Van Buren. A decisive stage had now been reached in the war west of the River. Should the Federals continue their penetrations, Arkansas and perhaps the entire Trans-Mississippi would be captured.[5]

General Theophilus H. Holmes (Portrait on Plate 5), commander of the Confederate Trans-Mississippi Department, tightened his defenses and managed temporarily to check the Federal invasion. It was doubtful that the Confederates could hold back the threatening armies, yet Holmes exhorted his commanders to do the best with what they had. Holmes had at his disposal about 27,335 effectives in two army corps.[6] The First Corps, now under the command of General T. C. Hindman (Portrait on Plate 6), was scattered along the Arkansas River watching Blunt. John S. Marmaduke's cavalry division and Allison Nelson's infantry division were with Hindman at Van Buren.[7] D. H. Cooper's Indian brigade (cavalry) was at Camp Steele in Choctaw country, perhaps twenty miles west of Fort Smith.[8] Patrolling the Arkansas near Clarksville were the Second Infantry Division and two unattached infantry brigades commanded by Brigadier General John S. Roane. The Second Corps, directed by Holmes himself, held a thin line running along the western bank of the White River, about forty-five miles east of Little Rock. Brigadier General H. E. McCulloch had three infantry brigades and W. H. Parsons' cavalry

[5] J. M. Schofield's report of Union operations in Missouri and Arkansas, April 10 to November 20, 1862, [n.d.], *Official Records*, ser. I, vol. XIII, 8, 9, 14, 17.

[6] *Ibid.*, 881; *ibid.*, ser. I, vol. XXII, pt. I, 903–904.

[7] *Ibid.*; T. H. Holmes to S. Cooper, November 25, 1862, *ibid.*, ser. I, vol. XIII, 927.

[8] Mabel W. Anderson, *Life of General Stand Watie: The Only Indian Brigadier General of the Confederate Army and the Last General to Surrender*, p. 20.

brigade at Brownsville, with heavy pickets thrown up near Helena watching Steele. Defending Little Rock were 4,000 or 5,000 infantry and cavalry commanded by Brigadier General T. J. Churchill. J. M. Hawes' cavalry brigade of Churchill's division guarded the White River in the vicinity of DeWitt.[9]

Most of these troops were, in Holmes' opinion, "a crude mass of undisciplined material." Over half were unarmed, and a large part of the remainder had only shotguns and squirrel rifles.[10] Could Arkansas be saved with such an army? Holmes did not think so. To make matters worse, the War Department had requested him to send 10,000 men to reinforce Pemberton at Vicksburg.[11] In answer he telegraphed Richmond on November 25 that if he were to help Pemberton "the valley of Arkansas will be taken possession of, and with it goes Arkansas and Louisiana," then Texas, and who knew what else, maybe even the whole Confederacy.[12] Earlier, Holmes had ordered Hindman to forget his "darling project" of carrying the war into Missouri, to hold onto northwestern Arkansas if he could, and to be ready to send help to Pemberton.[13] During the winter of 1862–1863, Confederate strategy in Arkansas was to be entirely defensive, unless events dictated otherwise.

In mid-November Federals in northwestern Arkansas again took the offensive. Leaving the Second and Third Divisions at Yellville, under the command of General F. J. Herron, Blunt marched the First Division of the Army of the Frontier down to Fayetteville.[14] His

[9] Holmes to Cooper, November 25, 1862, *Official Records*, ser. I, vol. XIII, 927.

[10] Holmes to Cooper, October 26, 1862, *ibid.*, p. 899.

[11] Holmes to Hindman, October 28, 1862, *ibid.*, p. 889; S. Cooper to Holmes, November 11, 1862, *ibid.*, p. 914.

[12] *Ibid.*, p. 928. Earlier, on November 12, the President informed the Secretary of War that he was opposed to moving Holmes east of the River. He hoped that under Holmes' leadership Marmaduke would be able to recapture Helena. *Ibid.*, pp. 914–915.

[13] Since August, Hindman had planned to enter Missouri with about 15,000 men. He wrote the War Department on August 5 that thousands of loyal Confederates in Missouri would flock to his banners and that with this powerful force he could "annihilate any force the enemy has or is likely to have on this side of the Mississippi." *Ibid.*, pp. 875, 889, 917, 918; David Y. Thomas, *Arkansas in War and Reconstruction 1861–1874*, pp. 153–154.

[14] S. R. Curtis to H. W. Halleck, November 24, 1862, *Official Records*, ser. I, vol. XXII, pt. I, 789. The number of effectives in the three divisions was 15,602. *Ibid.*, ser. I, vol. XIII, 807.

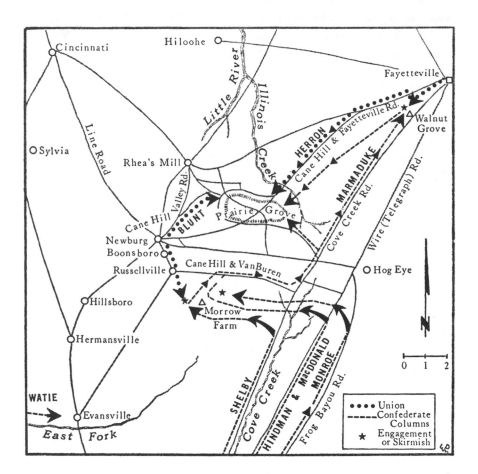

FIGURE 2

Union and Confederate lines of march during the Prairie Grove Campaign, December 3–6, 1862. Map copied and revised from a sketch in Ingersoll, *Iowa and the Rebellion*, p. 323. Neither Morrow Farm nor Walnut Grove can be located precisely; their positions on the map are, therefore approximate.

orders were to scatter the Confederate forces and wipe them out in detail.[15] After his cavalry had reconnoitered rebel installations, Blunt assured John Schofield, field general of Federal armies in Missouri, that with a little reinforcement he could crush Hindman and capture both Fort Smith and Van Buren. Little Rock would be next.[16]

The Confederates were also making plans. The militant Hindman had no taste for fighting a defensive war. Why should he wait for the Federals to attack? If he could strike them without delay, he might win a decisive victory and thus turn back the Federal army, whose skirmishers were now pestering him daily. He might then be able to invade Missouri, as he had planned to do in the summer. Throwing aside all caution, Hindman determined to take the offensive. He explained his plan to Holmes, who gave reluctant permission to undertake the campaign. Hindman's orders were to retire south of the Arkansas regardless of the outcome of the proposed operations.[17] Briefly, Hindman's strategy was this. He would send Marmaduke's cavalry on a diversion to Cane Hill to attract Blunt's attention while he marched the main army into the Union rear. With the element of surprise in their favor, Confederate forces could smash Blunt by front and rear assaults and then turn quickly to meet Herron, who at that point would probably be hastening to Blunt's aid.[18] A bold and daring plan this was, yet it might well succeed if Blunt were fooled by Marmaduke's movement to Cane Hill. The cavalry would be called upon to perform two of its basic tactical functions, namely, to seize important points for the main army, and to feint and deceive.

Cane Hill, Marmaduke's objective, was a ridge or elevation some

[15] Schofield's report for April 10 to November 20, 1862, *ibid.*, pp. 18–21; Schofield to Curtis, October 24, 1862, *ibid.*, p. 764; Schofield to Blunt, October 25, 1862, *ibid.* See also Thomas, *Arkansas in War and Reconstruction*, pp. 156–157; Wiley Britton, *The Civil War on the Border*, I, 385; Albert E. Castel, *A Frontier State at War: Kansas, 1861–1865*, p. 99. The phrase, "in detail," is military jargon meaning that the offensive force is going to defeat the opponent by scattering his units and destroying them individually.

[16] Blunt to Schofield, November 24, 1862, *Official Records*, ser. I, vol. XXII, pt. I, 790; Blunt to Schofield, November 26, 1862, *ibid.*, p. 792.

[17] Thomas, *Arkansas in War and Reconstruction*, p. 156; Robert R. Logan, "The Battle of Prairie Grove," *Arkansas Historical Quarterly*, XVI (Autumn, 1957), 259–260.

[18] Thomas, *Arkansas in War and Reconstruction*, p. 156; John N. Edwards, *Shelby and His Men: or, The War in the West*, p. 95.

eight miles in length and five miles in width, located in the south-western tip of Washington County, about thirty-five miles northeast of Van Buren. On top of the ridge were three almost adjoining hamlets—Russellville, Boonsboro, and Newburg—which extended northwest for about four miles along the road to Cincinnati. Valleys and hills flanked the ridge on both sides. Five flour mills near Newburg, and fertile farms in the valleys, producing good crops of wheat, corn, oats, potatoes, and apples, gave the area value in the eyes of both armies. In between Van Buren and Cane Hill lay the rugged Boston Mountains.[19]

Late in the evening, November 24, 1862, Quantrill's partisan company under Lieutenant W. H. Gregg left Van Buren and rode toward Newtonia to screen the movements of the cavalry division.[20] Less than an hour later Marmaduke's main column rode at a jingling trot along the "wire" or "telegraph" road which ran through Fayetteville. In the lead was J. O. Shelby's Iron Brigade, composed of B. F. Gordon's, G. W. Thompson's, and B. G. Jeans' regiments, B. F. Elliott's battalion of scouts, and Joseph Bledsoe's horse-drawn artillery. Next came C. A. Carroll's brigade, made up of J. A. Johnson's and J. C. Monroe's Arkansas regiments and J. C. Shoup's battery. Bringing up the rear was Emmett MacDonald's Missouri cavalry.[21] At dawn on November 25 the division dismounted at Cane Hill. Shelby's brigade pitched camp near Newburg, Carroll's and MacDonald's, at Boonsborough. Two hours later, after Gregg's company had also arrived at Cane Hill, Marmaduke sent out patrols to worry the Federals around Fayetteville and thus screen Hindman's main force, which was to move on the twenty-sixth or twenty-seventh.[22]

[19] T. C. Hindman to S. S. Anderson, December 25, 1862, *Official Records,* ser. I, vol. XXII, pt. I, 139; John M. Harrell, "Arkansas," *Confederate Military History,* X, 138; Edwards, *Shelby and His Men,* p. 95; Frank Moore, ed., *The Rebellion Record: A Diary of American Events . . . ,* VI, 69; Britton, *Civil War on the Border,* I, 396.

[20] Thomas, *Arkansas in War and Reconstruction,* p. 157; William E. Connelley, *Quantrill and the Border Wars,* p. 278; and John N. Edwards, *Noted Guerrillas,* pp. 156–158.

[21] Shelby's report, December 1, 1862, *Official Records,* ser. I, vol. XXII, pt. I, 55; Harrell, "Arkansas," *Confederate Military History,* X, 138.

[22] Edwards, *Shelby and His Men,* pp. 95–96. Edwards participated in the Cane Hill-Prairie Grove campaign as adjutant of Shelby's Fifth Missouri Cavalry.

At this point, as far as the Confederates knew, the campaign was unfolding according to plan. The truth was, however, that Blunt had not been fooled. Through spies and patrols, he had learned of the movements of both Hindman and Marmaduke. Blunt determined to march two of his three brigades at double-quick to Cane Hill, scatter Marmaduke, and then, with the aid of Herron's divisions, trap Hindman's army, which would, without its cavalry, be stumbling like a blindman toward Fayetteville. At dawn on the twenty-seventh he went after Marmaduke with 5,000 cavalry and infantry and thirty pieces of artillery. After making forced marches, Federal columns approached Cane Hill on the Fayetteville road at dawn on the twenty-eighth.[23]

An hour later a small body of Confederate cavalry reined up in front of headquarters tent, Shelby's brigade, and told the Colonel, who was having a quiet breakfast, that the Fayetteville road was swarming with Federals. Orders were shouted, soldiers assembled in line, mounted, formed in columns, and galloped up to a hill overlooking the Fayetteville road. There they dismounted to take position in line by regiments behind a long wooden fence. On the left was Thompson's regiment, on the right, Gordon's; Jeans' regiment and Bledsoe's two iron six-pounders, loaded with canister and grape shot, held the center. Elliott's scouts and Gregg's company, still mounted, were stationed on the flanks.[24] Several miles in the rear Marmaduke alerted Carroll's brigade and ordered it to form a second line across the road north of Boonsboro. Marmaduke had just sent MacDonald's regiment to Kidd's Mill, a few miles northeast of Carroll's position, when he heard the racket of canister and musketry sounding from the north.[25] He gathered his staff and galloped up to the front, arriving

[23] Blunt to Schofield, November 15, 1862, *Official Records*, ser. I, vol. XIII, 795; Blunt to Curtis, November 29, 1862, *ibid.*, ser. I, vol. XXII, pt. I, 42; Britton, *Civil War on the Border*, I, 385–386. Schofield had already ordered Herron to march to Blunt's aid (November 16, 1862). Herron, however, bungled the orders and remained at Yellville during the Cane Hill engagement. *Official Records*, ser. I, vol. XIII, 795.

[24] Shelby's report, *ibid.*, pp. 55–56; Edwards, *Shelby and His Men*, p. 95. Second citations of Federal and Confederate reports of the battle at Cane Hill will be without dates.

[25] C. A. Carroll's report, November 29, 1862, *Official Records*, ser. I, vol. XXII, pt. I, 55; Emmett MacDonald's report, November 30, 1862, *ibid.*, pp. 58–59; Harrell, "Arkansas," *Confederate Military History*, X, 138. Harrell

in time to see the Federal advance falling back from the hot fire delivered by Shelby's howitzers and musket. Initial success was with the Confederates, and Marmaduke, sitting placidly in his saddle behind Jeans' regiment, waited to see what the enemy would do.[26]

Blunt rallied his advance units and ordered his entire command to move up on the double-quick. Within the hour Union troops had formed in line of battle, and after an artillery barrage, commenced to make a general attack.[27]

Finding himself heavily outnumbered in men and artillery and threatened with encirclement, Marmaduke withdrew Shelby's brigade and MacDonald's regiment to Carroll's line at Boonsborough.[28] There was no time to deploy troops, for the Sixth Kansas Cavalry, supported by infantry and artillery, came rushing down the road with muskets blazing.[29] Monroe's Arkansans were thrown up as skirmishers and managed to check the Federals while the main column under Marmaduke galloped back to Russellville to draw up another defensive line.[30] The rest of Blunt's infantry marched up on the double-quick to support the advanced Kansas regiments, and 5,000 Federals, pushing aside Monroe, went after the Confederate main body. Knowing that he could not hold Cane Hill, Marmaduke decided to entangle Blunt in the Boston Mountains, several miles to the southeast. Shelby's brigade would act as rear guard to cover the withdrawal.[31]

The road on which the Confederates retreated ran for about three miles through a valley southeast of Boonsboro. Along it Shelby's troopers fought a brilliant rear guard action. Shelby's method was to arrange the thirty companies in his command in two columns on each side of the road. When the enemy approached within point-blank range, the two lead companies would open fire. Then each broke

---

participated in the Cane Hill-Prairie Grove operations as assistant adjutant general of Monroe's regiment of Carroll's Arkansas Brigade.

[26] Edwards, *Shelby and His Men*, p. 99; Shelby's Report, *Official Records*, ser. I, vol. XXII, pt. I, 56.

[27] Blunt's report, *Official Records*, ser. I, vol. XXII, pt. I, 43.

[28] Shelby's report, *ibid.*, p. 56; MacDonald's report, *ibid.*, p. 59.

[29] Blunt's report, *ibid.*, p. 44; T. E. Ewing's report, December 1, 1862, *ibid.*, p. 52; Edwards, *Shelby and His Men*, p. 99.

[30] Harrell, "Arkansas," *Confederate Military History*, X, 139; Carroll's report, *Official Records*, ser. I, vol. XXII, pt. I, 53; Shelby's report, *ibid.*, p. 57.

[31] Shelby's report, *Official Records*, ser. I, vol. XXII, pt. I, 57; Blunt's report, *ibid.*, p. 44.

PLATE 1

(above left) BEN McCULLOCH, Brigadier General. A celebrated Indian fighter who ordinarily wore a suit of black velvet rather than a uniform, he fell at Pea Ridge.

(above right) HENRY E. McCULLOCH, Brigadier General. Unlike his dashing brother, Henry was a taciturn, unassuming man who served in Texas during most of the war.

(below left) JAMES McINTOSH, Brigadier General. A West Point graduate, he commanded a cavalry brigade at Pea Ridge, where he was killed shortly after Ben McCulloch.

(below right) THOMAS J. CHURCHILL, Major General. Churchill raised the First Arkansas Mounted Rifles in 1861 and served as a division commander in the Red River Campaign.

Portraits from the collection of Ezra J. Warner.

PLATE 2

STAND WATIE, Brigadier General. A squat, fiery Cherokee with powerful pro-Southern sentiments, Watie was the only Indian brigadier general in the Confederate Army. *From the collection of Ezra J. Warner.*

PLATE 3

HENRY HOPKINS SIBLEY, Brigadier General. Pompous and pigheaded, with a weakness for the "bottle," Sibley led the Confederates to misfortune in New Mexico, then retired from active service. *From the collection of Ezra J. Warner.*

PLATE 4

EARL VAN DORN, Major General. Nephew of Andrew Jackson, Van Dorn commanded the district of Texas in 1861 and led Confederate forces at Pea Ridge, after which he rode east of the Mississippi. *From the collection of Ezra J. Warner.*

PLATE 5

THEOPHILUS H. HOLMES, Lieutenant General. Near-sighted and half deaf, "Granny" Holmes commanded the Trans-Mississippi Department during the fall and winter of 1862. *From the collection of Ezra J. Warner.*

PLATE 6

THOMAS C. HINDMAN, Major General. Hindman was an excellent organizer and a martinet to his subordinates. He commanded the Trans-Mississippi Department during the summer of 1862 and led the Confederates to defeat at Prairie Grove. *From the collection of Ezra J. Warner.*

PLATE 7

(above left) JOHN A. WHARTON, Major General. Entering the Confederate service as a member of Terry's Texas Rangers, Wharton saw action in the Red River Campaign. In 1865 he was killed in a duel with George W. Baylor.

(above right) XAVIER BLANCHARD DE BRAY, Brigadier General (commission as general not approved by President Davis). A native of France and graduate of St. Cyr, De Bray commanded the celebrated Twenty-Sixth Texas Cavalry.

(below left) JAMES F. FAGAN, Major General. Fagan led a cavalry division in Price's Missouri raid.

(below right) WILLIAM P. STEELE, Brigadier General. Steele led a regiment in Sibley's Army of New Mexico and commanded the Indian Territory during 1863.

Portraits from the collection of Ezra J. Warner.

PLATE 8

JOHN SAPPINGTON MARMADUKE, Major General. A Missouri aristocrat and the last major general appointed in the Confederate Army, Marmaduke was, aside from Jo Shelby, the main character in the story of Confederate cavalry west of the Mississippi. *From the collection of Ezra J. Warner.*

PLATE 9

JOSEPH ORVILLE SHELBY, Brigadier General. Commander of the famous Iron Brigade, Shelby was throughout the war the most able cavalry commander in the Trans-Mississippi. *From the collection of Ezra J. Warner.*

PLATE 10

STERLING PRICE, Major General. Debonair and highly popular with the Missouri troops, "Old Pap" commanded the unfortunate expedition into Missouri in 1864. *From the collection of Ezra J. Warner.*

PLATE 11

JOHN S. FORD, Colonel. "Rip" served almost all of the war in the Rio Grande Valley of Texas and led the Confederate cavalry at Palmetto Ranch, the last battle of the war. *Barker Texas History Center, University of Texas.*

PLATE 12

EDMUND KIRBY SMITH, Lieutenant General. A fairly good strategist, Smith commanded the Trans-Mississippi Department ("Kirby Smithdom") from 1863 to the end of the war. *From the collection of Ezra J. Warner.*

quickly and galloped to the head of its column, there to reload and make ready to repeat the maneuver. Thus the Federals always faced a solid rank with loaded muskets.[32]

At about 3:00 P.M. the Confederates reached a large mound-shaped hill at the base of the Boston Mountains. Here they dismounted and deployed in line to make another stand, but a barrage of Federal shells forced them to fall back to a stronger position in the mountains some four miles southeast of Cane Hill. There part of the division under Shelby was placed on a peak overlooking the road, while Carroll's brigade, the rest of Shelby's brigade, and MacDonald's regiment went back about a mile into the mountains to form a second line directly across the road. With Shelby were part of Bledsoe's battery, stationed on the summit and under the command of Lieutenant Dick Collins, several companies of Thompson's regiment led by M. W. Smith, part of Elliott's battalion commanded by a Captain Martin, and Gregg's company. Shelby dismounted all the horsemen and placed them in line along the north side of the mountain.[33] Just as Lieutenant Arthur McCoy planted the Stars and Bars squarely on the summit, the sun pierced through a break in the heavy clouds "and seemed to crest the waving banner with a crown of golden radiance." Certain of divine blessings, Shelby pointed to the blazing sky and shouted, "It is the sun of Austerlitz!"[34] But when the smoke of battle had cleared from the mountain and the Confederate flag lay buried beneath dirt and mangled bodies, Shelby would remember that it had been the Austrian sun for him.

Several hundred yards below the Confederates, Blunt's cavalry broke through the thick woods and stopped in a wide clearing. In a few minutes they were reinforced by the infantry. To the right of the clearing, on a slight elevation, General Blunt sat in his saddle survey-

[32] Edwards, *Shelby and His Men*, p. 100; Shelby's report, *Official Records*, ser. I, vol. XXII, pt. I, 57. According to Jay Monaghan, *Civil War on the Western Border, 1854–1865*, p. 259, this was the same trick that the Federal General Franz Siegel had used with artillery in the battle of Carthage, Missouri, July, 1861.

[33] Shelby's report, *Official Records*, ser. I, vol. XXII, pt. I, 57; Britton, *Civil War on the Border*, I, 390. Edwards says that Shelby had only Jeans' regiment on the mountain. *Shelby and His Men*, p. 101. The *Official Records*, ser. I, vol. XXII, pt. I, 57, show this to be a slip of the pen.

[34] Edwards, *Shelby and His Men*, p. 100.

ing the Confederate position and comparing it to his own. The Federal army was surrounded by trees and shrubbery, not to mention deep ravines and steep cliffs. He would not be able to use his field artillery to advantage; therefore, the mountain would have to be taken by storm. Blunt sent word to Colonel O. A. Bassett to dismount his Second Kansas Cavalry and open the attack from the center. The other units lined up to Bassett's right and left, forming a spearhead designed to smash through the Confederate center and roll back the left and right wings.[35]

In the initial attack at 5:00 P.M. the Federals dashed up the slope only to be pinned down by Confederate fire. The blue-coats soon fell back down the slope, but then reformed the line and renewed the attack.[36] Shelby, watching the oncoming troops, shifted three companies of Thompson's regiment to the center to receive the main shock and sent Gregg's company to the right to protect the flank. The two lines clashed and the fighting broke up into hand-to-hand grapplings. Over the "zip-zip" of Minie balls and the noise of cannon wailed the fierce war whoops of Union Indians (First and Third Indian Home Guard Infantry) and the screams of wounded men. Shelby seemed to be in a dozen places at once. He dashed up and down the line trying to reform his companies. The plume in his hat was carried away by a stray musket ball, and four horses, one after the other, were shot from beneath his legs.[37]

Outnumbered five to one, the Confederates fought stubbornly, but most of the "storm of lead and iron hail" they directed against the Union soldiers passed over their heads without doing much damage. The Federals could not be checked. In a final charge they carried the mountain, pushing Shelby's troops back to the second Confederate line held by Marmaduke.[38] Blunt marshaled his infantry and dis-

---

[35] Blunt's report, *Official Records*, ser. I, vol. XXII, pt. I, 45; Ewing's report, *ibid.*, p. 52; O. A. Bassett's report, December 2, 1862, *ibid.*, p. 50; W. T. Cloud's report, December 15, 1862, *ibid.*, p. 47; Britton, *Civil War on the Border*, I, 390–391. Britton was a member of the Sixth Kansas Cavalry which fought in the battles of Cane Hill and Prairie Grove.

[36] Blunt's report, *Official Records*, ser. I, vol. XXII, pt. I, 45; Shelby's report, *ibid.*, p. 57; MacDonald's report, *ibid.*, p. 59.

[37] Edwards, *Shelby and His Men*, p. 101; Shelby's report, *Official Records*, ser. I, vol. XXII, pt. I, 57; Blunt's report, *ibid.*, p. 45.

[38] *Ibid.*

mounted cavalry and sent them to scatter the rebels. Marmaduke decided once again not to undertake a general engagement and ordered a running retreat. And in this manner the Confederates fought through the mountains—skirmishing at one point, falling back, reforming, and skirmishing again.[39]

From the highest point in the mountains, the Cove Creek-Fayetteville road descended southward gradually into Cove Creek Valley, a narrow defile hemmed in by thickly wooded hills. Into this valley, shaped something like a funnel, rode Marmaduke's troops to make another stand. Carroll's brigade, up to now, had participated in little of the actual fighting. In each stand it had been given the inglorious assignment of holding a line in the rear. This was a vital formation in battle. A second line prevented complete rout of the first position and acted to check the charge of the enemy, once he had broken through the front line. Most of the volunteers, however, knew nothing of tactics; the only rule was to stand up and fight and keep on fighting until you were killed. One who went to the rear was a coward. And Shelby's horsemen, who had been up at the front since early morning, chided the Arkansans for being "cowards" and hiding in the rear. But now the Arkansans were to be given a chance to prove themselves. Marmaduke ordered them to cover the Confederate main body, which was quickly deploying in Cove Creek Valley. With bugles sounding they galloped up the road to meet the advance of Blunt's cavalry. The Federal advance could not be checked, and the Arkansans fell back down the road with bullets whizzing over their heads and 2,500 troops following in pursuit. At point-blank range, Shelby's and MacDonald's men rose up from both sides of the road, and the two forces blended, the noise of the fighting echoing up and down the valley. "The cheering of the white men," wrote a newspaper correspondent, "the shrill war-whoops of the Indians, the clashing of sabres, and the incessant roar of small arms, converted this remote mountain gorge into a perfect Pandemonium."[40]

Fighting stopped at nightfall. Federals wandered back up the road to reform at the mouth of the gorge; Confederates groped about in

[39] MacDonald's report, *ibid.*, p. 59; Shelby's report, *ibid.*, p. 57.
[40] Moore, *Rebellion Record*, VI, 185; Harrell, "Arkansas," *Confederate Military History*, X, 140; Carroll's report, *Official Records*, ser. I, vol. XXII, pt. I, 53–55.

the blackness searching for their outfits. A cold November wind began to blow and rain soon started to fall. A few men sought shelter under trees, but the rest dropped where they happened to be—on the road, in ditches, behind rocks—and fell asleep, the rain soaking their dirty uniforms and ruining their ammunition. They were too exhausted to care much about the weather, about anything except rest. Several hours later, at 5:00 A.M., November 29, Marmaduke led his soldiers back towards Van Buren.[41]

The battle at Cane Hill had extended for nine hours over fifteen miles of ridges, heavy timber and brush, and mountains and valleys. Both sides reported that fighting had been furious and bloody, but the actual losses were trifling in proportion to the numbers engaged. Eight Federals were killed and thirty-two wounded out of a total force of 5,000.[42] Confederate losses, out of a total engaged of 2,000 were not precisely reported, but they were not large, probably about the same as the Federal.[43] No doubt the number killed would have been much larger had the fighting occurred in open country. Trees and underbrush stopped much of the shot and shell and made it difficult to deploy artillery. This was of course an advantage for the Confederates, who were badly outgunned.[44]

Marmaduke's tactics also prevented a large casualty list. He understood that cavalry ordinarily was not a defensive force, that once it had lost the offensive it should fall back. And using this principle he retreated slowly from Cane Hill, making stands, but refusing to undertake a general engagement with unfavorable odds. Had he ordered his cavalry to attempt a decisive battle at Cane Hill, his division more than likely would have been wiped out.

Marmaduke halted his division at Dripping Springs and then rode over to Van Buren to inform Hindman that the first step of the campaign had failed. To the cavalryman's astonishment, the command-

[41] Moore, *Rebellion Record*, VI, 185; Edwards, *Shelby and His Men*, pp. 103–104; Shelby's report, *Official Records*, ser. I, vol. XXII, pt. I, 58; Blunt's report, *ibid.*, p. 46; Britton, *Civil War on the Border*, I, 394.

[42] Blunt's report, *Official Records*, ser. I, vol. XXII, pt. I, 46.

[43] Carroll reported that his brigade suffered only fourteen casualties. MacDonald gave his losses as five killed, seventeen wounded, and four missing. Nothing is known of Shelby's losses. *Ibid.*, pp. 55, 59; Thomas, *Arkansas in War and Reconstruction*, p. 161.

[44] Blunt's report, *Official Records*, ser. I, vol. XXII, pt. I, 46; Moore, *Rebellion Record*, VI, 185; Britton, *Civil War on the Border*, I, 394–395.

ing general's only reaction to defeat was to call for another attack. Marmaduke must get back to Dripping Springs and prepare the cavalry for a general advance on Cane Hill to be made by the entire First Corps.[45]

At dawn, December 3, Hindman started toward Cane Hill with 9,000 infantry, 2,300 cavalry, and twenty-two pieces of artillery. Want of shoes had compelled him to leave nearly 1,000 infantry at Van Buren.[46] Most of the effective army were clad in summer garments and suffered terribly from the bitter cold in the mountains.[47]

The line of advance followed three parallel roads that ran northward over the Boston Mountains to Fayetteville (see Figure 2). The main force, the infantry divisions of General Francis A. Shoup and General D. M. Frost, marched over the "wire" or "telegraph" road, with MacDonald's cavalry brigade in their front. About a mile to the west, Shelby's brigade trotted along the Cove Creek road to cover the left flank. Carroll's brigade (now commanded by Colonel J. C. Monroe), protecting the right flank, advanced down the Frog Bayou road, a mile east of the wire road. The plan of attack called for Shelby and Monroe to secure the Boston Mountains just south of Russellville and then to harass the Federals from the front while the infantry divisions and MacDonald's cavalry fell on their exposed flanks and rear. From the Indian Territory rode Stand Watie's Cherokees with orders to halt at Evansville, wait for the firing to commence, and then seize the flour mills west of Newburg. They were also to be prepared to attack Federal supply trains, should Blunt send his trains toward Cincinnati.[48]

Reports of Hindman's advance did not surprise Blunt. The day before, December 2, he had telegraphed Curtis, now commander of the Department of Missouri, that Hindman's army, 25,000 strong, was coming after him; at the same time he ordered Herron to reinforce him.[49] On the morning of the third he shifted a brigade to Rhea's Mill, eight miles north of Cane Hill, to guard supply trains from

[45] Edwards, *Shelby and His Men*, p. 111.
[46] Hindman's report, December 25, 1862, *Official Records*, ser. I, vol. XXII, pt. I, 138–139.
[47] Edwards, *Shelby and His Men*, p. 111.
[48] Marmaduke's report, December 16, 1862, *Official Records*, ser. I, vol. XXII, pt. I, 146; Hindman's report, *ibid.*, p. 139; Colonel Thomas L. Snead, "The Conquest of Arkansas," in *Battles and Leaders*, III, 449.
[49] *Official Records*, ser. I, vol. XXII, pt. I, 805.

Fayetteville. That afternoon the Second and Third Brigades with batteries were ordered to deploy across the Cane Hill-Van Buren road, two miles south of Russellville. When these dispositions were complete, pickets advanced to Morrow's farm and Reed's Mountain to cover the road to Van Buren.[50]

Meanwhile, Hindman's campaign met its first snag: intermittent rain and snow flurries delayed the progress of the main army, so that it advanced fewer than twenty miles in three days.[51] Shelby's cavalry, riding on ahead, reached Morrow's farm the night of December 5, and at dawn the next day drove Federal pickets back to the position held by Blunt's Second and Third Brigades.[52] That afternoon Monroe's Arkansas cavalry encountered Federal patrols near Reed's Mountain and scattered them with howitzer fire.[53] Hindman then rushed up Parsons' infantry brigade to support the gains of the cavalry, and by 7:00 P.M. the Confederates held a strong line in the mountains.[54] Across the Cove Creek Valley, Federal camp fires began to sparkle and smoulder.

While Hindman was pushing the remainder of his army through the mountains, reinforcements for Blunt were on the way. General Herron, moving the bulk of the Army of the Frontier back to Springfield, had received Blunt's telegraph at Wilson's Creek on December 4. By forced marches the General with six brigades, including 2,000 cavalry and thirty guns, reached Elk Horn on the fifth. That evening Herron's cavalry brigades rode ahead, and at 9:00 P.M. on the sixth reported to Blunt at Cane Hill.[55] At 3:00 A.M. on the seventh the rest

---

[50] Blunt's report, December 20, 1862, *ibid.*, p. 71.

[51] Hindman's report, *ibid.*, pp. 139–140.

[52] Shelby's report, December 11, 1862, *ibid.*, p. 149; Blunt's report, *ibid.*, p. 71; Edwards, *Shelby and His Men*, p. 112; Britton, *Civil War on the Border*, I, 400.

[53] Monroe's report, December 10, 1862, *Official Records*, ser. I, vol. XXII, pt. I, 153; Blunt to F. J. Herron, December 6, 1862, *ibid.*, pp. 812–813; Harrell, "Arkansas," *Confederate Military History*, X, 143.

[54] Hindman's report, *Official Records*, ser. I, vol. XXII, pt. I, 140; Marmaduke's report, *ibid.*, p. 147; Shelby's report, *ibid.*, p. 149.

[55] Herron's report, December 12, 1862, *ibid.*, p. 102; Curtis to J. C. Kelton, December 6, 1862, *ibid.*, p. 812; Wickersham's report, December 8, 1862, *ibid.*, p. 124; Blunt's report, *ibid.*, p. 72; Herron to Blunt, December 6, 1862, *ibid.*, p. 812; Charles H. Lothrop, *A History of the First Regiment Iowa Cavalry* ..., p. 89; Lurton Dunham Ingersoll, *Iowa and the Rebellion: A History of the Troops Furnished by the State of Iowa to the Volunteer Armies of the Union* ..., pp. 330–331; S. H. M. Byers, *Iowa in War Times*, p. 187.

of Herron's forces reached Fayetteville, where they bivouacked for the night.[56]

Herron's movements were unknown to General Hindman. The last news he had had placed Herron somewhere in the vicinity of Springfield—too far away to help Blunt. At dusk on December 6 Hindman assembled his generals at Morrow's farmhouse for final battle instructions. They gathered around a large table in one of the downstairs rooms and began to discuss the excellent possibilities of whipping Blunt. There were some differences of opinion on how the attack was to be carried out. Hindman insisted that Blunt should be attacked immediately. Marmaduke and James F. Fagan agreed. Shoup, Frost, and John S. Roane were undecided, fearing that inadequate supplies would result in disaster if the offensive were taken immediately. The commanding general argued pertinaciously and finally convinced the doubting officers that his plan would succeed. While the cavalry harried Blunt's right, he explained, the two infantry divisions would slide around his left flank and fall upon his rear, thus forcing him from his stronghold about Cane Hill.[57] Maps were being rolled up when a dispatch rider burst into the room with a message from Confederate headquarters at Little Rock:

General: I am instructed by Major-General Holmes to inform you that all the enemy's forces at Springfield, Mo., left that place on Thursday and Friday . . . and moved in the direction of Arkansas. . . . The force that left Springfield amounted to from 10,000 to 12,000. . . .[58]

Hindman knew that it was Herron and the rest of the Army of the Frontier. The original plan was scrapped and a new one contrived. Hindman would march his army in between the two Federal forces to prevent them from uniting, smash Herron, and then turn to defeat Blunt. Everything would depend upon speed and surprise.[59]

At midnight on the sixth Parsons' infantry moved back from the mountain line to Morrow's farm and fell into column behind Frost's

[56] Herron's report, *Official Records*, ser. I, vol. XXII, pt. I, 102; William Baxter, *Pea Ridge and Prairie Grove: or, Scenes and Incidents of the War in Arkansas*, pp. 179–181; Elsa Vaught, ed., *Diary of an Unknown Soldier, September 5, 1862 to December 7, 1862*, p. 41.

[57] Edwards, *Shelby and His Men*, p. 114; Hindman's report, *Official Records*, ser. I, vol. XXII, pt. I, 140.

[58] *Official Records*, ser. I, vol. XXII, pt. I, 902.

[59] Hindman's report, *ibid.*, p. 140.

division. Monroe's cavalry brigade was left near Russellville to skirmish vigorously as infantry, fool Blunt into thinking that his quarter was to be the center of attack, and thus prevent him from joining Herron. At 1:00 A.M. supply trains under a small guard moved to the rear on the telegraph road. These dispositions left Hindman with 10,000 effectives to contend with 6,000 under Herron, or with 11,000 should Herron and Blunt unite.[60]

At 3:00 A.M., Sunday, December 7, Hindman's long columns started toward Fayetteville, Marmaduke's division in the lead. Shelby's brigade was sent far ahead to seek out enemy pickets. At 4:00 A.M. the brigade passed the Hog Eye-Van Buren crossroads. Fayetteville lay six miles ahead. Bending forward in their saddles, the Missourians strained their eyes to catch the first fleeting glimpse of an enemy. Overhead, stars were twinkling, and a half-moon was sinking over the western horizon. The deathly still air carried not a sound except the dull, mechanical hoofbeats of the horses and an occasional squeak of leather. Over to Shelby's left MacDonald's brigade, comprising the First Texas Partisan Rangers, Lieutenant Colonel R. P. Crump, and M. L. Young's Missouri regiment, made its way through the brush about 200 yards west of the Cove Creek and Fayetteville road.[61] Shelby's column stopped momentarily while a squad from Gregg's company scouted the road ahead. "Halt! Who goes there?" rang out a strong voice. Several rifle shots flashed in the gloom and a Federal sentinel fell dead from his horse.[62] Harsh shouts and the popping of revolvers sounded from the left, and soon a small body of Federal cavalry came crashing through the thickets into the road, closely pursued by troopers from MacDonald's outfit. A "rebel yell" ripped through the air, and Shelby's men charged up the road, scattered the patrol, and swept down upon a Federal supply train guarded by a large detachment of cavalry. Elliott's and Jeans' troops hit the head of the column while Gregg's company fired at its rear. Screams of wounded Yankees, neighing of horses, and a whirlwind of musketry rose above the shouts of Union officers trying to steady their men.

[60] *Ibid.;* Monroe's report, *ibid.,* p. 154; Harrell, "Arkansas," *Confederate Military History,* X, 144; Edwards, *Shelby and His Men,* pp. 114–115.
[61] Marmaduke's report, *Official Records,* ser. I, vol. XXII, pt. I, 147; Shelby's report, *ibid.,* p. 149; MacDonald's report, December 11, 1862, *ibid.,* p. 154; Edwards, *Shelby and His Men,* p. 115.
[62] Edwards, *Shelby and His Men,* p. 116.

Blue-clad horsemen broke and fled with Shelby's troopers close on their heels.[63] In a few minutes MacDonald's brigade came upon the scene, stopped, and listened to the sound of thundering hooves fading in the distance. The road and clearing around them were strewn with rifles, pistols, and haversacks. The Missourians picked up weapons and canteens and then spurred their horses to full gallop and followed Shelby.[64]

In complete rout the enemy patrol kept running all the way back to Fayetteville, where they met Herron's divisions moving southward and set the entire army into confusion. "It was with the greatest difficulty," said Herron, "that we got them checked and prevented a general stampede of the battery horses; but after some hard talking, and my finally shooting one cowardly whelp off his horse they halted."[65] Herron's army, still somewhat confused, then deployed in line near Walnut Grove. Gray-clad cavalrymen emerged from the woods, dismounted, and prepared to assault. A battery of Missouri Light Artillery came up from the Union rear and began to argue with the Confederate cannon.[66]

Over on the Confederate left Marmaduke and his staff appeared. The general shouted an order, bugles sounded, and muskets began to flash all along the Confederate line. Soon, the tempo of artillery fire and the chatter of Federal small arms began to pick up. Where was the Confederate infantry? General Shoup had orders to follow up the cavalry as soon as it made contact with Herron. All along the Union line new troops were falling into position, and it appeared to Marmaduke that Herron had rallied his troops. Shoup still did not come. The Union line began to advance; there must be 5,000 coming in un-

[63] Shelby's report, *Official Records*, ser. I, vol. XXII, pt. I, 149–150; MacDonald's report, *ibid.*, p. 155; Lafayette Bunner to M. H. Brawner, December 11, 1862, *ibid.*, p. 114; Brawner to J. G. Clark, December 11, 1862, *ibid.*, p. 113; M. L. Young to F. B. Davidson, December 9, 1862, *ibid.*, p. 156; Ingersoll, *Iowa and the Rebellion*, p. 324.

[64] MacDonald's report, *Official Records*, ser. I, vol. XXII, pt. I, 155; R. P. Crump's report, December 9, 1862, *ibid.*, p. 157.

[65] Herron's report, *ibid.*, pp. 102–103; Herron's letter to a friend in Dubuque, Iowa, December 15, 1862, in Moore, *Rebellion Record*, VI, 69; Ingersoll, *Iowa and the Rebellion*, p. 324.

[66] Amos L. Burrows' report, December 9, 1862, *Official Records*, ser. I, vol. XXII, pt. I, 137; Joseph Foust to W. W. Orme, December 8, 1862, *ibid.*, p. 136; Britton, *Civil War on the Border*, I, 407.

broken front. Little could be done except retreat, and the cavalry mounted and galloped southward.[67]

Up to this point, Hindman's planning had been excellent, but now he failed to grasp the tactical opportunity. Instead of rushing the infantry to the support of Marmaduke and crushing the Federals in their confusion, he deployed his troops behind the Illinois River, near Prairie Grove, and waited for Herron to attack. Such passivity was certainly not typical of him, for he usually took advantage of any circumstance in his favor. If we may believe Major Edwards, the fault lay with the division commander, General Francis A. Shoup. Instead of following orders, Shoup "dilly-dallied" around, waiting an hour for Herron to attack, and then wasted another precious hour trying to find Hindman to tell him that the division was not strong enough to drive the enemy.[68] Yet Hindman did not reproach Shoup for his failure to support Marmaduke; in fact, he commended him for fine defensive dispositions. Thus Hindman must shoulder final responsibility for the failure to follow up the initial success of the cavalry. It may be that he did all that was possible under the circumstances. Most of his infantry were still far in the rear, and too exhausted to continue the march.[69]

Without reinforcements the cavalry had to fall back to Prairie Grove, where they dismounted and formed in line of battle on Shoup's right. Thus far the Confederate cavalry had performed with merit their basic tactical duties in the campaign. They had scouted enemy troop installations and routed pickets and patrols. They had screened the movements of the main army and protected the flanks and rear of marching infantry. Most important of all, they had set Herron's entire army in confusion. Now they prepared to fight on foot alongside the infantry.

The ridge on which the Confederates lay in wait for Herron ran east and west for about one mile. Heavy timber and thick underbrush made deployment of troops exceedingly difficult. Across the center

[67] Marmaduke's report, *Official Records*, ser. I, vol. XXII, pt. I, 147; Shelby's report, *ibid.*, p. 150; Herron's report, *ibid.*, p. 103; Herron's letter in Moore, *Rebellion Record*, VI, 69; Ingersoll, *Iowa in the Rebellion*, p. 324.

[68] Edwards, *Shelby and His Men*, p. 119.

[69] Hindman's report, *Official Records*, ser. I, vol. XXII, pt. I, 164; Thomas, *Arkansas in War and Reconstruction*, p. 165; Logan, "Battle of Prairie Grove," *Arkansas Historical Quarterly*, XVI, 262–263.

of the ridge ran the Fayetteville road. Clustered about the summit were a few deserted farmhouses and Prairie Grove Church, which was to be used as a Confederate field hospital. To the north of the ridge two cornfields, separated by the Fayetteville road, occupied a large valley. The Illinois River wound and twisted through the northern end of the valley, then flowed southwest toward the Arkansas River.[70] Hindman's plan in taking position upon the ridge was to let the enemy exhaust himself by continuous assaults.[71]

As Hindman and his staff stood on the steps of the church and watched, long lines of infantry trudged up the road. Some of the artillery harnesses had broken, and the heavy guns were being pulled by hand up the steep slope. A squad of cavalry scouts moved single file through the thick brush east of the infantry, dismounted, and formed a line near a deserted farmhouse. Suddenly, one of Hindman's staff officers ran into the churchyard, shouting and pointing westward toward Cane Hill. Dense columns of smoke rolling up into the sky indicated that Blunt had destroyed his stores and was moving to unite with Herron. Hindman now made what arrangements he could to meet the exigency. He ordered Frost's division to take a position on the western end of the ridge to meet Blunt, and sent word to Shoup and Marmaduke to be prepared for an assault from Herron.[72] By 11:00 A.M. Confederate dispositions were complete. On the left flank, near the Morton farm, was Roane's infantry brigade facing northwest. Immediately on Roane's right was M. M. Parsons' infantry brigade, with Perdell's battalion and the regiments of J. H. Caldwell, D. C. Hunter, A. E. Steen, and J. D. White from left to right in that order. Wesley Roberts' and C. B. Tilden's batteries were stationed on Parsons' left and right. Next was R. G. Shaver's brigade with its right flank resting on the west side of the Fayetteville road. Across this road and somewhat ahead of Shaver was Shoup's division with the brigades of Dandridge McCrae and J. F. Fagan and the batteries of H. C. West and W. D. Blocher. Fagan's right flank was located near the Borden farm. Holding the extreme right of the line were the

[70] Lothrop, *First Iowa Cavalry*, p. 90; Blunt's report, *Official Records*, ser. I, vol. XXII, pt. I, 74; Hindman's report, *ibid.*, p. 141; Moore, *Rebellion Record*, VI, 77; Ingersoll, *Iowa and the Rebellion*, p. 331.

[71] Thomas, *Arkansas in War and Reconstruction*, p. 165.

[72] Hindman's report, *Official Records*, ser. I, vol. XXII, pt. I, 141; Harrell, "Arkansas," *Confederate Military History*, X, 145.

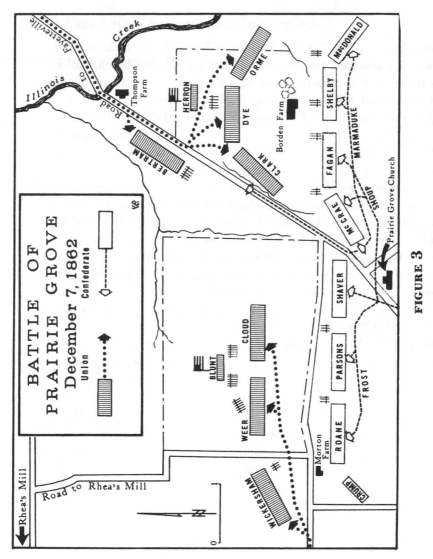

FIGURE 3

Map copied and revised from a drawing in *Battles and Leaders*, III, 449.

cavalry brigades of Shelby and MacDonald with Joseph Bledsoe's and Samuel Rufner's batteries—all under the command of General Marmaduke. Crump's First Texas Cavalry, normally a part of Mac-Donald's brigade, was shifted to the extreme left of the line. This completed the roster of Hindman's army. It totaled about 1,900 cavalry and 8,100 infantry and artillery.[73] Confederate positions, as well as those of the Federals, are shown in Figure 3.

While Marmaduke had contested Herron's advanced cavalry on the morning of the seventh, Monroe's cavalry attacking the Federals at Cane Hill had led Blunt to believe the entire Confederate army to be rolling down upon him. At 10:00 A.M. a cavalry patrol trotted into Blunt's headquarters at Newburg to tell the General that they had all been tricked. Hindman's army had been marching toward Fayetteville since midnight![74] Blunt then gathered his brigades and set out for Fayetteville via the valley road. A cavalry brigade had just been sent ahead when the booming of cannon was heard in the direction of Prairie Grove, five miles to the northeast. Blunt ordered his troops to march at double-quick. Perhaps they could still reach Herron in time.[75]

The booming that Blunt's troops heard came from Marmaduke's artillery, which were firing at an advanced unit of Herron's cavalry. The Federal horsemen soon turned their mounts and galloped back across the valley.[76] Certain that the cavalry was a feeler for Herron's army, Marmaduke rode from outfit to outfit, making final dispositions. Gordon's regiment was shifted to the right to support Bledsoe's battery. Thompson's regiment was placed on Bledsoe's left, just ahead and to the right of Fagan's brigade of Shoup's division. After ordering Gregg's company to join Gordon, Marmaduke instructed

[73] Charles W. Walker, "Battle of Prairie Grove," in *Publications of the Arkansas Historical Association*, II (1908), 357–358; Hindman's report, *Official Records*, ser. I, vol. XXII, pt. I, 141–142; Marmaduke's report, *ibid.*, p. 147; Shelby's report, *ibid.*, p. 150; MacDonald's report, *ibid.*, p. 135; H. C. West's report, December 9, 1862, *ibid.*, p. 158.

[74] Blunt's report, *ibid.*, p. 72, 73; J. M. Richardson's report, December 15, 1862, *ibid.*, p. 87; Britton, *Civil War on the Border*, I, 410.

[75] Blunt's report, *Official Records*, ser. I, vol. XXII, pt. I, 73–75.

[76] A. L. Burrow's report, December 9, 1862, *ibid.*, pp. 137–138; Britton, *Civil War on the Border*, I, 408–410.

MacDonald to mount his brigade and take position on the exposed right flank.[77]

Down in the valley Herron's infantry columns moved up to a small creek several hundred yards northwest of the Borden farm where they made ready for battle. At noon a line officer fired the signal gun, and with a roar Federal cannon swept the ridge with shell, shot, grape, and canister.[78]

Shelby's troops received the brunt of the fire. To avoid severe damage Shelby moved his brigade to the right and then shifted Thompson's and Jeans' regiments to support Blocher's advanced battery.[79]

Deciding to carry the ridge by storm, Herron unleashed his eager troops. They splashed through the creek, jogged across the cornfield, swept through a peach orchard beside the Borden farm, and broke into a dead run up the slope[80]—"like a stream that broke its banks," said a Confederate. "In unbroken front" they came, cheering, shouting, their muskets blazing.[81] They swept over the crest, shoving aside Thompson's regiment, flanking Jeans' regiment, and capturing Blocher's battery.[82]

Shelby, seeing that his advance line had crumbled, ordered Fagan's brigade to strike the Federal flank, brought up Gordon's regiment at double-quick, rallied part of Jeans' regiment, and led a countercharge against the advancing infantry. Surging forward, Confederates clubbed their way through to recapture Blocher's battery, then used

[77] Shelby's report, *Official Records*, ser. I, vol. XXII, pt. I, 150–151.

[78] Herron's report, *ibid.*, p. 105; W. W. Orme's report, December 10, 1862, *ibid.*, pp. 129–130; David Murphy's report, December 8, 1862, *ibid.*, p. 123; Daniel Huston's report, December 9, 1862, *ibid.*, p. 109; Herron to Curtis, December 12, 1862, *ibid.*, p. 103; J. G. Clark's report, December 14, 1862, *ibid.*, pp. 111–112; Herron's letter in Moore, *Rebellion Record*, VI, 69; Ingersoll, *Iowa in the Rebellion*, p. 324.

[79] Shelby's report, *Official Records*, ser. I, vol. XXII, pt. I, 151; Moore, *Rebellion Record*, VI, 69; Walker, "Battle of Prairie Grove," in *Publications of the Arkansas Historical Association*, II, 358.

[80] Ingersoll, *Iowa and the Rebellion*, pp. 325, 327; Herron to Blunt, December 12, 1862, *Official Records*, ser. I, vol. XXII, pt. I, 102; Moore, *Rebellion Record*, VI, 69.

[81] Edwards, *Shelby and His Men*, p. 121; Shelby's report, *Official Records*, ser. I, vol. XXII, pt. I, 151.

[82] Hindman's report, *ibid.*, p. 142; Moore, *Rebellion Record*, VI, 78; Walker, "Battle of Prairie Grove," in *Publications of the Arkansas Historical Association*, II, 358.

108

it to cut swaths in the Federal ranks.[83] The counterattack was driven home and Federal units fell back. Then straight through the Union center rode an officer waving his hat and pleading to his men to follow him back up the slope. The effect was electrifying. The blue-clad troops turned and followed their gallant officer. Then he fell from his horse, dead, and his command again dissolved midst shots, cries, confused running, and hand-to-hand strugglings. At this point Shoup's division, moving over to reinforce Shelby, dashed through the peach orchard and drove the Yankees back into the valley. Shelby reformed his units and they joined the southern tide that meant to engulf Herron's entire army.[84]

To meet the Confederates Herron rushed his artillery into the cornfield. The howitzers poured a murderous fire into the rebel ranks and checked the attack. Again it was Colonel Shelby's turn to rally his command. He made a stand in the peach orchard, where he was soon joined by fragments of McCrae's and Fagan's brigades. Over to their right MacDonald's troops pushed through dense thornbushes and turned the Federal left wing. Again Herron's infantry fell back to the cornfield and drew up in line beside the artillery. Momentarily there was a lull, then an artillery duel began.[85]

General Hindman watched the battle on his right wing from his headquarters at Prairie Grove Church. Seeing the lines heave and shudder in charge and countercharge, he directed that Shaver's brigade cross the road to reinforce Shelby, and ordered the other two brigades of Frost's division, still holding the Confederate left, to advance across the cornfield to strike Herron's exposed right flank. It was now 1:45 P.M. A roar of howitzers sounded from the west, and Hindman turned to see that Blunt's advance had arrived. He sent a second order to Frost to swing the brigades of Roane and Parsons around and engage Blunt,[86] but Frost's troops were already commit-

---

[83] Shelby's report, *Official Records*, ser. I, vol. XXII, pt. I, 151–152; Herron's report, *ibid.*, p. 106; Huston's report, *ibid.*, p. 109; Clark's report, *ibid.*, p. 111; W. M. Dye's report, December 10, 1862, *ibid.*, p. 116; Moore, *Rebellion Record*, VI, 78; Ingersoll, *Iowa and the Rebellion*, pp. 325, 327.

[84] Moore, *Rebellion Record*, VI, 69; Ingersoll, *Iowa and the Rebellion*, pp. 327, 331; Vaught, *Diary of an Unknown Soldier*, p. 42; Shelby's report, *Official Records*, scr. I, vol. XXII, pt. I, 151; Leake's report, *ibid.*, p. 121.

[85] Ingersoll, *Iowa and the Rebellion*, p. 327; Hindman's report, *Official Records*, ser. I, vol. XXII, pt. I, 142; Herron's report, *ibid.*, pp. 106–107; MacDonald's report, *ibid.*, p. 155; Britton, *Civil War on the Border*, I, 418–419.

[86] Hindman's report, *Official Records*, ser. I, vol. XXII, pt. I, 142.

ted to the attack originally ordered. Charging *en échelon* by brigades from the left, they swept over Federal cavalry and headed for the Fayetteville road to turn Herron's right wing. Suddenly, from the dense woods to the west came Federal infantry to crash into Frost's naked flank. Parsons' brigade was checked and pushed back several hundred yards to Roane's right and rear. Then a group of eager Texans—Crump's cavalry—rode around the Confederate left, rolled over two regiments of Federal cavalry, and turned a captured howitzer on the right flank of the assaulting infantry. Roane's brigade reformed and drove into the enemy front.[87]

Blunt's artillery got into position and forced the Confederates to pull back to a growth of oak timber on the southwestern end of the ridge. Blunt marshaled his infantry and artillery and sent them across the field to drive the rebels. As the Federals swept into the littered woods, volleys of buckshot and musket balls passed overhead; canister, dirt, gravel, twigs, pieces of bark flew everywhere.[88] Two regiments of Federal infantry slipped through the woods to the west and fell upon the exposed flank of Parsons' brigade. Again Crump's cavalry saved their fellow Confederates. Fighting on foot they skirted the Federal right flank, brushing aside a regiment of Kansas infantry and smashing into the front of the Federal flanking units. Parsons' brigade rallied and the Federal assault was turned back.[89]

For hours the fighting continued all along Prairie Grove valley. There was a constant rattling of musketry and booming of cannon as the contending armies swayed to and fro, each alternately advancing and retiring.[90] The heaviest fighting was at the peach orchard, rightly termed by one man the "slaughter point" of the battle.[91]

[87] *Ibid.*; Blunt's report, *ibid.*, p. 74; Lothrop, *First Iowa Cavalry*, p. 90; Moore, *Rebellion Record*, VI, 72.

[88] Blunt's report, *Official Records*, ser. I, vol. XXII, pt. I, 74–75; William Weer's report, December 12, 1862, *ibid.*, p. 89; Thomas Ewing's report, December 12, 1862, *ibid.*, p. 97; John W. Rabb's report, December 10, 1862, *ibid.*, pp. 99–100; Moore, *Rebellion Record*, VI, 75.

[89] Hindman's report, *Official Records*, ser. I, vol. XXII, pt. I, 142; Blunt's report, *ibid.*, p. 75; O. A. Bassett to Cloud, December 12, 1862, *ibid.*, p. 95; Moore, *Rebellion Record*, VI, 75; Lothrop, *First Iowa Cavalry*, p. 90; Britton, *Civil War on the Border*, I, 421–422.

[90] Blunt's report, *Official Records*, ser. I, vol. XXII, pt. I, 75; Hindman's report, *ibid.*, p. 142.

[91] Moore, *Rebellion Record*, VI, 70, 75, 78; Ingersoll, *Iowa and the Rebellion*, p. 331.

As twilight fell the fighting dwindled. At 7:00 P.M. a last attack of Federal infantry was directed against the line held by Frost. Crump's and Parsons' troops repulsed it, and the western end of the valley was quiet.[92] Over on the right of the Fayetteville road Federal and Confederate artillery argued in a last powerful flurry. Then the whole battlefield was silent.[93]

Down in the east end of the valley, Shelby's troops moved out of the cornfield and filed slowly back through the peach orchard. All around them, behind stumps, logs, and trees, lay the dead and wounded. A large Illinois soldier lay on his stomach, his crushed legs twisted under him. Deliriously, he called out to a Confederate passing by, "For the love of God, friend, kill me and put me beyond such intolerable misery." "Are you in yearnest?" replied the rough Missourian, "and may I have your overcoat and canteen?" "Yes, yes—everything," murmured the dying man. "Well, heer goes—shut yer eyes and hold yer breath—'twill be over in a minute." A rifle report echoed across the orchard. The body quivered. The Confederate gathered the promised articles, stared at the dead man for a moment, then turned and joined his outfit.[94]

After reaching the ridge, Shelby's horsemen lay down on the ground, their rifles at their sides, and looked down at the battlefield, listening. From every direction came cries of suffering men. The glare of a "cold battle moon" outlined twisted figures and spread a sinister glow across the field. A white hoarfrost hardened into ice the drops of water that seeped from the brows of the dead. Bobbing lights of burial parties moved like phantoms over the battleground. Daylight came slowly, and still all the dead were not buried and many of the wounded continued to cry for mercy. The horrors of that night would never be forgotten.[95]

At 6:00 A.M. Hindman and his generals held a council of war inside the church. They were undecided whether to resume the fighting or to retreat. According to an unsubstantiated report (actually false) General Schofield had arrived at Fayetteville with 7,000 men and would

[92] Hindman's report, *Official Records*, ser. I, vol. XXII, pt. I, 142; Lothrop, *First Iowa Cavalry*, p. 90; Moore, *Rebellion Record*, VI, 76.

[93] Ingersoll, *Iowa and the Rebellion*, p. 328; Herron's report, *Official Records*, ser. I, vol. XXII, pt. I, 107.

[94] Edwards, *Shelby and His Men*, pp. 122–123.

[95] *Ibid.*, pp. 126–127; Moore, *Rebellion Record*, VI, 75, 78.

soon reinforce Herron and Blunt. The Confederate wagons, thirty miles in the rear, could not be brought forward without danger of losing them. The men were destitute of food; ammunition was insufficient to fight another day; and battery animals were dying of starvation. In truth, there was no choice but to retreat. Fires were kindled all along the ridge to fool the enemy and blankets were wrapped around howitzer wheels to muffle their noise. Then the army slipped off the ridge and disappeared down the road leading to Van Buren.[96]

On paper, the battle of Prairie Grove was a draw. Neither side had been annihilated and both sustained about the same number of casualties. Total Union losses were 175 killed, 813 wounded, 263 missing: 1,251 casualties out of a total engaged of about 8,000. Some 3,000 cavalry, kept in the rear to guard supply trains, did not take part in the fighting.[97] Confederate losses out of 10,000 engaged of all arms, were 164 killed, 817 wounded, and 336 missing: a total of 1,317. Marmaduke's cavalry division, which fought at the peach orchard, probably sustained the heaviest proportionate losses.[98] Actually, during the course of the campaign, the cavalry had seen more action than either of the two infantry divisions. The work of the cavalry was commendable, though it did not of course compare with that of Stuart's famous cavalry in some of the larger eastern campaigns. It was largely because of Marmaduke's cavalry that the Confederates enjoyed what success they did at Prairie Grove.

Having been fought to a stalemate, the battle was in reality a defeat for the Confederates. They had failed in the whole purpose of the Cane Hill-Prairie Grove campaign, which had been to drive the enemy from Arkansas. On December 8 Hindman and the First Corps forded the Arkansas River and halted at a point just east of Van Buren. They remained there until December 28, when Blunt captured Van Buren and hastened the long-projected Confederate retreat to Little Rock. Northern Arkansas from Van Buren to Carrollton was now Union.

[96] Hindman's report, *Official Records*, ser. I, vol. XXII, pt. I, 142, 143–144.
[97] *Ibid.*, p. 86.
[98] Hindman's report, *ibid.*, p. 142.

RAIDING
FEDERAL MISSOURI

STRATEGIC USE OF CAVALRY

Cavalry in the Civil War was important not only for tactical duties but also for strategic operations. The use of mounted troops for raiding purposes was something new in warfare. In no European war before 1860 had cavalry operated as an independent force to strike the enemy behind the lines. The main objective of the cavalry raid was to damage the enemy's nexus of transportation and supply. Other important objectives were to acquire information and to force the enemy to weaken his armies at the front by increasing precautions behind the lines. A raid was also calculated to lower the morale of the opposing army and thus to destroy confidence in its commanders.

In its strategic role cavalry attained objectives less by force than by secrecy, celerity, and surprise. The leader had, therefore, to be bold, resourceful, and capable of judging accurately the potential of his horses and men. The troops themselves had to be well disciplined and strong enough to endure strenuous riding. Because it was next to impossible to provide raiding cavalry with any supply trains beyond pack animals to carry demolition material, the troops must live off the country, each soldier carrying only a minimum of clothing and equipment. During the expedition, detachments, except the minimum necessary to gather forage, to replace worn-out horses, and to guard against surprise, could rarely be made, for they might easily be lost from the main column.[1]

[1] First Lieutenant S. R. Gleaves, "The Strategic Use of Cavalry," *Journal of the U.S. Cavalry Association*, XVIII (July, 1907), 9, 18–25; George T. Deni-

The Confederates were the first to recognize the strategic importance of cavalry raids. As early as June, 1862, Jeb Stuart's remarkable cavalry force circled a large Federal army under McClellan and set the style for "the raid around the army." In the West the daring expeditions of Forrest and Morgan provided a constant worry for the Army of the Cumberland, and Van Dorn forced Federals to change their plan for capturing Vicksburg by destroying Grant's base of supplies at Holly Spring (December, 1862).

Confederates in the Trans-Mississippi were apparently slow to grasp the significance of the new role of cavalry. Not until after the Prairie Grove campaign—the last major Confederate offensive in the region—did the high command decide to employ cavalry in the strategic sense. The purpose here is to demonstrate by the series of Missouri raids in 1863 and 1864 the strategic role of Confederate cavalry in the Trans-Mississippi and to work out a little-known segment of operations in the region.

FOUR CONFEDERATE RAIDS
MARMADUKE'S FIRST RAID

After Prairie Grove, Marmaduke's cavalry went into camp at Lewisburg, on the Arkansas River, a hundred miles from Fort Smith. The morale of the division was dangerously low. The general feeling seemed to be that all had been lost at Prairie Grove. To make matters worse, disquieting rumors drifted through camp that Vicksburg was being assaulted and would probably fall before the winter's end. And Blunt's Army of the Frontier was poised in northwest Arkansas waiting for the winter thaws and a chance to strike at Little Rock.[2]

---

son, *A History of Cavalry from the Earliest Times*, pp. 394–395; Brigadier General Theodore H. Rodenbough, U.S.A. (retired), ed., *The Cavalry*, Volume IV of *Photographic History of the Civil War*, pp. 18–26; Major General J. F. C. Fuller, *Grant & Lee: A Study in Personality and Generalship*, pp. 276–277. For discussion of European opinion of cavalry for raiding purposes, see Jay Luvaas, *The Military Legacy of the Civil War: The European Inheritance*, pp. 2, 66, 85, 104, 114–115, 130, 136, 139, 141–146, 148, 153, 154, 157–158, 222–223, 237–244.

[2] John N. Edwards, *Shelby and His Men: or, The War in the West*, pp. 130–131; John M. Harrell, "Arkansas," *Confederate Military History*, X, 160; Wiley Britton, *The Civil War on the Border*, I, 442; and Colonel Thomas L. Snead, "The Conquest of Arkansas," in *Battles and Leaders of the Civil War*, III, 450.

Far downstream, at Little Rock, General Holmes and General Hindman met to discuss the possibilities of a cavalry raid into Missouri. Hindman had long favored such an operation; he meant to use his cavalry as a strategic force. He now proposed to send Marmaduke's division around to strike Blunt's rear, to attack Springfield, the Federal base of supplies, and to sever communications from St. Louis to Fayetteville. This would force the Army of the Frontier to move out of the valley of the Arkansas and dismiss plans for an offensive toward Little Rock. Holmes consented to Hindman's scheme, and on December 30 dispatched the order to General Marmaduke.[3]

The cavalrymen responded to the order with alacrity and high hopes. A raid into Missouri might afford them an opportunity to visit their homes.[4] On the morning of December 31, the division, 2,370 strong, set out for Missouri. In the lead was Shelby's Iron Brigade with its famous battle flag fluttering in the freezing wind. James C. Monroe's Arkansans and Joseph Bledsoe's guns followed in column, the dull hoofbeats of the horses blending strangely with the clanging of the artillery. Emmett MacDonald's Missouri brigade brought up the rear.[5] (See Figure 4 for a map of the raid.)

At the base of the Boston Mountains the division split, Shelby's brigade moving west while MacDonald's and Monroe's rode toward Yellville. Monroe received at Yellville an order from Hindman to withdraw from the raid and attack Federal entrenchments along Van Buren Creek. Marmaduke then complained that he must have more troops, and Holmes allowed him to order Colonel Joseph C. Porter to take command of White's Missouri cavalry, encamped at Pocahontas, and form a junction with the main column at Hartville on January 8.[6] Porter, a cautious man who liked to make careful preparations, did not move until January 2.[7]

Meanwhile, Shelby and Marmaduke swung back through the Bos-

[3] Holmes to R. C. Newton, February 8, 1863, *Official Records*, ser. I, vol. XXII, pt. I, 199; Marmaduke to Newton, January 18 and February 1, 1863, *ibid.*, pp. 194–195; Britton, *Civil War on the Border*, I, 444–445; John C. Moore, "Missouri," *Confederate Military History*, IX, 111.

[4] Edwards, *Shelby and His Men*, p. 132; Britton, *Civil War on the Border*, I, 445.

[5] Marmaduke's report, February 1, 1863, *Official Records*, ser. I, vol. XXII, pt. I, 196; Shelby's report, January 31, 1863, *ibid.*, p. 200. Second citations to reports of Marmaduke's first Missouri raid will be without dates.

[6] Marmaduke's report, *ibid.*, p. 196.

[7] Porter's report, February 3, 1863, *ibid.*, p. 205.

FIGURE 4

(Porter's column, which followed the return route, is not shown.)

ton Mountains, and on January 4 met MacDonald at Yellville. Next day the column moved north, forded the White River at Dubuque, and rode toward Springfield, Missouri. Scouts informed Marmaduke that the garrison there was weakly defended and could be destroyed with little difficulty. After sending word to Porter to advance from Hartville to Springfield with all speed, Marmaduke divided his force into two columns, one under himself and the other under Shelby. Shelby rode through the Ozarks, burning several forts and destroying a few bridges. At dawn on January 8 his men encountered Federal pickets on the outskirts of Springfield. A few hours later MacDonald and Marmaduke joined him, and the united force prepared to assault the town.[8]

Dismounted and formed in line of battle, the cavalrymen swept through the streets of Springfield and drove the Federals into four breastworks in the heart of the city. Black smoke billowed up into the sky as Confederate artillery sprayed the forts and surrounding buildings with grape and canister. Twice Confederate assaults on the forts were repulsed by 3,000 determined Yankees. At 2:30 P.M., after a short artillery duel, Confederates undertook a third and final assault. As they ran down the streets, Federals jumped from behind their breastworks and the lines blended. Most of the fighting consisted of hand-to-hand grapplings in streets, behind fences, on roof tops, and from house to house. One of the first soldiers to fall was the Federal Commander with a critical wound in his right shoulder.[9] Neither side could gain anything, and with nightfall came the trumpeting of Confederate bugles sounding retreat. Gray cavalrymen moved out of Springfield, leaving twenty dead and carrying as many of the twelve wounded as they could. As the troops lay on their arms that night, they watched flames from the burning town leap into the sky and

[8] Marmaduke's report, *ibid.*, p. 196; Shelby's report, *ibid.*, pp. 200–201; G. W. C. Bennett's report, January 29, 1863, *ibid.*, pp. 207–208.

[9] Shelby's report, *ibid.*, p. 201; C. B. Holland to W. D. Wood, January 11, 1863, *ibid.*, pp. 182–183; B. Crabb to S. R. Curtis, January 10, 1863, *ibid.*, pp. 183–187; Bennett's report, *ibid.*, pp. 208–209; E. B. Brown to Curtis, January 8, 1863, *ibid.*, pp. 179–181; Frank Moore, ed., *The Rebellion Record: A Diary of American Events* . . . , VI, 350; Britton, *Civil War on the Border*, I, 447.

listened to the shouts of Federals struggling to bring the fire under control.[10]

Behind the Confederate lines Marmaduke and his colonels reviewed their situation. The fighting that day had gone badly, and the men were exhausted. Porter had not arrived; picked riders, who had been sent to look for him, reported at sundown that he could not be found. One officer suggested that they should leave Springfield; by now every Federal in Missouri was probably marching to reinforce the town. The discussion ended at midnight and the officers returned to their outfits. They would make further plans the next morning.[11]

Daybreak of January 9 came cold and clear after a cloudy night. Confederates shouldered their rifles and prepared to open the second day of the battle for Springfield. Then an order came to mount in columns. Marmaduke had decided not to continue the fight, and within the hour the horsemen were riding along the road to Rolla. Again the force split, Shelby moving through Sand Spring, burning forts and bridges, and MacDonald trotting toward Marshfield. On January 10 the two columns made a junction at Marshfield and shortly afterward were joined by Porter. The stolid colonel explained to Marmaduke that his march toward Springfield had been delayed by heavy Federal resistance at Hartville and Hazelwood. Marmaduke determined to attack these garrisons and then to return to Arkansas.[12]

Federals were out in force now and were preparing to give Marmaduke a warm welcome at Hartville. The garrison there consisted of about 1,000 cavalry and infantry; reinforcements for them—Herron's two divisions of the Army of the Frontier—were on their way from Arkansas.[13] At dusk on January 11 Federal patrols fired upon Porter's brigade, which formed the Confederate advance, and a heated skirmish flared.

---

[10] Shelby's report, *Official Records*, ser. I, vol. XXII, pt. I, 201–202; Holland to Wood, January 11, 1863, *ibid.*, pp. 182–183; Crabb to Curtis, January 10, 1863, *ibid.*, pp. 183–187; Moore, *Rebellion Record*, VI, 351; Edwards, *Shelby and His Men*, pp. 136–141.

[11] Marmaduke's report, *Official Records*, ser. I, vol. XXII, pt. I, 197.

[12] *Ibid.*; Shelby's report, *ibid.*, p. 203; Bennett's report, *ibid.*, p. 209; Porter's report, February 3, 1863, *ibid.*, pp. 205–206.

[13] Warren to Curtis, January 12, 1863, *ibid.*, pp. 187–188; Warren to N. P. Chipman, January 16, 1863, *ibid.*, pp. 189–191; Curtis to Brown, January 16, 1863, *ibid.*, p. 179.

At dawn, January 12, Shelby and MacDonald took up a position on Porter's left, and down the road they saw infantry coming up on the double-quick to support the Federal advance. For about an hour Confederates peppered away at the Federals and got peppered in return; then the Federals ran back down the road. Marmaduke's men mounted and pursued them to Hartville. There the two forces took up positions on the opposite ends of town, and began to exchange volleys of musketry and canister. Then the Confederates attacked. Above the racket of small arms could be heard shouts of the men and the screams of wounded horses.[14] Every captain but four in Shelby's brigade fell dead. Shelby himself had two horses shot under him; the glittering cavalry badge on his hat stopped a bullet. General Marmaduke and his horse went down but somehow Marmaduke extricated himself and took cover in a grove of trees. Colonel Porter, leading his brigade against the Federal right, was torn from his saddle by an artillery shell and died an hour later. On the Confederate right, Colonel Emmett MacDonald rallied a hundred stragglers and led them in a magnificent charge against a Federal artillery emplacement. A spray of canister caught the colonel squarely in the chest and stomach. Shelby ran up to the dying officer, bent over and whispered that they were going to win. MacDonald's eyes brightened momentarily and then glazed as his body stiffened. His death was a tragic loss to the division, and he would be missed in the fighting to the end of the war.[15]

The battle was as yet undecided. At dusk Marmaduke ordered a final attack. Gordon swept down the Federal right while Thompson and Shanks drove up the center. The enemy regiments fell back grudgingly to take up a stronger position inside the city. The battle ended at dark with a last flurry of musketry. The Confederates had lost twelve dead, ninety-six wounded, and three missing; Federal casualties were seven dead, sixty-four wounded, five taken prisoner, and two missing.[16]

At midnight a Confederate aide galloped in to report to Marma-

[14] Warren to Chipman, January 16, 1863, *ibid.*, p. 189; Shelby's report, *ibid.*, pp. 203–204; C. W. Dunlap to Curtis, January 22, 1863, *ibid.*, pp. 191–192; Porter's report, *ibid.*, p. 206; Bennett's report, *ibid.*, pp. 209–210; Britton, *Civil War on the Border*, I, 458–462.

[15] Edwards, *Shelby and His Men*, pp. 143–145; Moore, "Missouri," *Confederate Military History*, IX, 114.

[16] *Ibid.*; Shelby's report, *Official Records*, ser. I, vol. XXII, pt. I, 204–205.

duke that enemy cavalry were approaching from the west and that Herron's infantry were coming up from the southwest. Marmaduke decided to fall back to Arkansas.[17]

The retreat was one of acute suffering. A raging storm on January 19 lasted ten hours, leaving ice and huge snowdrifts. Many wounded, unable to endure the grueling march, dropped off, one by one, and waved to the column as it disappeared down the icy road.[18]

After eluding a regiment of Federal cavalry at the state line, the raiders followed the meandering White River and on January 25 made camp at Batesville, Arkansas.[19] Casualties of the expedition totaled about 136. Two hundred horses had been abandoned on the roadside to die, their riders marching on foot during the remainder of the raid; all the horses were badly jaded. Many troops had been frostbitten, some of them so severely that amputations were necessary. Because supply trains were snowbound for weeks in the mountains, the soldiers had to bivouac upon the snow without tents, cooking utensils, or change of clothing.[20]

Had the raid achieved its purpose? Marmaduke in his report said that:

I think I may safely state that the object of the expedition was fully accomplished, and more. Blunt's Army of the Frontier counter-marched to save Springfield; a long chain of forts, strong in themselves, built at great expense and labor, which overawed and kept in subjection the country, were razed to the ground, and the heart of the people revived again at the presence of Confederate troops.[21]

General Holmes agreed that the raid had been successful and commended Marmaduke for gallantry and excellence in command. He told Colonel R. C. Newton that his aristocratic looking brigadier "is the only officer I have who is fitted for a large cavalry command."[22]

Marmaduke's raid was a landmark in the employment of mounted

[17] Marmaduke's report, *ibid.*, p. 197; Britton, *Civil War on the Border*, I, 464-465.
[18] Edwards, *Shelby and His Men*, p. 147; Shelby's report, *Official Records*, ser. I, vol. XXII, pt. I, 204; Marmaduke to R. C. Newton, January 18, 1863, *ibid.*, p. 195.
[19] Marmaduke's report, *ibid.*, pp. 197-198.
[20] Shelby's report, *ibid.*, p. 204; Edwards, *Shelby and His Men*, p. 147.
[21] Marmaduke's report, *Official Records*, ser. I, vol. XXII, pt. I, 198.
[22] Holmes to R. C. Newton, February 8, 1863, *ibid.*, pp. 198-199.

troops west of the Mississippi. For the first time cavalry in the region had operated as an independent striking force to carry the war to the heart of the enemy.

THE CAPE GIRARDEAU RAID

Early in 1863 the War Department reshuffled the Trans-Mississippi high command. Major General Edmund Kirby Smith (Portrait on Plate 12), who had earned a reputation as Confederate commander of east Tennessee, was sent across the River to take charge of the Department.[23] General Holmes was demoted to command the district of Arkansas.[24] General Hindman, now more unpopular than ever, was relieved of command of the First Corps on January 30 and ordered to report to Vicksburg.[25]

When Kirby Smith set up his headquarters at Shreveport on March 7, he began to review the dispositions of his troops. The army totaled 26,047 men.[26] The First Corps, composed of 8,475 poorly armed infantry, was at or near Lewisburg. Marmaduke's cavalry, encamped at Batesville, was the only Confederate force in northern Arkansas. William Steele had perhaps 4,884 cavalry west of Fort Smith.[27] Holmes' Second Corps still held Little Rock, but Frederick Steele's Yankees were now advancing west from Helena and Federal gunboats were operating on the lower Arkansas and White rivers. Civil government in the state had largely disappeared and Holmes' military rule was weak. Bushwhacking, burning, assassination, pillage, and violence prevailed in the northern part of the state.[28]

Even though his army was badly scattered and fighting defensively at every point, Kirby Smith with enthusiasm and a soldier's spirit of conquest gazed northward toward Missouri. Perhaps after Confederate forces had been consolidated and the enemy driven out of Arkansas, he could send an army of invasion into the state. Smith was not just dreaming. By his request "Old Pap" Sterling Price had been

[23] Special Orders No. 11, January 14, 1863, *ibid.*, pt. II, 772; General Orders No. 23, March 18, 1863, *ibid.*, p. 803.

[24] S. Cooper to Kirby Smith, February 9, 1863, *ibid.*, p. 786.

[25] Special Orders No. 25, *ibid.*, p. 780.

[26] *Ibid.*, ser. IV, vol. II, 530.

[27] *Ibid.*, ser. I, vol. XXII, pt. II, 832–833, 793.

[28] David Y. Thomas, *Arkansas in War and Reconstruction, 1861–1874*, pp. 189–190, 197.

FIGURE 5

transferred from Mississippi to the Department and was now in command of Hindman's old corps. Perhaps this tall, handsome, popular Missourian would be the ideal officer to lead such an invasion.[29]

Capture and permanent occupation of Missouri, however, were not Smith's immediate objectives. He must first attempt to push Blunt and Steele out of Arkansas, drive the Federals out of Louisiana, help Pemberton clear the Mississippi of Union forces and keep the River open for southern trade.[30] Yet Kirby Smith did not completely rule out a Missouri operation. Marmaduke had proposed a plan which he thought might work—a cavalry diversion into Missouri. As Marmaduke pointed out, this would draw off the Federals in northern Arkansas and thus relieve some of the pressure on Vicksburg and Little Rock. Confederates might then be able to deal with the disorder and vandalism in northern Arkansas, concentrate on keeping the Mississippi in Confederate hands, and prepare to make an invasion of Missouri later in the year, perhaps in the fall.[31]

In mid-March Marmaduke travelled to Little Rock to confer with Holmes on specific objectives. The division was to sweep through the Iron Mountains, destroying telegraphs, bridges, and forts as it went, and then swing across to the eastern side of the state to demolish the strategic Federal supply depot at Cape Girardeau. Both Smith and Holmes hoped that Marmaduke could also pick up in Missouri a large number of recruits.[32]

Marmaduke returned to Batesville early in April and began to concentrate his forces at Eleven Points River.[33] There were new outfits and new officers in the division now. A brigade from Texas under

[29] Special Orders No. 58, February 17, 1863, *Official Records*, ser. I, vol. XXII, pt. II, 791; T. C. Reynolds to J. A. Seddon, February 5, 1863, *ibid.*, pp. 782–783; Seddon to J. C. Pemberton, February 6, 1863, *ibid.*, pp. 783–784.

[30] Seddon to Kirby Smith, March 18, 1863, *ibid.*, pp. 802–803; Jefferson Davis to Kirby Smith, May 8, 1863, *ibid.*, pp. 834–835.

[31] Holmes to Marmaduke, February 16, 27, March 5, 1863, *ibid.*, pp. 788, 790, 794; Edwards, *Shelby and His Men*, p. 151.

[32] Edwards, *Shelby and His Men*, p. 151; Bennett H. Young, *Confederate Wizards of the Saddle: Being Reminiscences and Observations of One Who Rode with Morgan*, p. 541; Thomas, *Arkansas in War and Reconstruction*, p. 194.

[33] Marmaduke's report, May 20, 1863, *Official Records*, ser. I, vol. XXII, pt. I, 285. Second citations to reports of Marmaduke's Cape Girardeau expedition will be without dates.

Colonel George Washington Carter comprised the Nineteenth Texas, Colonel N. M. Burford; the Twenty-First Texas, Lieutenant Colonel D. C. Giddings; Reves' Partisan Company; Major C. L. Morgan's squadron; and Captain J. A. Pratt's four-gun battery. These men were inexperienced, but they had courage and endurance.[34] On April 9 Colonel John Q. Burbridge had formed a Missouri brigade composed of his own regiment, Colonel R. C. Newton's Fifth Arkansas Cavalry, and Lieutenant Colonel S. G. Kitchen's Missouri battalion.[35] In command of MacDonald's old brigade was a stolid and competent Missourian, Colonel Colton Greene. The four brigades that made up the division (the fourth was Shelby's)[36] numbered 5,086 with eight pieces of artillery, two of them Parrot guns attached to Bledsoe's battery of Shelby's brigade. Unfortunately, 1,200 of the men were unarmed and 900 were without horses, but Marmaduke felt compelled to take them along lest they desert if left behind. He hoped that guns and horses could be captured on the march.[37] Even allowing for the unarmed and the unmounted, the column would be a powerful one, larger than any that Wheeler, Morgan, or Forrest had thus far employed in their spectacular raids.[38]

On April 19 the division rode at an easy gait for Rolla, Missouri, some 180 miles north of Batesville. Because the country along the line of march was denuded of corn and oats—even grass was scarce—movement was in two columns, one under Shelby, the other under Carter.[39] (See Figure 5 for a map of the raid.)

Marmaduke's first objectives were the garrisons at Patterson, lightly defended by 600 militia, and Bloomfield, commanded by the notorious John McNeil, known to Confederates as the "butcherer"

[34] Young, *Confederate Wizards of the Saddle*, p. 541.

[35] S. G. Kitchens' report, May 7, 1863, *Official Records*, ser. I, vol. XXII, pt. I, 298–299; J. Q. Burbridge's report, May 11, 1863, *ibid.*, p. 296.

[36] Greene's brigade, all Missouri troops, consisted of the regiments of Lieutenant Colonel Leonidas C. Campbell and Colonel W. L. Jeffers, and Colonel M. L. Young's battalion. Shelby's brigade, also Missouri troops, comprised the regiments of Colonel Beal G. Jeans, Colonel B. Frank Gordon, and Colonel George W. Thompson, and the battalions of Major Benjamin Elliott and Major David Shanks.

[37] Marmaduke's report, *Official Records*, ser. I, vol. XXII, pt. I, 285.

[38] Young, *Confederate Wizards of the Saddle*, p. 542.

[39] Marmaduke's report, *Official Records*, ser. I, vol. XXII, pt. I, 285; Thompson's report, May 15, 1863, *ibid.*, p. 289.

because of his alleged brutality to citizens and prisoners. McNeil had some 2,000 infantry and cavalry.[40]

The plan of operations called for demonstrations by Shelby's column, now moving west, to create the illusion of a Confederate invasion of Missouri via Thomasville, and Houston, and west of Rolla. The enemy might thus be drawn from northern Arkansas and southwestern Missouri and the garrisons at Patterson, Ironton, and Bloomfield thrown off their guard. Carter's column, composed of Carter's and Greene's brigades, was to take a shorter, less travelled route, strike Patterson, and join Shelby near Ironton. Both columns were then to smash McNeil.[41]

Carter's and Greene's brigades, riding via Doniphan, reached a hamlet thirty miles from Patterson at 4:00 A.M. on April 20. There Colonel Carter sent a detachment of 450 men and two pieces of artillery under Lieutenant Colonel Giddings to clear out Federal patrols along the road to Patterson. The detachment reached Patterson at dawn and surprised a large body of Federal cavalry trotting back home after an uneventful night of patrolling. Instead of letting these men go and avoiding a lot of gunfire which would scare off the Federal garrison, the inexperienced Texans undertook to fight them in a stand-up battle.[42] The Federal garrison commander, hearing the firing and shouting, set fire to his stores and led his force at a gallop to Bloomfield.[43] Giddings' men pursued him for a few miles, killed a few stragglers, and then returned to Patterson. At dusk Shelby's brigades, having completed their demonstrations around Thomasville and Houston, rode into Patterson. After a short rest, the combined columns struck out for Bloomfield.[44]

The next morning, April 21, Marmaduke again split his force. Carter advanced directly on Bloomfield. Marmaduke and Shelby rode for Fredericktown, ten miles southeast of Pilot Knob, to intercept

[40] Marmaduke's report, *ibid.*, p. 286; Young, *Confederate Wizards of the Saddle*, pp. 543–544; Moore, "Missouri," *Confederate Military History*, IX, 131.

[41] Marmaduke's report, *Official Records*, ser. I, vol. XXII, pt. I, 286.

[42] Carter's report, May 5, 1863, *ibid.*, p. 300; Greene's report, May 15, 1863, *ibid.*, p. 303; Marmaduke's report, *ibid.*, p. 286.

[43] Edwin Smart to J. W. Davidson, April 21, May 9, 1863, *ibid.*, pp. 263, 264–265.

[44] Marmaduke's report, *ibid.*, p. 286; Thompson's report, *ibid.*, p. 300; Burbridge's report, *ibid.*, pp. 296–297.

McNeil if he attempted to escape to Ironton. After fording the treacherous St. Francis River, Shelby's column on the evening of April 22 reached Fredericktown, capturing there a small militia force.[45] Meanwhile, Carter's troops bogged down in the Mingo Swamps, several miles northwest of Bloomfield, and lost an entire day extricating wagons and artillery from the mud. On the evening of April 23 a detachment from Burbridge's brigade under Lieutenant Colonel William J. Preston dashed into Bloomfield to find only smouldering ruins. The day lost in the swamps had given McNeil time enough to burn the town and retreat toward the Mississippi River. Preston learned from a citizen that McNeil was headed for Cape Girardeau. After the remainder of the troops came up, Carter formed them in a two-column front, and they rode east hoping to cut off McNeil at Williams' Ferry. But blowing rain and slushy roads forced them to give up the chase. At noon on April 24 McNeil and his troops filed unmolested into Cape Girardeau.[46]

In the meantime Shelby's column, ignorant of the fact that McNeil had escaped Carter, remained in the vicinity of Ironton. Late on April 23 a raiding detachment of ninety-three men slipped out of Fredericktown and during the next two days destroyed a bridge over Big Creek and wrecked long stretches of the St. Louis Railroad. On their return march they spotted a large body of enemy cavalry moving quietly toward Fredericktown. The battle flag of the First Iowa, fluttering at the head of the column, revealed it to be part of Davidson's division (under General William Vandever) of the Army of the Frontier. The Confederates hid in the woods and, after the Federals had passed, struck out for Dallas at a killing gallop, overtaking Shelby's column as it crossed the Castor River near Bloomfield.[47] Shelby then marched his men through rain and darkness to a junction with Carter near Old Jackson before dawn on April 26. Cape Girardeau lay four miles away.[48]

It was raining in torrents now, and water stood inches deep on the

---

[45] Marmaduke's report, *ibid.*, pp. 286–287; Thompson's report, *ibid.*, p. 289.

[46] Carter's report, *ibid.*, pp. 300–301; Greene's report, *ibid.*, p. 303.

[47] Muse's report, May 14, 1863, *ibid.*, p. 294; Charles H. Lothrop, *A History of the First Regiment Iowa Cavalry . . .* , pp. 107–108.

[48] Marmaduke's report, *Official Records*, ser. I, vol. XXII, pt. I, 286–287; Thompson's report, *ibid.*, p. 290.

road to Cape Girardeau. Through this slush rode the Confederate column bent on driving McNeil from the city whose lights flickered in the distance.[49] McNeil had a strong natural position. A chain of hills encircled the town on the west, and on these hills were four forts, heavily armed with field artillery and rifled cannon. The Mississippi River wound around the east side of town. The place looked to be almost impregnable, and Marmaduke decided not to attempt to storm it, at least for the time being. He sent Shelby's brigade to drive in the enemy pickets and to skirmish lightly with the forts. At 8:00 A.M. Thompson's regiment, leading Shelby's advance, encountered stiff resistance and took up a position in a field at the base of the chain of hills. The rest of Shelby's brigade quickly came up to its support. Lieutenant Colonel David Shanks' battalion formed on the left of the Jackson-Cape Girardeau road, which cut through the field and passed over the heights into the town. Shanks' left flank rested on the edge of a thick growth of timber. Immediately on Shanks' right was Thompson's regiment. Next was Captain Dick Collins' battery with one gun on the road and the other three in line in a small field on the right. In the woods on Collins' right was Colonel Beal G. Jeans' regiment. Colonel B. Frank Gordon's regiment held the extreme right of the Confederate line.

At midmorning Federal field guns opened up and raked the Confederates with shell and canister. Suddenly there emerged from the forest an uneven line of Federal infantry which began to fire at Gordon's troops. The skirmishing promised to become a respectable battle as artillery fire was "constant and terrific" and Minie balls were "hissing a treble to the music of the roar." At noon Carter's and Greene's brigades fell into position on Shelby's left, but by now General Marmaduke had agreed with Colonel Thompson that to charge the fortifications would definitely be "wanton butchery and slaughter." Leaving forty casualties on the field, the division wheeled about and fell back to Old Jackson, where it encamped for the night.[50]

At dusk two young girls, both loyal Confederates, wandered onto

[49] Thompson's report, *ibid.*, p. 290; Young, *Confederate Wizards of the Saddle*, p. 546.

[50] Thompson's report, *Official Records*, ser. I, vol. XXII, pt. I, 290–291; McNeil's report, May 12, 1863, *ibid.*, pp. 258–259; Marmaduke's report, *ibid.*, p. 287; Carter's report, *ibid.*, p. 301; Moore, *Rebellion Record*, VI, 561–563.

the battlefield to care for the wounded. Two bodies were found, hunched and twisted over the wheels of a disabled cannon. Crying softly, the two girls dug a grave with their hands and buried the dead. Afterward, they helped the walking wounded back to Cape Girardeau, where the wounded placed themselves at the mercy of John McNeil.[51]

During the afternoon McNeil had been reinforced by two steamboat loads of troops, bringing his total to perhaps 3,500. He had also received word that General Vandever with 5,000 cavalry (the force encountered by the Confederate detachment the day before) was closing in on Marmaduke from the direction of Fredericktown. Thus when the Confederates retreated, McNeil determined to take the offensive. At 8:00 P.M. Federal cavalry and infantry with drums beating and bugles blowing tramped out of Cape Girardeau along the road to Jackson.[52] Then at midnight Vandever's cavalry slipped unobserved down the Jackson and Fredericktown road and moved stealthily into the woods to encircle Newton's regiment, which was encamped some four miles beyond Jackson. Vandever's men crept out of the timber to assail the sleeping Confederates. Everywhere there were shouts, flashes, humming bullets, and men thrashing about in the darkness. Newton's troops were completely routed. Whooping and firing their pistols in the air, Federals swept into Burbridge's camp and put his brigade into great disorder. It appeared that they would rout the entire Confederate division. Colonel Burbridge managed, however, to rally two companies and check Vandever's furious assailants for the better part of an hour.

The noise having aroused Marmaduke, he ordered Shelby and Greene to take their brigades to find out what the commotion was about. Through broken lines of troops streaming back to Jackson, they made their way to Burbridge's position and opened a brisk fire upon the enemy. All the Confederates then fell back to Jackson, where they formed a second line on the outskirts of town. General Marmaduke, learning of McNeil's advance from the east, ordered his brigade commanders to gather their men and prepare to retreat. At 4:00

[51] Edwards, *Shelby and His Men*, pp. 157–158.

[52] McNeil to Curtis, April 26, 1863, *Official Records*, ser. I, vol. XXII, pt. I, 255; Curtis to H. W. Halleck, April 26, 1863, *ibid.*, p. 252; Vandever to Curtis, April 24, 1863, *ibid.*, p. 272; Vandever to Davidson, April 27, 1863, *ibid.*, p. 274; Moore, *Rebellion Record*, VI, 563.

A.M. a series of lightning flashes revealed a long column of Confederate cavalry slipping out of Jackson and moving off toward Bloomfield.[53]

With Shelby covering the retreat, the division rode down southern Missouri along the Cape Girardeau and Kitchens' Mill road. After crossing and destroying the White Water bridge, it reached Bloomfield on April 28. While the division fell back slowly from Bloomfield, skirmishing with McNeil and Vandever at every advantageous point,[54] a small detail of picked men worked feverishly for two days and a night to construct a "trembling, crazy bridge" across the St. Francis at Chalk Bluff. Made of huge logs cabled on both banks and supported in the middle by a log barge and an unwieldy raft, it rose up and down on the swirling water.[55]

The division reached the St. Francis on May 1, formed a semicircular battle line on the northern bank, and contested the Federals while artillery and horses moved across the bridge. Before long a body of enemy cavalry drove into Carter's exposed right flank and forced his brigade against Gordon's right. Shelby shifted Thompson's regiment from left to right to support Carter, and the Confederates drove back the assailants. Then one by one the regiments pulled out of the line and moved across the shaky bridge, consuming eight hours in the crossing. Just after Thompson's regiment arrived safely on the southern bank, Federals appeared at the edge of the woods on the opposite side. A Confederate sliced the moorings with his saber, and the bridge was swept downstream.[56] Here the Federal pursuit ended.[57]

[53] Marmaduke's report, *Official Records*, ser. I, vol. XXII, pt. I, 287; Curtis to Halleck, April 26, 27, 28, 1863, *ibid.*, pp. 252–253; Burbridge's report, *ibid.*, pp. 296–297; Thompson's report, *ibid.*, p. 291.

[54] Marmaduke's report, *ibid.*, pp. 287–288; Thompson's report, *ibid.*, p. 291; Carter's report, *ibid.*, p. 301; Greene's report, *ibid.*, pp. 303–304.

[55] Young, *Confederate Wizards of the Saddle*, p. 561; Moore, "Missouri," *Confederate Military History*, IX, 133.

[56] Marmaduke's report, *Official Records*, ser. I, vol. XXII, pt. I, 278; Thompson's report, *ibid.*, pp. 292–293; Carter's report, *ibid.*, pp. 302–303; Greene's report, *ibid.*, pp. 303–304; Burbridge's report, *ibid.*, pp. 297–298.

[57] William Vandever to Davidson, April 29, 1863, *ibid.*, p. 274. The Federal pursuit consisted of the First Wisconsin Cavalry, the Second Missouri State Militia, two detachments of enrolled Missouri militia, and Welfey's battery. These were under McNeil. The two brigades under Vandever comprised: First Brigade —Third Missouri Cavalry, Third Missouri State Militia Cavalry, Third Iowa Cavalry, First Iowa Cavalry, the Thirteenth Illinois Infantry, Stranger's section

One enemy had been eluded, but an even worse foe was yet to be conquered—the impenetrable swamps lying southwest of the St. Francis. On May 6 the division entered the swamps, following the Cache River which wound southward in a "devious, sluggish, sickly way." Artillery, baggage, and ammunition wagons bogged in the mire. Horses and mules that refused to move despite coaxing and lashing were left to die in the mud. After seventy-two hours of sleepless nights, of attacks by swarms of mosquitoes, of alternate rain and sticky heat, of squirming through miles of oozing mud, the men emerged from the sloughs, looking more "like an army of denizens of a semi-amphibio subterranean world than one of men and animals."[58]

On May 31 the raiders dismounted at Jacksonport, Arkansas. The wounded were cared for and the horses turned to pasture. The troops, having pitched camp, set about cleaning their arms, repairing their trappings, washing and mending their mud-caked uniforms.[59] The raid had cost the division 30 killed, 60 wounded, and 120 missing. One hundred and fifty new recruits compensated somewhat for the losses.[60]

In terms of strategic objectives, Marmaduke's second Missouri raid was a complete failure. The Federal supply depot at Cape Girardeau had not been damaged, and the Army of the Frontier was moving once again into northern Arkansas. The main fault lay with Confederate planning. To send cavalry and light artillery against a town as heavily fortified as Cape Girardeau approached the insane. Raiding cavalry should never undertake a siege. Its main purpose was to strike isolated garrisons, small forts, towns, and then run and strike again. Marmaduke committed his first serious mistake before the raid began. A cardinal principle of a raid was to collect, well in advance, information about what would be encountered, but Marmaduke allowed himself to remain ignorant of road conditions, the forces available to the

of Hauch's battery, Lindsay's section of enrolled Missouri militia; Second Brigade—First Nebraska Infantry, Second Missouri State Militia Cavalry. McNeil to Davidson, May 12, 1863, *ibid.*, pp. 257, 259. Total casualties in Union forces operating against Marmaduke from April 17 to May 2 were twenty-two killed, thirty-seven wounded, and fifty-one missing. *Ibid.*, p. 253.

[58] Thompson's report, *ibid.*, p. 293; Burbridge's report, *ibid.*, p. 298; Young, *Confederate Wizards of the Saddle*, pp. 562–563.

[59] *Ibid.*, p. 562.

[60] Marmaduke's report, *Official Records*, ser. I, vol. XXII, pt. I, 288.

enemy, and the strength of the four forts at Cape Girardeau. Marmaduke made another blunder in taking along numerous supply wagons. To strike successfully, raiding cavalry must travel light and live off the land. Marmaduke's trains slowed his march, and, by bogging down in the Mingo Swamps, they prevented the Confederates from capturing McNeil. The difficulty in moving them across the St. Francis had almost caused disaster on the retreat.

SHELBY'S RAID

In mid-July of 1863 Federal armies in Missouri, encouraged by the Union victories at Vicksburg and Gettysburg, swarmed across the Arkansas line. One pincer led by General Cloud and General Blunt captured Fort Smith, "the key to the northwest," and began to advance down the Arkansas against negligible opposition. A second pincer—6,000 cavalry under Brigadier General J. W. Davidson—captured Jacksonport and drove Marmaduke's cavalry division back to Little Rock. Davidson's objectives were to annihilate Marmaduke, gain possession of as much of the state as possible, and open communications with Blunt and Cloud.[61]

General Sterling Price, in temporary command of Arkansas while Holmes recovered from illness, watched the Federal advances uneasily. With Blunt at Lewisburg, and Davidson's cavalry moving down the prairies toward Little Rock, Price ordered an evacuation of the city. On September 11, as Price's 8,000 troops retreated to Arkadelphia, Davidson's army entered Little Rock; the capital and half the state were now under Federal control.[62]

A week later, Colonel Shelby (Portrait on Plate 9) rode to Confederate headquarters at Arkadelphia, where he outlined to Price and Marmaduke a bold plan of attack on Federal Missouri. Shelby's superiors endorsed the plan and presented it to Holmes and Smith for approval.[63] The objectives of the raid, as formulated by Shelby, were to strike a series of rapid blows that might prevent the Federals from transferring large numbers of troops to reinforce Rosecrans at Chat-

[61] Frederick Steele to Schofield, September 12, 1863, *ibid.*, p. 475; Marmaduke to J. T. Belton, December ?, 1863, *ibid.*, pp. 526–527; Thomas, *Arkansas in War and Reconstruction*, p. 209.

[62] Price to Belton, November 20, 1863, *Official Records*, ser. I, vol. XXII, pt. I, 520–522.

[63] Edwards, *Shelby and His Men*, p. 196.

tanooga; to recruit a brigade of cavalry; and to keep alive in loyal Confederates their opposition to Federal rule. Establishment of a permanent base in the state was not expected, but the raid might lead to an all out invasion during the following spring.[64]

On the morning of September 21, Shelby's brigade, now encamped at Arkadelphia, received from General Price the final order to proceed. The troops spent the rest of the day making their preparations. The day of marching, September 22, came warm and pleasant. General Price and Thomas C. Reynolds, Confederate governor of Missouri, walked to the edge of town to watch the raiders pass by. The force consisted of detachments from three regiments, Elliott's battalion of scouts, a section of light artillery under Lieutenant D. Davis, and twelve light ammunition wagons—a total of 600 men. After the last wagon had passed Price, an officer shouted an order and the column halted. Colonel Shelby reined up in front of his commander and saluted with difficulty. A shoulder wound received in the battle for Little Rock still bothered him. *"You must not fail,"* Price told him, "the buff sash of a Confederate Brigadier awaits the successful issue." Shelby nodded his head, spun about, spurred his horse to full gallop, and shouting and waving his hat ordered his little army forward. Price would not see nor hear from these troops for over a month.[65] (See Figure 6 for a map of the raid.)

After riding hard for four days, the column reached the Ouachita Mountains at dusk on September 26. The next morning Captain "Tuck" Thorp's scouts encountered and scattered several Federal partisan companies. That afternoon Thorp fell upon 200 of the First Arkansas Infantry (Federal) twelve miles south of the Arkansas and drove them into a grove of timber. Shank's and Gordon's troops moved around the Federals' flanks and "rode them down," said Shelby proudly, "like stubble to the lava tide." Booty consisted of three wagons of commissary stores.

At dusk the column forded the Arkansas, shallow and treacherous with shifting sands, and, after resting two hours, rode all night, reaching Ozark by 10:00 A.M. on September 28. During the next two days,

[64] *Ibid.*, pp. 195–196; Harrell, "Arkansas," *Confederate Military History*, X, 191; Moore, "Missouri," *ibid.*, IX, 141–149; Daniel O'Flaherty, *General Jo Shelby: Undefeated Rebel*, p. 191; Joseph H. Parks, *General Edmund Kirby Smith, C.S.A.*, p. 314.

[65] Shelby's report, November 16, 1863, *Official Records*, ser. I, vol. XXII, pt. I, 670; Edwards, *Shelby and His Men*, p. 197.

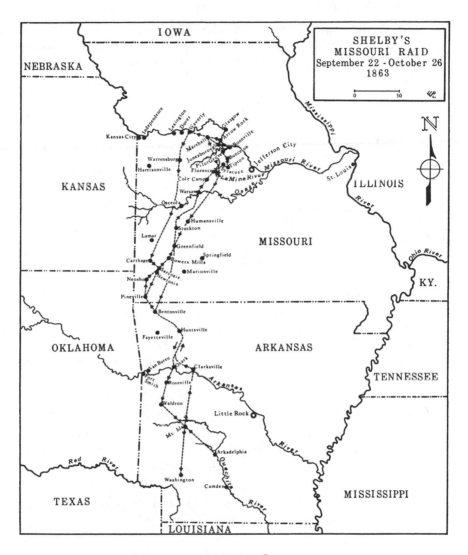

FIGURE 6

the raiders rode through Huntsville, destroyed the telegraph wire along the Fayetteville road, and at nightfall on September 30 encamped at Bentonville. The next day they stopped at McKissick's Springs, where they were joined by Colonel DeWitt C. Hunter with 200 men recently recruited in Arkansas and Missouri. At Pineville on October 2 another 400 troops under Colonel John T. Coffee were added. The force was now 1,200 strong.

On October 3 the Confederates reached Neosho and prepared to attack a body of mounted Federal militia. Shelby sent Coffee's regiment on a detour to gain the rear of the town. Then he ordered Gordon to shift his troops to the right and extend his right flank to connect with the left of Coffee. Shanks was sent to turn the Federal right. Bugles blew the charge and Shelby with men from Hunter's and Hooper's outfits, covered by Davis' artillery, swept down the streets of Neosho.[66] The Federal cavalry—180 men under Captain C. B. McAfee—sought cover in a brick courthouse, loopholed for musketry.[67] Confederate cannon were wheeled into position and joined the fight with a boom. A shell struck the courthouse. It seemed to mushroom and then its walls crumbled in fragments around torn and twisted bodies. A half hour later the Stars and Bars fluttered over Neosho and six burning subsistence wagons, fired by Confederate torches.[68] Riding out of Neosho that evening, the raiders travelled all night to reach Sarcoxie at daybreak on October 4. Heavy guerrilla warfare during the past year had reduced the town to smouldering foundations and fire-scarred chimneys.

Moving by night and resting by day, the column pushed on to Oregon, or Bower's Mills, scattered a small body of militia, and then dashed through the streets of Greenfield at dawn on October 5. The garrison at Greenfield having fled, the Confederates set fire to the fort and ordnance stores. Then they rode to Stockton, where they routed a few militia units and burned another fort.[69]

Next day the cavalry skirmished lightly at Humansville and en-

[66] Shelby's report, *Official Records*, ser. I, vol. XXII, pt. I, 671–672. Second citations to reports of Shelby's raid will be without dates.

[67] C. B. McAfee to J. Edwards, October 10, 1863, *ibid.*, pp. 656–657.

[68] Shelby's report, *ibid.*, p. 672; C. B. Eno to J. Edwards, October 5, 1863, *ibid.*, p. 658. Federal losses were four killed and two wounded.

[69] Shelby's report, *ibid.*, p. 672; Charles Sheppard to J. Edwards, October 6, 1863, *ibid.*, p. 660; Edwards to Schofield, October 7 and 8, 1863, *ibid.*, p. 653; Wick Morgan to McNeil, October 6, 1863, *ibid.*, p. 659.

camped that night ten miles west of Warsaw. In the morning, they found at Warsaw 200 Federal cavalry drawn up to dispute the crossing of the Hackberry Ford. Shelby sent Gordon's regiment along the road to Osceola to attack from the north and ordered Elliott's battalion to move to the Confederate right to charge in from the east. Shelby then dismounted a body of men under Lieutenant Colonel James C. Hooper and sent them across the ford to break the Federal center. Hooper was supported on his left and right by Hunter and Shanks respectively. Within half an hour the Federals were routed, leaving to the Confederates thirty wagons, large quantities of foodstuffs and arms, and a number of prisoners.[70]

After passing through Cole Camp and Florence, the raiders captured Tipton on the morning of October 10. That afternoon a detachment of 100 men under Captain James Wood blew up the $400,000 bridge across the La Mine. From Tipton Shelby sent out demolition patrols to destroy the telegraph and railroad toward St. Louis. For thirty miles they tore up rails, demolished bridges, burned ties, cut wire, and wrecked water tanks and cattle stops. Part of the command attacked Syracuse, scattering Federal militia, and then joined the main column as it started for Boonville.[71]

Having encountered no opposition at Bunceton or Pilot Grove, the raiders moved slowly along the road to Boonville. Suddenly, from distant foliage, there appeared a puff of white smoke, and the noise of cannon was heard. The spatter of skirmishing fire followed. There was a hoarse cheering, and several hundred infantry moved onto the road to dispute the right of way. The Confederates formed in column, eight deep, charged, and dispersed the enemy.[72]

The night of October 10 came with an electrical storm and a cloudburst. At daybreak the weather cleared and the sun shone brightly on the column as it galloped through the vacant streets of Boonville. That afternoon the Confederates reached the Missouri River, where they scattered a Federal regiment guarding the ferry. The men, seeing the enemy in retreat, forgot their exhaustion and began to jump and

[70] Shelby's report, *ibid.*, pp. 672–673; J. Philips to E. B. Brown, October 31, 1863, *ibid.*, p. 638.

[71] Shelby's report, *ibid.*, p. 673; Kelly to Hall, October 22, 1863, *ibid.*, p. 635; William Gentry to Brown, October 31, 1863, *ibid.*, p. 637; George H. Hall to Henty Suess, October 23, 1863, *ibid.*, p. 634.

[72] Shelby's report, *ibid.*, pp. 673–674; Crittenden's report, October 26, 1863, *ibid.*, p. 644.

shout. Soon there was a whistle, a black wisp of smoke, and a steamboat moved sluggishly around a bend in the river. The Confederates opened fire, and the boat turned about and crept down river toward Jefferson City.[73]

Up to this point the raiders had ridden across Missouri almost unmolested. But now the Federals were preparing to track them down. General E. B. Brown had consolidated his scattered militia units at Jefferson City and was leading 1,600 troops on forced marches toward Boonville.[74] On the afternoon of October 11, Federal advance elements encountered Confederate pickets on the outskirts of Boonville.[75] Skirmishing continued through the night. At dawn the Federals attacked and drove the Confederates back to the Marshall-Boonville road.[76] Shelby formed his regiments into column and led them west to the La Mine Creek, where he prepared an ambush. Leaving two companies on the east bank as decoys, he placed the rest of the force in the woods across the stream. When the Federals approached, the two decoy companies yelled and fired their revolvers and then waded the creek and ran through the timber. The Federals, certain of easy victory, dashed into the water only to be caught in midstream by musketry from the hidden Confederates. Seven men pitched forward and drifted along with the current, coloring the water with a reddish tint. The ambush forced Brown to pursue more cautiously for the next few hours, but at dusk he pressed Shelby heavily at the crossing of the Blackwater, near Jonesborough. At 10:00 P.M. the Confederates halted for the night within six miles of Marshall. A scout reported all quiet at Arrow Rock.[77]

At daybreak on October 13 the Confederate column rode toward Marshall to find 1,000 militia cavalry drawn up for battle on a high

---

[73] Shelby's report, *ibid.*, p. 674; Crittenden to Lucien J. Barnes, October 12, 1863, *ibid.*, p. 642; Crittenden's report, *ibid.*, p. 645.

[74] These were the Fourth Missouri State Militia, the Fifth Provisional Enrolled Militia, the Seventh Missouri State Militia, and the First Missouri State Militia Battery. Brown to Schofield, October 13, 1863, *ibid.*, pp. 623–624; Brown to Greene, October 28, 1863, *ibid.*, p. 627.

[75] Lazear to Brown, October 19, 1863, *ibid.*, p. 629.

[76] Shelby's report, *ibid.*, p. 674; Brown to Schofield, October 13, 1863, *ibid.*, pp. 623–624.

[77] Shelby's report, *ibid.*, pp. 674–675; Lazear to Brown, October 19, 1863, *ibid.*, pp. 630–631; Brown to Greene, October 27, 1863, *ibid.*, p. 627.

ridge with a deep ravine in their front.[78] Deciding to rout these troops before Brown struck his rear, Shelby ordered a charge. In this attack Hooper formed the left, the artillery, supported by Elliott and Gordon, the center, and Hunter and Coffee, the right. For two hours the Federals held their ground. Then in a powerful charge the Confederates doubled the Federal left wing back upon the right and drove into Marshall, raking the streets with revolver fire. Suddenly, over the noise of small arms came the booming of field howitzers. Brown's column was coming into action from the north. A hundred Federal infantry hit Shanks' rear and a hand-to-hand engagement ensued which lasted two hours. The Federals, unable to drive Shanks, split into two wings, crossed a creek above and below him, and streamed around both his flanks. Shanks, keeping his ranks well closed, retreated step by step, beating back the assailants with accurate fire and finally finding safety inside Marshall. The Federals then began to surround the town.

Heavily outnumbered, Shelby decided to run for it. The rifled cannon, its axle broken in two, was spiked and left to the enemy. Formed by regiments, the column slipped out of the southern end of town and instantly met a storm of shell from Federal cannon. The enemy had now almost surrounded the invaders. The Confederates with revolvers popping scattered the Federals, and Coffee's, Gordon's, and Elliott's units and the wagons broke into the clear. The head of Hunter's regiment, however, became tangled in thick underbrush and the outfit was unable to close up its ranks. A regiment of enemy cavalry drove in between Hunter and the rear of Gordon's unit. Hunter's troops, now separated from the main column, turned abruptly to their right and riding at a gallop, outdistanced the enemy.[79] The retreat south continued with the raiding force split into two columns.

For eight miles along the road to Waverly, Shelby was sorely pressed by Federal cavalry.[80] Formed in a two-column front, the Confederates skirmished at every natural position and kept the pursuers

[78] Shelby's report, ibid., p. 675; Kelly to Hall, October 22, 1863, ibid., p. 635; Gentry to Brown, October 31, 1863, ibid., p. 637.

[79] Shelby's report, ibid., pp. 675–677; J. F. Philips to Brown, October 19, 1863, ibid., pp. 639–641; Gentry to Brown, October 31, 1863, ibid., p. 637; Lazear to Brown, October 19, 1863, ibid., p. 631; Brown to Greene, October 27, 1863, ibid., p. 627; Brown to Schofield, October 13, 1863, ibid., p. 624.

[80] Philips to Brown, October 19, 1863, ibid., p. 640.

in check. At 3:00 P.M. on October 13, the column rode through Waverly and reached Hawkins' Mill that night. Shelby ordered his empty ammunition wagons to be sunk in the Missouri River. During the next six days the column rode through Warrensburg, scattering 2,000 militia, through Vernon and Barton counties, skirmished at Carthage, crossed the Springfield road three miles east of Keytesville, and reached the Arkansas border on October 20.

Meanwhile, the other column under Hunter crossed the railroad four miles south of Tipton, forded the Osage at Duroc, and fought a detachment from the Second Arkansas (Federal) two miles south of the River. As the Confederates rode through Humansville and Greenfield, they demolished twenty Federal wagons, wrecked several miles of newly laid track, and damaged the railroad from Sarcoxie to Marionville. On the morning of October 20 they crossed into Arkansas and joined Shelby. The united column now retreated in a devious zigzag march, eluding their pursuers and reaching a point near Huntsville on October 23.[81]

On news of the Confederate retreat a division of 3,000 eager Federal infantrymen marched out of Fayetteville to intercept Shelby's raiders in the Buffalo Mountains. There they skirmished with the Confederate rear guard. The Federal pursuit ended at Clarksville, where the Confederates forded the Arkansas and headed south.

For the next week the raiders rode through a severe rain and snow storm. On November 3, they halted at Washington, exhausted, cold, and starving.[82] A great raid was over.

Shelby's report claimed that they had in forty-one days and 1,500 miles of riding killed and wounded 600 Federals and captured and paroled as many more;[83] destroyed ten forts, nearly $800,000 worth

[81] Shelby's report, *ibid.*, pp. 676–677; A. A. King, Jr., to John McNeil, October 17, 1863, *ibid.*, p. 655; Brown to Schofield, October 13, 1863, *ibid.*, p. 624.

[82] Shelby's report, *ibid.*, p. 677; Young, *Confederate Wizards of the Saddle*, pp. 220–221.

[83] Federal casualty reports, though not accurately given, certainly do not substantiate this claim. Brown gave his losses as five killed, twenty-six wounded, and eleven captured and missing; a total loss of forty-two. Brown to O. D. Greene, October 28, 1863, *Official Records*, ser. I, vol. XXII, pt. I, 628. McAfee reported that he lost six men in the action at Neosho. He surrendered 180. McAfee to J. Edwards, October 10, 1863, *ibid.*, p. 657. Only eight men of Philips' command were captured at Warsaw. Philips to Brown, October 19,

of property, and a million dollars worth of supplies; seized 300 wagons, forty stand of colors, 1,200 rifles and revolvers, and 6,000 horses and mules. He had found

the people of Missouri, as a mass, true to the South and her institutions, yet needing the strong presence of a Confederate army to make them volunteer. The southern, southwestern, and some of the middle counties of Missouri are completely desolated. In many places for 40 miles not a single habitant is to be found, for on the road we met delicate females fleeing southward, driving ox teams, barefooted, ragged, and suffering for even bread.

Besides the damage inflicted, Shelby asserted proudly that the presence of his raiders in Missouri had prevented 10,000 troops from being sent to reinforce Rosecrans, who had on September 22 suffered a major defeat at Chickamauga.[84]

All this was accomplished by 1,200 men, at a cost, according to Shelby, of only 150 killed and wounded left along the way—a brilliant demonstration of the power of a column of cavalry operating strategically. General Price praised Shelby, declaring proudly to everyone that his young officer was worthy of his brigadier general's commission.[85] And the men themselves loved to say: "You've heard of . . . Jeb Stuart's Ride around McClellan? Hell, brother, Jo Shelby rode around MISSOURI!"

> Ho Boys! Make a Noise!
> The Yankees are afraid!
> The river's up, hell's to pay—
> Shelby's on a Raid![86]

The mistakes made in the planning and execution of Marmaduke's second raid had been carefully avoided in Shelby's expedition. Shelby

---

1863, *ibid.*, p. 639. Nothing is known of Federal losses in the other skirmishes, but they were not large. Total casualties were probably about 240 in killed, wounded, missing, and captured.

[84] Shelby's report, *ibid.*, p. 678. Shelby's claim that his column prevented reinforcements from going to Rosecrans could not be substantiated in Federal documents. Jay Monaghan, *Civil War on the Western Border, 1854–1865*, p. 291, and O'Flaherty, *General Jo Shelby*, p. 191, accept Shelby's word without question.

[85] Young, *Confederate Wizards of the Saddle*, p. 221.

[86] This song was called "Shelby's Mule." Henry Clay McDougal, *Recollections, 1844–1909*, p. 205.

had collected intelligence on the strength of Federal garrisons in the southern and middle counties of Missouri and on road conditions. His objectives and line of march had been determined from this information. Shelby's column, travelling with a minimum of supplies, struck rapidly and never undertook a pitched battle. Cornered at Boonville and again at Marshall, the raiders retreated, splitting when necessary into two columns to baffle and confuse the pursuit.

PRICE'S RAID

There was little evidence that northern Arkansas was a battle front during the winter of 1863–1864. Yankee and Confederate pickets were content with watching each other and occasionally gossiping about a variety of subjects that ranged from the going price of horses to the course of the war. But with spring came the end of peaceful coexistence and an increasing clamor among Confederate commanders for a new move against Little Rock. General Sterling Price (Portrait on Plate 10), who had taken command of the district of Arkansas on March 14, 1864, clamored the loudest. He urged Kirby Smith to crush Federal forces in northern Arkansas and then undertake the all out invasion of Missouri that Confederates had been contemplating since 1862.[87] Although Smith was friendly to such an enterprise, he was not disposed to try it immediately. Intelligence reports had substantiated the rumors of a Yankee build-up in the Red River country above New Orleans. This could mean invasion. Price's corps must make defensive preparations to meet the Federal offensive when it came.[88]

Confederates did not have long to wait. In March, 1864, General Nathaniel P. Banks with some 27,000 men (including A. J. Smith's veteran infantry corps of Sherman's army) and a fleet of gunboats moved up the Red River. The objective of the expedition was to sweep into Texas and then stamp out all Confederate resistance in the Trans-Mississippi. On March 23 a second Federal army—10,400 troops under General Frederick Steele—tramped out of Little Rock heading south toward a junction with Banks at Shreveport.

Smith's forces acted quickly to meet the exigency. In Louisiana

[87] Price to Smith, March 8, 1864, *Official Records*, ser. I, vol. XXXIV, pt. II, 1029.

[88] Smith to Price, March 15, 1864, *ibid.*, pp. 1043–1044.

General Richard Taylor's indomitable army of about 13,000 met Banks at Sabine Crossroads (April 8) and Pleasant Hill (April 9) and threw his forces back down the Red River. The second Yankee column advancing down Arkansas butted against an insurmountable obstacle—the Confederate cavalry divisions of John S. Marmaduke, S. B. Maxey, and James F. Fagan. Barely escaping disaster at Camden, and again at Jenkin's Ferry, Steele's army now marching north reached Little Rock and safety on April 13. By the first of June, 1864, the Red River campaign had been written off as a complete flop and Kirby Smith had gained as a result relative freedom of action in the Trans-Mississippi region.[89]

Smith was now ready to invade Missouri. On June 3 he told Price to use his friends in Missouri to collect information on road conditions, available Union forces, and the possibility of gaining recruits.[90] Smith then disclosed his plans to Governor Thomas C. Reynolds and President Davis, pointing out that a successful Missouri campaign would bolster waning Confederate fortunes in the East.[91] By mid-July Price had found that his home state was very susceptible to invasion. Most of the Federal garrisons had been removed. The people by and large were still loyal to the South. Price requested that he be allowed to head the enterprise, expressing his ardent desire to plant Confederate colors in Missouri soil where thousands would flock to his banners.[92]

Then began a curious series of events in which Taylor, presumably under orders from General Braxton Bragg, attempted unsuccessfully to move two infantry divisions into Mississippi. Since Smith at first made no objection to the movement, it seems that he may never have seriously planned an all out invasion of Missouri.[93] In August he wrote President Davis that although an offensive into Missouri had been abandoned a cavalry expedition was still being considered.[94]

Even before Taylor tried to cross the River, Smith instructed Price

[89] The best study of the campaign is Ludwell H. Johnson, *Red River Campaign: Politics and Cotton in the Civil War*. Note particularly the discussion on pages 170–205 of Confederate cavalry operations against Steele.

[90] *Official Records*, ser. I, vol. XXXIV, pt. IV, 642–643.

[91] *Ibid.*, pt. I, 482; ser. I, vol. XLI, pt. II, 1011, 1014, 1020.

[92] *Ibid.*, 1023–1024.

[93] For a discussion of these events, see Parks, *Kirby Smith*, pp. 403–431.

[94] *Official Records*, ser. I, vol. XLI, pt. I, 113.

to prepare all the cavalry in his command for a raiding expedition. The commanding general had decided long ago that Major General Price, the ranking Missourian in the Confederate Army, was the best man to lead such a campaign. Price was very popular with the men, who fondly called him "Old Pap."[95] His name was linked in the public mind with earlier expeditions into Missouri, although he had not accompanied them, hence the familiar saying that Missouri weather comprised five seasons—"spring, summer, fall, Price's raid, and winter."[96] The fact that Price had had no experience in cavalry command apparently was given little consideration.[97]

Price had been a leader of infantry troops throughout most of his military career. As a Confederate general, he had won some distinction in western Tennessee and in the Red River Campaign. Though he strove to be a good soldier, certain aspects of his personality impaired his ability to lead combat troops. He was slow and lethargic and was guilty of procrastination and indifference to matters of discipline. Such traits would weigh heavily in the outcome of the proposed expedition.[98]

On August 4, 1864, Price received the final order to proceed. "Make St. Louis the objective point of your movement," Smith told him. Rapid marching "will put you in possession of that place, its supplies and military stores, and will do more toward rallying Missouri to your standard than the possession of any other point." Should retreat become necessary, Price was to come back through Kansas and the Indian Territory, gathering horses, cattle, mules, and military supplies.[99] There was no mention of how long the cavalry was to stay in Missouri. Plans were elastic, designed to enable the raiders to take

[95] Walter B. Stevens, *Missouri the Center State, 1821–1915*, I, 340 ff.; W. L. Webb, *Battles and Biographies of Missourians: or, The Civil War Period of Our State*, pp. 208–209.

[96] Paul B. Jenkins, *The Battle of Westport*, p. 36.

[97] Rumor had it that Smith had approached General S. B. Buckner about leading the expedition, but Buckner refused because he had never led cavalry troops. Edwards, *Shelby and His Men*, p. 378.

[98] See Thomas C. Reynolds' "Memoir" published in the (Marshall) *Texas Republican*, December 17, 1864, in *ibid.*, pp. 466–474; Howard L. Conrad, ed., *Encyclopedia of the History of Missouri*, V, 229; Allen Johnson and Dumas Malone, eds., *Dictionary of American Biography*, XV, 216; Ezra J. Warner, *Generals in Gray: Lives of the Confederate Commanders*, pp. 246–247.

[99] *Official Records*, ser. I, vol. XLI, pt. II, 1040.

FIGURE 7

advantage of events as they occurred. Thus the operation, as Kirby Smith conceived it, was to be simply a cavalry raid, like the ones that Marmaduke and Shelby had made the year before. Primary consideration was to be given to recruits, horses, destruction of supply depots, and diversion of enemy troops.

Sterling Price, however, had different notions about over-all objectives. The military goals were important, to be sure, but even more important were political objectives—elections and state government. With the aid and encouragement of Governor Reynolds, who would accompany the expedition, Price hoped to bring Missouri back into the Confederacy.[100]

Two weeks passed before Price got James F. Fagan's and John S. Marmaduke's divisions ready to move. On August 28 they left Camden and during the next week averaged barely sixteen miles a day —very poor marching time for cavalry, indicating that Price was oblivious to the vital elements of speed and surprise necessary to take St. Louis.[101] Precious time was consumed making eloquent speeches along the way and ensuring the comfort of the commanding general, who forsook his horse in order to travel in a carriage (which was scarcely conducive to swift cavalry movement). The raiders forded the Arkansas on September 6 and rode leisurely to Pocahontas, where they were joined by Shelby's brigade which had been in northeastern Arkansas recruiting under the nose of Federal militia garrisons.[102] (See Figure 7 for a map of the raid.)

Price spent the next four days at Pocahontas reorganizing his cavalry into three distinct divisions, including a new one for Shelby.[103] Thus the last Missouri expedition was to be made by a corps of cavalry, similar in organization to the force that had operated under Stuart, or those now operating under Sheridan, Forrest, and Wheeler. But the power of Price's force was greatly reduced in that it included nearly 4,000 unarmed men as well as seven regiments and one bat-

[100] Norman Potter Morrow, "Price's Missouri Expedition, 1864," p. 58. This is the most detailed account of the raid.

[101] Cyrus R. Peterson and Joseph M. Hanson, *Pilot Knob: The Thermopylae of the West*, p. 33.

[102] Price's report, December 28, 1864, *Official Records*, ser. I, vol. XLI, pt. I, 626 (second citations to reports of Price's raid will hereafter be without dates); Edwards, *Shelby and His Men*, p. 470; Jenkins, *Battle of Westport*, p. 24.

[103] For details see Appendix C.

144

talion of mounted infantry which had no training in cavalry tactics. Even allowing for these, Price's column of 12,000 horsemen was the most powerful body of cavalry ever mustered in the Trans-Mississippi.

From Pocahontas, the three divisions travelled separately to facilitate the collection of forage. They crossed the state line on September 21. The rendezvous point was Fredericktown, some twenty-one miles southeast of Pilot Knob.[104]

As Price neared Fredericktown, General W. S. Rosecrans, commanding the Department of Missouri with headquarters at St. Louis, sensed that this was something more than an ordinary raid. His scouts placed Confederate strength at 20,000 plus. Was it an all out invasion? He alerted all militia garrisons in southeastern Missouri and began concentrating regular units at St. Louis. Fortunately for the Yankees, he managed to get reinforcements in the form of A. J. Smith's infantry corps, which had come up the Mississippi on its way to Virginia.[105]

When news that Smith had joined Rosecrans reached the Confederates, Price concluded that attack on St. Louis was now out of the question. He would leave his present line of march and move on Pilot Knob, located eighty miles southeast of St. Louis and lightly defended by militia under Brigadier General Thomas Ewing, Jr.[106]

Confederate columns reached Pilot Knob at noon on September 27. While Shelby's and Fagan's troops surrounded Fort Davidson, which protected the city, Marmaduke's horsemen took a position in a dry creek bed a mile or so to the north. The initial attack of the fort at 2 P.M. was promptly repulsed by murderous artillery fire. The raid was clearly off to a poor start. The soldiers complained bitterly as morale dropped to a dangerous low. That evening Price held a war council in which he made plans for a second attack. Afterwards he gave his demoralized army something of a pep talk.[107]

Inside the fort, the Federals, thinking that Price had well over

[104] Jenkins, *Battle of Westport*, p. 34.

[105] *Official Records*, ser. I, vol. XLI, pt. III, 25, 117, 132, 164, 174.

[106] Price's report, *ibid.*, pt. I, 630; Morrow, "Price's Missouri Expedition," p. 82.

[107] Shelby's report, December ?, 1864, *Official Reports*, ser. I, vol. XLI, pt. I, 655; Proceedings of a Court of Inquiry Convened at Shreveport, La., April 21, 1865—May 3, 1865, *ibid.*, p. 103. Confederate losses were about 425 in killed and wounded.

20,000 men, decided to get out while they still could. Leaving a detachment to blow up the powder magazine, they slipped unobserved out of the fort and galloped northwest to reach Rolla at sundown on September 28.[108]

Meanwhile, the Confederates, unaware of the evacuation, renewed the assault at dusk on September 27. A loud explosion inside the fort (the Yankee detachment detonating the powder magazine) convinced the attackers that they must proceed cautiously. An hour or so later they discovered, to their disgust and embarrassment, that not a Federal was to be found in the Pilot Knob vicinity. As Shelby and Marmaduke set out in pursuit of the fleeing Federals, Price counted his booty—sixteen cannon, most of them useless, some small arms, and nearly 10,000 rations.[109]

The time between Price's capture of Pilot Knob on September 28 and his occupation of Lexington on October 19 might truthfully be termed the "picnic period" of the expedition. It was filled with many "bright hours of pleasure and enjoyment" as speeches were made and small militia garrisons routed. The rate of march was leisurely. Ten days were consumed in covering the 166 miles from Pilot Knob to Jefferson City.[110]

From Richwoods, on September 30, Price's army rode north through St. Clair, Union, and Washington, then turned northwest toward Jefferson City, the capital of the state. Marmaduke and Shelby rejoined the column on October 1. With occasional side forays, the force pushed on to occupy Linn some eighty miles west of St. Louis. The next day, October 3, demolition parties destroyed railroad bridges across the Meramec, Moselle, and Gasconade rivers and tore up miles of railroad track. After uniting, the raiders rode to the Osage River, where they encountered and dispersed a small body of enemy militia. Moving on, the Confederates found at the Moreau Creek near Jefferson City several hundred Federals who were ready for a fight. The Southerners dismounted and opened a brisk fire on the blurred figures crouching in the tall weeds along the opposite bank of the

[108] Ewing's report, October 20, 1864, *ibid.*, pp. 445–452; Peterson and Hanson, *Pilot Knob*, p. 100.

[109] *Official Records*, ser. I, vol. XLI, pt. I, 710; pt. III, 960–961; Webb, *Battles and Biographies of Missourians*, p. 213; Moore, "Missouri," *Confederate Military History*, IX, 181.

[110] Shelby's report, *Official Records*, ser. I, vol. XLI, pt. I, 656; Webb, *Battles and Biographies of Missourians*, p. 215.

creek. In the ensuing battle, Colonel David Shanks, highly esteemed commander of the Iron Brigade, was killed. Brigadier General M. Jeff Thompson, a tall, muscular Missourian known as the "Missouri Swamp Fox," took command of the celebrated organization and led it against the Yankees, forcing them to retreat at a run. All the Confederates then moved across the creek and encamped just outside Jefferson City at twilight on October 7. In a war council held that night, Price and his officers decided that the fortifications about Jefferson City were impregnable. The next morning the cavalry resumed the march west.[111] Thus the second major political objective of the expedition was abandoned (the first had been St. Louis) and Governor Reynolds was highly provoked at being denied the chance to have an inauguration in the capital. He would have many nasty things to say about Price in a court of inquiry held after the campaign was over.[112]

As Price moved up the Missouri River, the Yankees made feverish preparations to chase him. From St. Louis came Smith's 9,000 infantry marching at quick time. At Jefferson City, General Alfred Pleasonton, who once had commanded the cavalry of the Army of the Potomac, hurriedly organized all the horsemen present, about 4,100, into three brigades and struck out after Price, overtaking him at dusk on October 8 at the crossing of the Moreau Creek near Russellville. Skirmishing lasted throughout the night. At dawn a Yankee brigade drove hard into the flank of Marmaduke's division, threatening to put the entire force into great disorder. Then the Union troops inexplicably withdrew (the Federal commander, John Sanborn, had called off the attack so that his hungry men could go back to get something to eat).

Hours later Federal cavalry returned to the Russellville area only to find that Price had ridden westward. The Yankees followed, keeping well to the south of the raiders in order to intercept and delay should they suddenly turn south and head for Arkansas. Meanwhile, Smith's infantry was moving up fast from Jefferson City.[113]

[111] Price's report, *Official Records*, ser. I, vol. XLI, pt. I, 630–631; Shelby's report, *ibid.*, pp. 653–654; John B. Clark's report, December 19, 1864, *ibid.*, pp. 679–681; Rosecrans' report, December 7, 1864, *ibid.*, pp. 308–311.

[112] Edwards, *Shelby and His Men*, pp. 395 ff.; *Official Records*, ser. I, vol. XLI, pt. I, 701–726.

[113] Moore, "Missouri," *Confederate Military History*, IX, 182; [Richard J. Hinton], *Rebel Invasion of Missouri and Kansas, and the Campaign of the Army of the Border . . .*, p. 113.

Price's present objective was to move toward Kansas occupying en route the forts at Boonville, Sedalia, Lexington, and Independence. His army still moved "in the atmosphere of a prolonged picnic,"[114] and did not increase the rate of march even when rear guard action began to pick up. Having failed to send out reconnaissance patrols, Price had no idea of the hostile forces building up in his rear. He knew even less of what lay ahead. At Kansas City General Samuel R. Curtis, commanding the Department of Kansas, had gathered several thousand militia and was moving down to meet the invading column.

And slowly, ever slowly, moved Price's unwary army. It occupied Boonville on October 9, rested three days, then broke up into smaller, more mobile units to terrorize the country along the Missouri River from Arrow Rock to Glasgow. At dusk on October 18 the united force encamped at Waverly, twenty-six miles east of Lexington.

As the Confederates slept, General James G. Blunt marched the "right wing" of Curtis' Army of the Border from Pleasant Hill to Lexington, rested for an hour or so, and then set out for Waverly hoping to intercept Price.

The picnic was now over. On the morning of October 19 the first contact was made between elements of the two forces about five miles southeast of Lexington. This engagement was the beginning of five days of continuous action in which Price had to fight most of the time facing in opposite directions. In the initial engagement, Shelby's division leading the Confederate advance forced Blunt to retreat in good order toward Independence. Shelby sensed trouble and told his men that there will be "heavy work for us all in the future."[115] Instead of chasing Blunt, Price moved his army about two thirds of the distance from Lexington to Independence and on October 20 encamped for the night on the eastern bank of the Little Blue River.[116]

[114] Morrow, "Price's Missouri Expedition," p. 106. Unless otherwise cited, the discussion of the events from October 8 to October 20 when Price reached Lexington are based on these documents: *Official Records*, ser. I, vol. XLI, pt. I, Price's report, pp. 625 ff.; Shelby's report, pp. 652 ff.; Clark's report, pp. 678 ff.; Colton Greene's report, December 18, 1864, p. 687; Jackman's report, November 30, 1864, p. 671; Thompson's report, November 24, 1864, pp. 663 ff.; Rosecrans' report, p. 307 ff.; Pleasonton's report, November 1, 1864, pp. 336 ff.; Sanborn's report, November 13, 1864, pp. 385 ff.; Philips' report, November 7, 1864, pp. 350 ff.; McNeil's report, November 23, pp. 371 ff.

[115] Shelby's report, *ibid.*, p. 657.

[116] Price's report, *ibid.*, p. 633.

Meanwhile, Pleasonton with a thousand horsemen caught up with Sanborn's two brigades at Dunksburg, five miles southeast of Lexington, and the united cavalry force, totaling about 8,500 men, headed for Independence. Not far behind were Smith's infantry marching at a killing pace toward Chapel Hill, about twenty-two miles southeast of Independence. At the same time Curtis moved his entire army of fifteen thousand troops (including Blunt's force) down to a point a few miles above the Little Blue River.[117] The Confederate invading column was now caught in a neat vice.

At this point Price should have turned south and raced for Arkansas. But overconfident and ignorant of the enemy forces closing in on him, he pushed across the Little Blue on October 21. Marmaduke's division ran abruptly into a large Yankee force and a heated skirmish flared. The fighting soon became so intense that Price had to send Shelby to help. Fighting on foot as infantry, according to Price's orders, the Confederates forced their way into Independence and the battle of the Little Blue was over. The next day the raiders set out for the Big Blue, Westport, and disaster.[118]

At the Big Blue the Confederates found Curtis' army holding a line which extended fifteen miles from the mouth of the stream to a point near Hickman's Mills. Shelby's incomparable horsemen attacked immediately and drove the Yankees back to the state line. There Curtis rallied his divisions and counterattacking strongly recaptured by nightfall all the positions lost to Shelby. An hour later Curtis learned that Pleasonton's cavalry was moving up fast on Price's left flank and rear. Curtis decided to attack at dawn.[119]

The Yankee horsemen under Pleasonton had encamped at Lexington on October 20, ridden hard the next day, and at dawn on October 22 fell upon Price's rear guard under Fagan on the Little Blue. Part of Marmaduke's division galloped back to assist only to be engulfed by streams of retreating Confederates closely pursued by Yankee cavalry. Marmaduke rallied a brigade and charged forward. But overborne by numbers, outflanked on right and left, the brigade

---

[117] Sanborn's report, *ibid.*, pp. 388–389.

[118] Edwards, *Shelby and His Men*, p. 435; Moore, "Missouri," *Confederate Military History*, IX, 189.

[119] Curtis' report, *Official Records*, ser. I, vol. XLI, pt. I, 484–485; Morrow, "Price's Missouri Expedition," p. 127.

dissolved almost immediately and the rear of Price's army gave way in panic and utter rout. Marmaduke himself escaped only through a display of masterful horsemanship.

Nightfall rescued the Southerners from destruction. Pleasonton withdrew his horsemen to a point near the Little Blue. Price and Marmaduke gathered their scattered outfits and encamped at Westport; there they were joined by Shelby's division which had fought Curtis to a standstill on the Big Blue.[120]

With one minor defeat on their record and Yankee forces in their front and rear, the Confederates prepared to fight it out on October 23. The day "dawned upon us clear, cold, and full of promise," recalled Shelby, as the three divisions marched out of Westport to deploy in line of battle, with Shelby on the left and Fagan in the center, facing north, and Marmaduke on the right, facing due east. In front of Shelby and Fagan lay Brush Creek and a heavy growth of timber. The open farm country south of the creek was studded with stone fences. As was said, Curtis planned to advance due south from his position above the Big Blue, but Shelby's division attacked first and was able to drive the Federal advanced elements back across Brush Creek. Curtis rushed up reinforcements and counterattacked, but Shelby held his ground and appeared to be in no great danger when he learned that Yankee cavalry had swamped the Confederate right, thus exposing his rear and right flank as well as that of Fagan. Shelby rode up and down the lines imploring his men to fight harder. A second message bore ominous news. Fagan had been scattered. Union artillery began to pound Shelby's flanks at close range. There was a blast of bugles and hundreds of yowling Yankees charged his front. Nothing was left but "to run for it" and the battle became a "pell-mell gallop, every man for himself."

Shelby managed to rally a few regiments at a point two miles below the battlefield. Fighting desperately the horsemen fell back to Santa Fe, where they were able to check the Yankees and end the battle of Westport.[121] This defeat delivered the decisive blow that crushed Con-

[120] Edwards, *Shelby and His Men*, p. 396; [Hinton], *Army of the Border*, p. 115.

[121] Curtis' report, *Official Records*, ser. I, vol. XLI, pt. I, 480 ff.; Blunt's report, *ibid.*, pp. 572 ff.; Shelby's report, *ibid.*, pp. 658 ff.; Clark's report, *ibid.*, pp. 684 ff. Good over-all accounts of the battle of Westport may be found in Mor-

federate hopes of winning something in the West that would compensate for losses in the East.

The remnants of Price's divisions regrouped about Shelby's position at Santa Fe and set out for Arkansas on October 24. Fortunately for them the enemy pursuit was anything but prompt and vigorous. Smith's infantry, having arrived at Westport after the battle was over, angled south in hopes of cutting off the retreat, but the men were dead tired and many began to drop off along the line of march. As Smith called off his pursuit, a few cavalry units charged after Price but accomplished little.

With the only chance of escape depending upon rapid movement, Price directed a retreat that one might expect of a worn-out infantry column. He refused to abandon his unmanageable wagon train and insisted on frequent rest stops. To make matters worse he picked up along the way a large number of refugee families whose assorted vehicles carrying loads of household possessions gave the unwieldy retreating column the appearance of a circus caravan rumbling slowly across the Missouri prairies heading south.[122]

By this time Curtis had organized his pursuit and was bearing down on the retiring Confederates. He caught them in the misty, early morning hours of October 25 on the banks of the Marais-des-Cygnes River, near the settlement of Trading Post. Marmaduke's and Fagan's divisions were driven back with heavy casualties; Generals Marmaduke and Cabell, some 500 troops, and a number of field guns were captured.[123] Price, riding in an ambulance at the front of the army, heard the commotion at the rear and decided to investigate. On the way back he met "the divisions of Major Generals Fagan and Marmaduke retreating in utter and indescribable confusion, many of them having thrown away their arms. They were deaf to all entreaties or commands, and in vain were all efforts to stop them."[124] Once again

---

row, "Price's Missouri Expedition," pp. 110–138, and Jenkins, *Battle of Westport*, pp. 86–157. Union casualties out of a total engaged of some 23,500 were about 1,000 in killed and wounded. Confederates lost about the same number out of a total engaged of about 8,000.

[122] Edwards, *Shelby and His Men*, pp. 440, 470; Moore, "Missouri," *Confederate Military History*, IX, 191.

[123] Frederick W. Benteen's report, November 3, 1864, *Official Records*, ser. I, vol. XLI, pt. I, 637; Curtis' report, *ibid.*, pp. 493–495.

[124] Price's report, *ibid.*, p. 637.

Shelby saved the day and the army. With Thompson's brigade and one other regiment he galloped through broken lines of troops to form a battleline just north of the Little Osage. Yankees were everywhere. Shelby's force fell back to form a second line along some low hills to the south. The action that followed was a remarkable exhibition of cavalry delaying tactics. From the second position, Shelby's horsemen, firing constantly, retired about nine miles to a hill north of the Marmaton River. Here Jackman's Brigade galloped up to attack, opening its ranks to let Shelby's exhausted cavalry through. All the cavalry then made a desperate stand just north of the Marmaton River. After about an hour of vicious close-quarter fighting the Federals withdrew. Price then gave the order to burn most of the wagons[125]—an order that should have been issued days before.

The next day, October 27, the Confederates marched fifty-six miles and resembled for the first time since the beginning of the expedition a column of raiding cavalry. The Federals rode equally hard. Marching day and night they caught Price again at Newtonia, Missouri, on October 28. The battle that followed was indecisive, but as was usually the case, both sides claimed the victory. Here the active Yankee pursuit ended and with it the last of heavy hostilities in the Trans-Mississippi west.[126]

From Newtonia, on October 29, Price's demoralized army made its way into northwestern Arkansas, bypassed Fayetteville, and in early November encamped near Boonsborough. After sending the brigades of Dobbin, Freeman, and McCray to recruit in areas in Arkansas where they had raised their outfits, Price took the rest of the cavalry through Choctaw country and into Texas. The march was one of extreme suffering due to the lack of food and clothing and to an epidemic of smallpox. The remnants of the once proud cavalry corps staggered into Bonham, Texas, on November 23, and over a week later reached Laynesport, Arkansas.

Upon reaching Smith's headquarters, Price submitted a vague and misleading report that tried to picture his expedition as a tremendous success. He had marched over 1,400 miles, fought more than forty engagements, captured and paroled some 3,000 prisoners, collected a large number of military supplies, and destroyed "miles and miles

[125] *Ibid.*, pt. IV, 1013.
[126] Curtis' report, *ibid.*, pt. I, 507–515; Price's report, *ibid.*, pp. 637–638.

of railroad" and property valued at ten million dollars—all this at a cost of only 1,000 men including the wounded left in Missouri. Furthermore, he had brought with him "at least 5,000 new recruits" and others "were arriving in large numbers daily." Although he stated accurately enough the size of the corps when it rode into Missouri, Price avoided mention of the number of men he had when he returned. He felt that "in my opinion the results flowing from my operations in Missouri are of the most gratifying character," but he neglected to list the great loss of supplies and matériel on the retreat. In his conclusion the general returned to the lost dream: "Recruits flocked to our flag in . . . numbers. . . . I am satisfied that could I have remained in Missouri this winter the army would have been increased 50,000 men."[127]

But Price was not fooling anyone. The raid had been a failure and no amount of equivocal reporting could make it out to be otherwise. All of the major objectives had been abandoned, a number of good cavalry officers lost to the enemy, and the incompetence of the commanding general made glaringly evident. After the raid it was said that Kirby Smith himself considered "Price as a military man 'absolutely good for nothing.' "[128] In truth the expedition had proved that Price, having never been on a cavalry raid, lacked that ability to judge the potential of his men and horses which came only with experience. Not recognizing that mobility was the key to successful cavalry operations, he had concentrated on problems of supply and had been reluctant to live off the country. Finally, using tactics that were natural for an infantry commander, he had undertaken at Westport a full-scale battle with a superior Union army. In so doing he had violated a cardinal principle of the cavalry raid. To complete the list of mistakes, his retreat had been badly conducted and the cavalry corps allowed to melt away by desertion.

But not all the blame can be placed on Price. As the commanding general of the Department who chose Price to lead the operation, Edmund Kirby Smith must shoulder final responsibility for the blunders that brough defeat and shattered dreams. Had he given the command to one of the experienced cavalry generals, the redoubtable

---

[127] Price's report, *ibid.*, p. 640.
[128] Reynolds to Waldo P. Johnson, March 2, 1865, Thomas C. Reynolds Papers, Library of Congress.

Jo Shelby for instance, the raid might have been more successful. Price himself said after the Missouri enterprise that Shelby was "the best cavalry officer I ever saw."[129]

Price's raid was the last operation in which the cavalry in the Department operated as a strategic force. The four Missouri raids taken as a whole had formed the basis of Confederate strategy in Arkansas from 1862 onward. Forced on the defensive after Prairie Grove, Confederates called on their cavalry to prevent the capture of Arkansas. Deep strikes into Union territory compelled the Federals to strengthen their garrisons behind the lines at the expense of their armies at the front. The Confederate ability to roam about destroying supply depots and burning forts may have impaired the fighting spirit of Union troops and lowered their confidence in their commanders.

The raids of Marmaduke, Shelby, and Price were not so spectacular as Morgan's Christmas raid (1862–1863) or his expedition into Ohio and Indiana (summer, 1863), nor did they compare in daring with Stuart's exploits. Yet the same purpose was accomplished in all cases: the raiders forced a Federal army temporarily to dismiss offensive movements and they spread terror and destruction behind enemy lines.

[129] Price's report, *Official Records*, ser. I, vol. XLI, pt. I, 639. Morrow has an excellent evaluation of the campaign. "Price's Missouri Expedition," pp. 160–172.

CLOSING SCENES

In December, 1864, Kirby Smith became convinced that all his cavalry units, except a picked few, should be dismounted and transferred to the infantry. This decision stemmed mainly from two things: (1) the failure of Price's expedition, which proved that Missouri was now invulnerable to cavalry thrusts; and (2) the surplus of mounted troops in the Department. Of the 40,987 soldiers at Smith's disposal, 22,795 were cavalry.[1] On December 9 Smith ordered J. Bankhead Magruder, then commander of Arkansas, to reorganize Price's corps, dismounting all except Shelby's and one other brigade.[2] Magruder warned his superior that the order would cause many of the stragglers still drifting in from Missouri and the hundreds of troops on furlough to decide not to return to their commands.[3] Smith, however, insisted that the cavalry should be reduced to a minimum and the order to Magruder stood. It was likely that his army would never again be able to take the offensive and therefore a large offensive cavalry force was not needed. Smith then instructed General John A. Wharton, now commanding Green's cavalry division, to dismount nine of his regiments, leaving only the best-disciplined and best-equipped regiments as cavalry. Horses of dismounted troops were to be sent to the artillery service.[4]

[1] *Official Records*, ser. IV, vol. III, 989; John M. Harrell, "Arkansas," *Confederate Military History*, X, 277.

[2] *Official Records*, ser. I, vol. XLI, pt. IV, 1103–1104.

[3] Magruder to W. R. Boggs, December 12, 13, 1864, *ibid.*, pp. 1107–1108, 1111.

[4] *Ibid.*, ser. I, vol. XLVIII, pt. I, 1351–1352.

By March 7, 1865, Smith's policy was beginning to show results. The General wrote the President that the cavalry in the Department had been reduced to 17,000 and that 6,000 of these were in the process of being dismounted.[5]

While the departmental command concerned itself with the reorganization of the army, a Confederate cavalry force under Colonel John S. "Rip" Ford (Portrait on Plate 11) fought the Yankees in the last battle of the war, at Palmetto Ranch near the Rio Grande several miles east of Brownsville. On the evening of May 11, some 300 Federals from Brazos Island moved onto the mainland in a blinding rainstorm. After a circuitous march through the chaparral the column at 8:30 A.M. the next day met a Confederate battalion led by Captain W. N. Robinson at Palmetto Ranch. After about an hour of skirmishing the Confederates retreated into the thickets leaving to their protagonists a number of horses and cattle and some supplies. Having set fire to the ranch, the Yankees retired to White Ranch, where they bivouacked for the night. Sometime during the early morning of May 13, about 200 reinforcements under Colonel Theodore H. Barrett reached the Union camp. [6]

Meanwhile, Robinson's cavalry had taken a position about a mile above Palmetto Ranch. At 10 P.M., May 12, a rider set out for Brownsville to get help. For the next twelve hours or so the Confederates skirmished lightly with Federal pickets near Palmetto.[7]

When Colonel Ford and General James E. Slaughter, over-all Confederate commander in the valley, got Robinson's message they had barely 300 men at Brownsville. The rest of the command, about 1,000 men, was badly scattered over the subdistrict. The two officers held a conference in which they made plans to meet the exigency. While Slaughter concentrated the scattered forces at Brownsville, Ford with the available troops and six field guns moved toward the battle front.[8]

At 3 P.M., May 13, Ford's column reached Robinson's new position

[5] *Ibid.*; Harrell, "Arkansas," *Confederate Military History*, X, 276–277.

[6] David Branson's report, May 18, 1865, *Official Records*, ser. I, vol. XLVIII, pt. I, 267–268; Theodore H. Barrett's report, August 10, 1865, *ibid.*, pp. 265–266.

[7] John Salmon Ford, Memoirs, VII, 1174–1180; John S. Ford's article in San Antonio (Texas) *Express*, October 10, 1890.

[8] John S. Ford's report in Oran M. Roberts, "Texas," *Confederate Military History*, XI, 126; Ford, Memoirs, V, 1031–1033.

in a thicket on the riverbank about two miles north of Palmetto. A Federal offensive was about to open. Ford quickly deployed his horsemen in line of battle. A battalion under Captain D. W. Wilson held the Confederate right; a section of Captain O. G. Jones' battery of light artillery, the center; and Giddings' battalion and two infantry companies, all under Robinson, the left.[9] A bugle blared over the swell; a loud cheer came from the woods; and the Yankees came swarming through the thickets. Over the noise of exploding shells and humming bullets could be heard the shouts of officers exhorting their men to die. Soon the Federals retired to regroup and try again to overrun the Confederate position.[10]

During the momentary lull, Rip Ford determined impulsively to counterattack and rode up and down the line shouting: "Men, we have whipped the enemy in all our previous fights! We can do it again!"

"Rip! Rip!" His soldiers shouted back.

Ford raised his six-shooter.

A piercing Texan yell resounded across the chaparral.

"Forward!"

"Charge!"[11]

The Confederates surged forward shooting at everything that moved. The Yankee skirmish line melted away. Wilson's yipping troops hit the Union left. A regiment of Federal Negroes broke and fled. Robinson's horsemen swept over the Union right. The entire Federal line dissolved and within minutes the battle was a near rout. Many of the Yankees were captured, some run down by Confederate horsemen, and other chased into the muddy waters of the Rio Grande. The enemy commanders managed to rally part of the Thirty-Fourth Indiana and some of the Negro troops several hundred yards above the ruins of Palmetto. Robinson's cavalry swooped around the Union left flank. Colonel Barrett ordered a retreat, and the Yankees, throw-

[9] W. H. D. Carrington's report in John Henry Brown, *History of Texas from 1685 to 1892*, II, 432; Dudley G. Wooten, ed., *A Comprehensive History of Texas*, II, 560.

[10] Branson's report, May 18, 1865, *Official Records*, ser. I, vol. XLVIII, pt. I, 268; Barrett's report, August 10, 1865, *ibid.*, p. 266; Ford, Memoirs, VII, 1180–1188.

[11] Carrington's report in Brown, *History of Texas*, II, 436.

ing up skirmishers to check the Confederate pursuit, marched at quick time back toward Brazos Island.[12]

Ford's Texans followed the Federals for seven miles to Cobb's Ranch, just above Brazos Island. Knowing that his men and horses were much too exhausted to continue the pursuit, Ford shouted: "Boys, we have done finely. We will let well enough alone and retire."[13] Just then a Confederate column riding at a gallop reached the scene—General Slaughter with Cater's Battalion under Captain W. H. D. Carrington. Slaughter and Ford engaged in rather strenuous argument over whether or not the attack should be renewed. Ford insisted that his men were too tired to fight. Slaughter disagreed and ordered Carrington to renew the firing as the Yankees attempted to cross the Boca Chica. By this time Brazos Island had been alerted and Barrett's command greatly reinforced. The Federals were strong enough to hold off any attack that Slaughter could muster.

At dusk the firing began to dwindle. An artillery shell burst near a youthful Confederate. Swearing loudly, the boy fired his rifle at the shadows of the island and the shooting part of the Civil War was over.[14]

The next day, Colonel Ford learned from a prisoner taken during the battle that General Lee had surrendered at Appomattox over a month before and that the Federal officers at Brazos Island, having received the news, had moved toward Brownsville expecting Confederate capitulation. The skirmish with Robinson on May 12, the prisoner continued, had been an accident, the ensuing battle, a mistake. Ford and his lieutenants denied this story (the Yankee army later

[12] Ford's report in Roberts, "Texas," *Confederate Military History*, XI, 127–128; Barrett's report, August 10, 1865, *Official Records*, ser. I, vol. XLVIII, pt. I, 266; Wooten, *Comprehensive History of Texas*, II, 560. Hubert Howe Bancroft, *History of the North Mexican States and Texas*, II, 475.

[13] Ford, Memoirs, V, 1032–1033.

[14] Carrington's report in Brown, *History of Texas*, II, 433–435. With respect to the numbers engaged and the casualties sustained, the accounts of the battle come nowhere near general agreement. Federal losses out of about 800 engaged all told were probably 30 killed and wounded and 113 taken prisoner. Confederate casualties must have been more than five slightly wounded, as reported. Carrington stated in his report (*ibid.*, p. 435) that after it was all over the Confederates took time out to bury their dead. It is likely that out of some 1,300 total troops engaged, Confederates lost about the same in killed and wounded as the Yankees.

advanced a view of the battle supporting this denial) and insisted that Union forces had come off Brazos Island looking for trouble, and certainly they had found it.[15] This dispute has never been settled to the satisfaction of both sides. But the motives behind the last battle were actually insignificant as the final chapter of the Civil War was coming to a close.

The news of Lee's surrender spread rapidly, disheartening loyal Confederates west of the Mississippi.[16] At Opelousas, Louisiana, war-weary people began to rejoice in the thought of giving up the Confederacy.[17] Citizens in Arkansas and Texas displayed a similar reaction on news of the surrender of the Army of Tennessee at Greensboro, North Carolina.[18]

Some soldiers, however, remained to the end loyal to the Confederacy, God, and Jeff Davis. "If our people," wrote W. W. Heartsill of the Lane Rangers, "and our TROOPS would come to the rescue as they should do: if they would unite as one man; the Trans-Mississippi could defy the combined powers of all Yankeedom." The men of the Lane Rangers shared Heartsill's patriotism. On May 9, at Millican, Texas, they met with Company I of Morgan's Texas Cavalry Regiment and drew up a resolution:

Resolved—that we, the members of the "WP Lane Rangers," are as fully determined to stand by our colors, and endure any privations and offer any sacrifices as we were when we first rallied with patriotic devotion to the standard of our country.[19]

Cavalry units stationed in Louisiana also remained loyal to the Confederacy.[20] "It is . . . a tribute to the cavalry branch of the serv-

---

[15] Ford's article in San Antonio (Texas) *Express*, October 10, 1890; Benson John Lossing, *Pictorial History of the Civil War in the United States of America*, III, 180.

[16] Richard Taylor, *Destruction and Reconstruction: Personal Experiences of the Late War*, pp. 271–272.

[17] Sergeant Edwin H. Fay to his wife, May 14, 1865, in *This Infernal War: The Confederate Letters of Sgt. Edwin H. Fay*, p. 448.

[18] Sarah Katherine (Stone) Holmes, *Brokenburn: The Journal of Kate Stone, 1861–1868*, pp. 333, 340, 344–345.

[19] William W. Heartsill, *Fourteen Hundred and Ninety-One Days in the Confederate Army: or, Camp Life, Day by Day, of the W. P. Lane Rangers from April 19, 1861, to May 20, 1865*, pp. 239, 241–242.

[20] Taylor, *Destruction and Reconstruction*, pp. 271, 272.

ice," wrote Andrew B. Booth, "that they showed up as well as they did under these very trying conditions; when so many of their comrades in arms, especially those in other branches of the service, had weakened and left—unmindful of their duty to remain subject to the end."[21]

But cavalry outfits in other areas had by mid-May lost their patriotism. Dissatisfaction among Texas troops erupted into open disregard for discipline and organization. On May 16 Magruder wired Smith that troops at the Galveston garrison had mutinied.[22] The next day Smith decided to transfer his headquarters from Shreveport to Houston, and setting out across Texas he was confronted every day with the evidence that his army was crumbling to pieces before him. Fully half the troops in the Western Subdistrict of Texas had deserted. The remaining half, implacably refusing to bring back the deserters, agreed that "it is useless for the Trans-Mississippi Department to undertake to do what the Cis-Mississippi Department had failed to do." Other Texas cavalry, though remaining quiet, were reported to be waiting for "what they considered to be the inevitable result, viz., surrender." Magruder did all that he could. Finally, in exasperation, he requested that Smith allow the troops to return home by regiments "with as little damage to the community as possible."[23]

On the night of May 19, officers of the Nineteenth and Twenty-Sixth Texas Cavalry met at Hempstead, Texas, and agreed to disband. Each company was to retain its original organization and return home to protect citizens from "roving bands of thieves and robbers."[24] By May 21 everything in Texas had crumbled. John H. Forney's division had broken up, and Wharton's would probably go within the next twenty-four hours. Smith left Crockett and set out for Hemp-

[21] Andrew B. Booth, *Records of Louisiana Confederate Soldiers and Louisiana Confederate Commands*, I, 5–6.

[22] *Official Records*, ser. I, vol. XLVIII, pt. II, 1308. On May 11 Magruder had ridden to Galveston and appealed to the troops to stay at their post. According to a newspaper correspondent, the soldiers listened silently and respectfully, but without "manifestation or enthusiasm." Four days later they grabbed their gear and headed for home. Galveston (Texas) *Tri-Weekly News*, May 15, 1865.

[23] Magruder to Smith, May 16, 1865, and J. E. Slaughter to Magruder, May 19, 1865, *Official Records*, ser. I, vol. XLVIII, pt. II, 1308, 1313–1314: Joseph H. Parks, *General Edmund Kirby Smith, C.S.A.*, p. 472.

[24] Heartsill, *Fourteen Hundred and Ninety-One Days*, p. 244.

stead to try to prevent the disbanding of the cavalry units. He was confronted at Huntsville with mobs of "disorderly soldiery thronging the roads." Before he could get to Hempstead all the cavalry and infantry had disbanded and control over troops was gone. The next day, May 22, Smith was a general without an army.[25] The "bright dream" of the Confederacy was over. "Our Armies," recorded W. W. Heartsill, "are scattered to the four units of the Heavens. Our cause is lost, ! LOST!! ... Yes, I could fall down in the dust and weep over our great misfortune, our great calamities."[26] Many troops, however, were glad to be civilians again and were anxious to get home to a real bed, good cooking, and honest work.

General Simon Bolivar Buckner surrendered the Army of the Trans-Mississippi to E. R. S. Canby on May 26, 1865. A few Arkansas and Texas cavalry regiments, unwilling to lay down their arms, pushed through the sagebrush of the hostile Sioux country and on into the wild territory of Montana. Five hundred Missouri horsemen, equally determined to continue the war, rode through Texas, crossed the Rio Grande, and moved into Mexico. Among them were Jo Shelby, "Old Pap" Sterling Price, Tom Hindman, and even Kirby Smith himself. It is said that the troopers carried along their bullet-ridden flags, burying them in the Rio Grande before crossing into Mexico.[27]

On news of the disintegration of Kirby Smith's army, William C. Quantrill conceived a plan to eclipse his sacking of Lawrence, the outstanding bushwhacking victory of the war. With his loyal company he would ride to Washington and assassinate President Lincoln. Disguised in blue uniforms as the Fourth Missouri Cavalry (Federal), the band moved east. At the Kentucky line the determined horsemen found to their dismay that Booth had beaten them to their objective. Soon afterwards, on May 10, Quantrill was killed in a skirmish with Federal militia, just below Louisville.[28]

By the end of May, all Confederate forces but one had either surrendered or fled from the Department. Truculent old Stand Waite, too

---

[25] Parks, *Kirby Smith*, p. 473.

[26] Heartsill, *Fourteen Hundred and Ninety-One Days*, p. 245.

[27] John N. Edwards, *Shelby and His Men: or, The War in the West*, pp. 543–551.

[28] William E. Connelley, *Quantrill and the Border Wars*, pp. 465, 475.

stubborn to admit defeat, kept up a mild resistance in the Indian Territory until June, when he and his Indian cavalry, still dressed in tattered Confederate gray, rode into Doaksville and gave themselves up.[29]

[29] Stand Watie to his wife, June 23, 1865, in Edward Everett Dale and Gaston Litton, eds., *Cherokee Cavaliers: Forty Years of Cherokee History as Told in the Correspondence of the Ridge-Watie-Boudinot Family*, p. 228.

162

APPENDICES

APPENDIX A

LIST OF CONFEDERATE CAVALRY REGIMENTS AND
BATTALIONS FROM THE TRANS-MISSISSIPPI

The "First Colonel," or "First Commander," in each entry designates the initial commander of the outfit. Names following the first colonel or first commander are subordinate officers and, in the case of colonels, later commanders.

ARKANSAS[1]

FIRST BATTALION, Arkansas Cavalry
First Commander: Major William H. Brooks

FIRST BATTALION, Arkansas and Louisiana Cavalry
First Commander: Major G. W. Buckner

FIRST REGIMENT, Arkansas Cavalry (successor to DeRosey Carroll's First Arkansas State Cavalry)
First Colonel: Charles A. Carroll
Johnson, J. A., Lieutenant Colonel
Thompson, Lee L., Lieutenant Colonel, later Colonel

FIRST REGIMENT, Arkansas Cavalry (Fagan's Regiment, Monroe's Regiment)

First Colonel: James F. Fagan, later Major General
Davis, M. D., Major
Monroe, James C., Colonel
O'Neil, James M., Major
Reiff, A. V., Major, later Lieutenant Colonel

FIRST REGIMENT, Arkansas Mounted Rifles
First Colonel: Thomas J. Churchill (later Brigadier General)
Campbell, William P., Major
Galloway, Morton G., Lieutenant Colonel, later Colonel
Harper, Robert W., Major, later Colonel

[1] Compiled from *Official Records*; Colonel V. Y. Cook, "List of General and Field Officers, Arkansas Troops, C.S.A., and State Troops," in *Publications of the Arkansas Historical Association*, I (1906), 411–421; United States War Department, *List of Field Officers, Regiments and Battalions in the Confederate Army, 1861–1865*, pp. 8–14; John M. Harrell, "Arkansas," *Confederate Military History*, X; Fay Hempstead, *A Pictorial History of Arkansas from Earliest Times to the Year 1890*, pp. 363–427.

Laswell, George S., Major, later Lieutenant Colonel

Matlock, Charles H., Lieutenant Colonel

Ramseur, Lee M., Major, later Lieutenant Colonel

Reynolds, Daniel H., Major, Lieutenant Colonel, later Colonel

Wells, George W., Major, later Lieutenant Colonel

SECOND BATTALION, Arkansas Cavalry
First Commander: Major W. D. Barnett

SECOND REGIMENT, Arkansas Cavalry (formed from Phifer's Battalion and other independent Arkansas cavalry companies)
First Colonel: W. F. Slemons
Cochran, Thomas M., Lieutenant Colonel

Reid, T. J., Major
Somerville, William J., Major
Withers, H. A., Lieutenant Colonel

SECOND REGIMENT, Arkansas Cavalry (Morgan's Regiment)
First Colonel: Thomas J. Morgan
Bull, John P., Major, later Lieutenant Colonel
Coarser, John W., Lieutenant Colonel
Portis, William N., Major

SECOND REGIMENT, Arkansas Mounted Rifles
First Colonel: James McIntosh (later Brigadier General)
Brown, Henry K., Major, later Lieutenant Colonel
Eagle, James P., Major
Embry, Benjamin T., Lieutenant Colonel, later Colonel
Flanagin, Harris, Colonel
Gipson, William, Major
Smith, James T., Lieutenant Colonel
Williamson, James A., Lieutenant Colonel, later Colonel

THIRD REGIMENT, Arkansas Cavalry (called First Arkansas Mounted Volunteers at organization, July 29, 1861, changed to Third Arkansas, January 15, 1862; included three companies of Williamson's infantry battalion)
First Colonel: Solon Borland
Blackwell, William H., Major
Danley, Benjamin F., Lieutenant Colonel
Earle, J. F., Major
Earle, Samuel G., Colonel
Gee, James, Lieutenant Colonel
Henderson, M. J., Major, later Lieutenant Colonel
Shall, David F., Major

FIFTH REGIMENT, Arkansas Cavalry
First Colonel: Robert C. Newton
Bull, John P., Lieutenant Colonel
Smith, John, Major

SIXTH BATTALION, Arkansas Cavalry
First Commander: Major David G. White

SEVENTH BATTALION, Arkansas Cavalry
First Commander: Major J. N. Cypert

SEVENTH REGIMENT, Arkansas Cavalry
First Colonel: John F. Hill
Adams, J. L., Major
Basham, Oliver, Lieutenant Colonel, later Colonel
Ward, J. C., Major

THIRTEENTH BATTALION, Arkansas Cavalry
First Commander: Major J. L. Witherspoon

BABER'S REGIMENT, Arkansas Cavalry
First Colonel: Milton D. Baber

BUSTER'S BATTALION, Arkansas Cavalry (for service in Indian Territory)
First Commander: Lieutenant Colonel M. W. Buster

166

CARLTON'S REGIMENT, Arkansas Cavalry

First Colonel: Charles H. Carlton

Peoples, S. J., Major

Thompson, R. H., Lieutenant Colonel

CHRISMAN'S BATTALION, Arkansas Cavalry

First Commander: Major Francis M. Chrisman

CRAWFORD'S REGIMENT, Arkansas Cavalry (also referred to as First Regiment, Arkansas Cavalry)

First Colonel: William A. Crawford

Kilgore, Dawson L., Lieutenant Colonel

Walker, John W., Major

DOBBIN'S REGIMENT, Arkansas Cavalry (also referred to as First Regiment, Arkansas Cavalry)

First Colonel: Archibald S. Dobbin

Corley, Samuel, Major

FORD'S BATTALION, Arkansas Cavalry

First Commander: Lieutenant Colonel Barney Ford

Wolf, E. O., Major

GORDON'S REGIMENT, Arkansas Cavalry (successor to Carroll's Regiment and Thompson's Regiment)

First Colonel: Anderson Gordon

Arrington, John A., Major

Fayth, William H., Major

GUNTER'S BATTALION, Arkansas Cavalry

First Commander: Lieutenant Colonel Thomas M. Gunter

Woosley, James, Major

HARRELL'S BATTALION, Arkansas Cavalry

First Commander: Lieutenant Colonel John M. Harrell

Bishop, J. W., Major

McMURTREY'S BATTALION, Arkansas Cavalry

First Commander: Lieutenant Colonel E. L. McMurtrey

MATLOCK'S BATTALION, Arkansas Cavalry (dismounted July 11, 1862)

First Commander: Lieutenant Colonel Charles H. Matlock

POE'S BATTALION, Arkansas Cavalry (This outfit consisted of part of the Eleventh Arkansas Infantry, deserters, and absentees.)

First Commander: Major James T. Poe

STIRMAN'S BATTALION, Arkansas Cavalry (successor to First Battalion, Arkansas Cavalry)

First Commander: Lieutenant Colonel R. Stirman

WRIGHT'S REGIMENT, Arkansas Cavalry

First Colonel: John C. Wright

Bowie, James W., Lieutenant Colonel

Wright, George M., Major

TOTALS: Regiments   15
Battalions   15

INDIAN TERRITORY[2]

FIRST BATTALION, Cherokee Cavalry (Meyer's Battalion)

First Commander: Major Benjamin W. Meyer

[2] Compiled from *Official Records*; United States War Department, *List of Field Officers, Regiments and Battalions in the Confederate Army*, pp. 27–28; Annie H. Abel, *The American Indian as Slaveholder and Secessionist*; Volume I of *The Slaveholding Indians*, pp. 240–253; Harrell, "Arkansas," *Confederate Military History*, X, 70, 98, 198.

167

FIRST BATTALION, Cherokee Cavalry (Bryan's Battalion)
First Commander: Major J. M. Bryan

FIRST REGIMENT, Cherokee Mounted Rifles
First Colonel: Stand Watie, later Brigadier General
Bell, James M., Lieutenant Colonel, later Colonel
Boudinot, E. C., Major
Howland, E. J., Major
Parks, Robert C., Lieutenant Colonel
Taylor, Thomas F., Lieutenant Colonel
Thompson, Joseph F., Major, later Lieutenant Colonel
Vann, Clem. N., Lieutenant Colonel

SECOND REGIMENT, Cherokee Mounted Rifles
First Colonel: William P. Adair
Bell, James M., Lieutenant Colonel (transferred to First Regiment, Cherokee Mounted Rifles)
Brewer, O. H. P., Lieutenant Colonel
Hammock, Porter, Major
Harden, J. R., Major
Vann, John, Major

SECOND REGIMENT, Cherokee Mounted Rifles (also referred to as Drew's Regiment and First Regiment, Cherokee Cavalry)
First Colonel: John Drew
Pegg, Thomas, Major
Ross, William P., Lieutenant Colonel

FRYE'S BATTALION, Cherokee Cavalry
First Commander: Major Moses C. Frye
Scales, Joseph A., Major

FIRST BATTALION, Chickasaw Cavalry
First Commander: Lieutenant Colonel Joseph D. Harris
Reynolds, Lemuel M., Major

FIRST REGIMENT, Chickasaw Cavalry
First Colonel: William L. Hunter
Hays, Abram B., Major
Martin, Samuel H., Lieutenant Colonel

SHECO'S BATTALION, Chickasaw Cavalry
First Commander: Lieutenant Colonel Martin Sheco
Nail, Jonathan, Major

FIRST BATTALION, Choctaw Cavalry
First Commander: Major J. W. Pierce

FIRST REGIMENT, Choctaw Cavalry (also called First Choctaw War Regiment; formed from Battice's Battalion)
First Colonel: Simpson N. Folsom
Battice, F., Lieutenant Colonel

FIRST REGIMENT, Choctaw Cavalry
First Colonel: Sampson Folsom
Hawkins, David F., Lieutenant Colonel

THIRD REGIMENT, Choctaw Cavalry (formed from First Choctaw Battalion)
First Colonel: Jackson McCurtain
Page, John, Major
Lewis, Tom, Lieutenant Colonel

FIRST REGIMENT, Choctaw and Chickasaw Mounted Rifles
First Colonel: Douglas H. Cooper
Jones, Willis J., Major
Le Flore, Mitchell, Major
Loering, Sampson, Major
Riley, James, Lieutenant Colonel
Walker, Tandy, Lieutenant Colonel (transferred to Second Regiment, Choctaw and Chickasaw Mounted Rifles)

SECOND REGIMENT, Choctaw and Chickasaw Mounted Rifles
First Colonel: Tandy Walker

168

FIRST REGIMENT, Creek Cavalry
First Colonel: Daniel N. McIntosh
Chekote, Samuel, Lieutenant Colonel
Derrysaw, Jacob, Major
McHenry, James, Major
McIntosh, William R., Lieutenant Colonel

SECOND REGIMENT, Creek Cavalry (formed from First Battalion, Creek Cavalry)
First Colonel: Chilly McIntosh

Barnett, Timothy, Major, later Colonel
Hawkins, Pink, Lieutenant Colonel

FIRST BATTALION, Seminole Cavalry
First Commander: Lieutenant Colonel John Jumper
Cloud, George, Major

OSAGE CAVALRY BATTALION
First Commander: Major Broken Arm

TOTALS: Regiments 11
Battalions 8

LOUISIANA[3]

FIRST REGIMENT, Louisiana Cavalry
First Colonel: John S. Scott
Nixon, James O., Lieutenant Colonel
Schlater, Gervais, Major
Taylor, J. M., Major

FIRST REGIMENT, Louisiana Partisan Rangers (formed from Wingfield's Ninth Battalion and three companies of east Louisiana cavalry)
First Colonel: James H. Wingfield
DuBond, [given name unknown] Major
Amacker, P. O., Lieutenant Colonel

SECOND BATTALION, Louisiana State Cavalry
First Commander: Lieutenant Colonel H. M. Farrot

SECOND REGIMENT, Louisiana Cavalry
First Colonel: William G. Vincent
Blair, James D., Major, later Colonel
Breazeale, Overton, Major

Breazeale, Winter W., Major, later Lieutenant Colonel
Logan, George D., Major
McWaters, J., Lieutenant Colonel
Thompson, James M., Major

THIRD REGIMENT, Louisiana Cavalry (formed from Chambliss' Battalion and other independent Louisiana cavalry companies; broken up in January, 1863, and not included in totals)
First Colonel: J. Frank Pargoud
Capers, Richard L., Major
Chambliss, Samuel L., Lieutenant Colonel

FOURTH REGIMENT, Louisiana Cavalry
First Colonel: A. J. McNeil

FOURTH REGIMENT, Louisiana Cavalry (also referred to as Fifth Regiment)
First Colonel: Richard L. Capers

[3] Compiled from *Official Records*; Louisiana Adjutant General, *Annual Report, 1891*, pp. 34–41; Andrew B. Booth, comp., *Records of Louisiana Confederate Soldiers and Louisiana Confederate Commands*; United States War Department, *List of Field Officers, Regiments and Battalions in the Confederate Army*, pp. 30–35; Adjutant General M. Grivot, "Report to the Louisiana Legislature Upon State Troops, for the Years 1860, '61 and '62," in [Napier Bartlett], *A Soldier's Story of the War: Including the Marches and Battles of the Washington Artillery, and of Other Louisiana Troops*, pp. 237–259.

FIFTH REGIMENT, Louisiana Cavalry (also referred to as Third Regiment, formed from Thirteenth Battalion Partisan Rangers)
First Colonel: Isaac F. Harrison

SIXTH REGIMENT, Louisiana Cavalry
First Colonel: William Harrison
Johnson, W. W., Colonel

SEVENTH REGIMENT, Louisiana Cavalry
First Colonel: Louis Bush
Bringier, Amedee, Lieutenant Colonel
Mouton, William, Major

EIGHTH REGIMENT, Louisiana Cavalry (formed from Thirteenth Battalion and three independent companies)
First Colonel: Benjamin W. Clark
Caldwell, R. J., Major
Wyche, R. E., Major

EIGHTEENTH BATTALION, Louisiana Cavalry (also called Tenth Battalion)
First Commander: Lieutenant Colonel Haley M. Carter
Sherburne, H. Newton, Major

BAYLISS' BATTALION, Louisiana Cavalry
First Commander: Lieutenant Colonel W. H. Bayliss

CHAMBLISS' BATTALION, Louisiana Cavalry
First Commander: Lieutenant Colonel Samuel L. Chambliss

GOBER'S REGIMENT, Louisiana Cavalry
First Colonel: Daniel C. Gober

POWER'S REGIMENT, Louisiana Cavalry (often called Fourth Regiment, consisted of seven Louisiana companies, three Mississippi companies)
First Colonel: Frank P. Powers
McKowen, John C., Lieutenant Colonel

ZOUAVE BATTALION, Louisiana Cavalry
First Commander: Lieutenant Colonel M. A. Coppens
Coppens, George A., Lieutenant Colonel
De Bordenave, Fulgence, Major
Hyllested, Waldemar, Major

TOTALS: Regiments 11
Battalions 5

MISSOURI[4]

FIRST BATTALION, Missouri Cavalry (First Indian Brigade)
First Commander: Major Thomas R. Livingston
Pickler, J. F., Major
Piercey, A. J., Major
FIRST REGIMENT, Missouri Cavalry
First Colonel: Elijah Gates

Chiles, Richard B., Lieutenant Colonel
Law, George W., Major, later Lieutenant Colonel
Lawther, Robert R., Major
Maupin, William D., Lieutenant Colonel
Parker, William D., Major

[4] Compiled from *Official Records*; United States War Department, *List of Field Officers, Regiments and Battalions in the Confederate Army*, pp. 42–47; United States Record and Pension Office, *Organization and Status of Missouri Troops, Union and Confederate, during the Civil War*; John C. Moore, "Missouri," *Confederate Military History*, IX.

FIRST REGIMENT, Missouri Cavalry (formed from Elliott's scouting battalion)
First Colonel: Benjamin F. Elliott
McDaniels, W., Major, later Lieutenant Colonel
Walton, Thomas H., Major, later Lieutenant Colonel

FIRST REGIMENT, Northeast Missouri Cavalry (consolidated with Second Northeast Missouri Cavalry, April 4, 1863)
First Colonel: Joseph C. Porter
Blanton, William C., Lieutenant Colonel
Major, Elliott E., Major

SECOND REGIMENT, Missouri Cavalry (formed from Fourth Battalion)
First Colonel: Robert McCulloch, Jr.
Couzens, William H., Major
Hyams, Samuel M., Jr., Lieutenant Colonel
Smith, John J., Major

SECOND REGIMENT, Northeast Missouri Cavalry (consolidated with First Northeast Missouri Cavalry, April 4, 1863)
First Colonel: Cyrus Franklin
McCullough, Frisby H., Lieutenant Colonel
Smith, Raphael, Major

THIRD REGIMENT, Missouri Cavalry
First Colonel: D. Todd Samuel

THIRD REGIMENT, Missouri Cavalry (formed from Sixth Battalion)
First Colonel: Colton Greene
Campbell, L. A., Major, later Lieutenant Colonel
Campbell, Leonidas C., Lieutenant Colonel
Surridge, James, Major

FOURTH REGIMENT, Missouri Cavalry (formed from Preston's Battalion)
First Colonel: John Q. Burbridge

Preston, William J., Lieutenant Colonel
Smith, Dennis, Major

FIFTH REGIMENT, Missouri Cavalry
First Colonel: Joseph Orville Shelby, later Brigadier General
Blackwell, Y. H., Major, later Lieutenant Colonel
Gordon, B. Frank, Lieutenant Colonel, later Colonel
Kirtley, George G., Major

SIXTH REGIMENT, Missouri Cavalry (also referred to as Southwest Regiment and Eleventh Regiment)
First Colonel: John T. Coffee
Hooper, James C., Lieutenant Colonel
Nichols, George W., Major
Smith, Moses E., Major
Thompson, George W., Lieutenant Colonel, later Colonel

SEVENTH REGIMENT, Missouri Cavalry (also called Tenth Regiment)
First Colonel: Solomon G. Kitchen
Ellison, Jesse, Lieutenant Colonel
Walker, James A., Major

EIGHTH REGIMENT, Missouri Cavalry
First Colonel: William L. Jeffers
Parrott, James, Major
Ward, Samuel J., Lieutenant Colonel

TENTH REGIMENT, Missouri Cavalry (also called Lawther's Regiment, formed from Young's Eleventh Battalion, December 14, 1863)
First Colonel: Robert R. Lawther
Bennett, George W. C., Major
Young, Merritt L., Lieutenant Colonel

TWELFTH REGIMENT, Missouri Cavalry (successor to Jackson County Cavalry)
First Colonel: David Shanks
Bowman, Samuel, Major
Erwin, William H., Lieutenant Colonel
Vivien, H. J., Major

FOURTEENTH BATTALION, Missouri Cavalry
First Commander: Major Robert C. Wood

CLARK'S REGIMENT, Missouri Cavalry (Clark's Recruits)
First Colonel: H. E. Clark

FREEMAN'S REGIMENT, Missouri Cavalry
First Colonel: Thomas R. Freeman
Love, Joseph B., Lieutenant Colonel
Shaver, M. V., Major

FRISTOE'S REGIMENT, Missouri Cavalry
First Colonel: Edward T. Fristoe
Norman, Matthew J., Major
Tracy, J. H., Lieutenant Colonel

HUNTER'S REGIMENT, Missouri Cavalry
First Colonel: DeWitt C. Hunter

JACKSON COUNTY REGIMENT, Missouri Cavalry
First Colonel: Upton Hays

Gilkey, Charles A., Major, later Lieutenant Colonel

Jeans, Beal G., Lieutenant Colonel, later Colonel

Shanks, David, Major, later Lieutenant Colonel

MACDONALD'S REGIMENT, Missouri Cavalry (reduced to Young's Battalion, which later was merged into Lawther's Tenth Regiment)
First Colonel: Emmett MacDonald
Bennett, George W. C., Major
Young, Merritt L., Lieutenant Colonel

REVES' BATTALION, Missouri Cavalry
First Commander: Major Timothy Reves (later Colonel)

SNIDER'S BATTALION, Missouri Cavalry (Northeast Cavalry Battalion)
First Commander: Major Henry G. Snider

TOTALS: Regiments   20
           Battalions   4

TEXAS[5]

FIRST BATTALION, Texas State Cavalry
First Commander: Lieutenant Colonel D. D. Holland
Taylor, Joseph, Major

FIRST REGIMENT, Arizona Brigade (formed from First Battalion, Arizona Brigade)
First Colonel: William P. Hardeman
Hardeman, Peter, Lieutenant Colonel, later Colonel
Looscan, Michael, Major

Riordan, Edward R., Lieutenant Colonel

Terrell, Alexander W., Major

FIRST REGIMENT, Texas Cavalry (formed from Taylor's Eighth Battalion and Yager's Third Battalion)
First Colonel: Augustus C. Buchel
Myers, Robert A., Major
Yager, William O., Lieutenant Colonel

[5] Compiled from *Official Records*; Lester N. Fitzhugh, comp., *Texas Batteries, Battalions, Regiments, Commanders and Field Officers Confederate States Army, 1861–1865*, pp. 4–23; United States War Department, *List of Field Officers, Regiments and Battalions in the Confederate Army*, pp. 71–78; Dudley G. Wooten, ed., *A Comprehensive History of Texas*, II, 572–630; Oran M. Roberts, "Texas," *Confederate Military History*, XI; Harry M. Henderson, *Texas in the Confederacy*, pp. 123–144.

FIRST REGIMENT, Texas Mounted Rifles (reduced to Eighth Battalion)
First Colonel: Henry E. McCulloch, later Brigadier General
Barry, James B., Major
Burleson, Edward, Major
Frost, Thomas C., Lieutenant Colonel

FIRST REGIMENT, Texas Partisan Rangers
First Colonel: Walter P. Lane, later Brigadier General
Burns, A. D., Major
Crump, R. P., Lieutenant Colonel
Saufley, William P., Major

FIRST REGIMENT, Texas State Cavalry
First Colonel: Tignal W. Jones
Coleman, J. J. (G.?), Major
Stidham, G. W., Lieutenant Colonel

SECOND REGIMENT, Arizona Brigade (formed from Second Battalion, Arizona Brigade)
First Colonel: George W. Baylor
Hunter, Sherod, Major
Mullen, John W., Lieutenant Colonel

SECOND REGIMENT, Texas Cavalry
First Colonel: John S. "Rip" Ford
Baylor, John R., Lieutenant Colonel
Donelson, John, Major
Nolan, Matthew, Major
Pyron, Charles L., Major, later Lieutenant Colonel, Colonel
Spencer, William A., Major
Walker, James, Lieutenant Colonel
Waller, Edward, Jr., Major

SECOND REGIMENT, Texas Partisan Rangers
First Colonel: B. Warren Stone
Chisum, Isham, Lieutenant Colonel, later Colonel
Miller, Crill, Lieutenant Colonel
Throckmorton, James W., Major
Vance, James G., Major

SECOND REGIMENT, Texas State Cavalry (formed from Second Battalion, Texas State Cavalry)
First Colonel: Gid Smith
Carter, J. C., Lieutenant Colonel
McLean, James B., Major

THIRD BATTALION, Texas State Cavalry
First Commander: Lieutenant Colonel J. M. Morin
Scoggins, L. G., Major

THIRD REGIMENT, Arizona Brigade (formed from Third Battalion, Arizona Brigade)
First Colonel: Joseph Phillips
Madison, George T., Lieutenant Colonel
Ridley, Alonzo, Major

THIRD REGIMENT, Texas Cavalry (South Kansas-Texas Regiment)
First Colonel: Elkanah Greer, later Brigadier General
Barker, J. J. A., Major
Boggess, Giles S., Major, later Colonel
Chilton, George W., Major
Cumby, Robert H., Lieutenant Colonel, later Colonel
Harris, J. A., Major
Lane, Walter P., Lieutenant Colonel
Mabry, Hinchie P., Lieutenant Colonel, later Colonel
Stone, Absalom B., Major

THIRD REGIMENT, Texas State Cavalry
First Colonel: T. J. M. Richardson
Dunaway, George O., Lieutenant Colonel
Rogers, L. M., Major

FOURTH BATTALION, Texas State Cavalry
First Commander: Lieutenant Colonel William C. Tait
Townes, E. D., Major

FOURTH REGIMENT, Arizona Brigade
First Colonel: Spruce M. Baird
Riordan, Edward, Major

173

Showalter, Daniel, Lieutenant Colonel

FOURTH REGIMENT, Texas Cavalry
First Colonel: James Reily
Hampton, George J., Major, later Lieutenant Colonel
Hardeman, William P., Lieutenant Colonel, later Colonel
Lesueur, Charles M., Major
Raguet, Henry W., Major
Scurry, William R., Lieutenant Colonel

FOURTH REGIMENT, Texas State Cavalry
First Colonel: J. B. Johnson
Cook, H. W., Major
Easley, Sam A., Lieutenant Colonel

FIFTH REGIMENT, Texas Cavalry
First Colonel: Tom Green, later Brigadier General
Lockridge, Samuel A., Major
McNeill, Henry C., Lieutenant Colonel
McPhaill, Hugh A., Major
Shannon, Denman W., Major, later Lieutenant Colonel

FIFTH REGIMENT, Texas Partisan Rangers (formed from Randolph's Ninth Battalion and Martin's Tenth Battalion)
First Colonel: Leonidas M. Martin
Mayrant, William H. (N.?), Major
Weaver, William M., Lieutenant Colonel

SIXTH BATTALION, Texas Cavalry (dismounted)
First Commander: Lieutenant Colonel Robert S. Gould
Veser, William W., Major

SIXTH REGIMENT, Texas Cavalry
First Colonel: B. Warren Stone
Griffith, John S., Lieutenant Colonel

Ross, Lawrence S., Major, later Colonel, Brigadier General
Wharton, Jack, Major, Lieutenant Colonel, later Colonel
White, Robert M., Major
Wilson, Stephen B., Major

SEVENTH REGIMENT, Texas Cavalry
First Colonel: William P. Steele, later Brigadier General
Bagby, Arthur P., Lieutenant Colonel, later Colonel
Herbert, Philemon T., Lieutenant Colonel
Hoffman, Gustave, Major
Jordan, Powhatan, Major, later Lieutenant Colonel
Sutton, J. S., Lieutenant Colonel

EIGHTH REGIMENT, Texas Cavalry (Terry's Texas Rangers)
First Colonel: Benjamin F. Terry
Christian, Samuel P., Lieutenant Colonel
Cook, Gustave, Colonel
Evans, Marcus Legrand, Major, later Lieutenant Colonel
Ferrell, Stephen C., Lieutenant Colonel
Jarmon, William R., Major
Harrison, Thomas, Colonel, later Brigadier General
Lubbock, Thomas S., Lieutenant Colonel
Rayburn, Leander M., Major
Walker, John G., Lieutenant Colonel, later Major General
Wharton, John A., Colonel, later Major General

NINTH REGIMENT, Texas Cavalry
First Colonel: William B. Sims
Bates, James C., Major
Berry, Thomas G., Lieutenant Colonel
Dodson, J. N., Lieutenant Colonel
Jones, Dudley William, Lieutenant Colonel, later Colonel

Quayle, William, Lieutenant Colonel

Townes, Nathan W., Major, later Colonel

TENTH REGIMENT, Texas Cavalry

First Colonel: Matthew F. Locke

Barton, James M., Lieutenant Colonel

Craig, Washington de LaFayette, Major, later Lieutenant Colonel

Earp, C. R., Colonel

Ector, Wiley B., Major

Redwine, Hulum D. E., Major

ELEVENTH BATTALION, Texas Cavalry and Infantry (Spaight's Battalion)

First Commander: Lieutenant Colonel Ashley W. Spaight

Irvine, J. S., Major

ELEVENTH REGIMENT, Texas Cavalry

First Colonel: William C. Young

Bone, Henry F., Major

Bounds, Joseph Murphy, Lieutenant Colonel, later Colonel

Burks, John C., Colonel

Diamond, James J., Lieutenant Colonel, later Colonel

Hooks, Robert W., Lieutenant Colonel, later Colonel

Mayrant, John W., Major

Messick, Otis M., Major, later Lieutenant Colonel, Colonel

Nicholson, Andrew J., Lieutenant Colonel

Puryear, John B., Major

Reeves, George R., Colonel

TWELFTH REGIMENT, Texas Cavalry

First Colonel: William H. Parsons

Burleson, Andrew Bell, Lieutenant Colonel

Mueller, John W., Lieutenant Colonel

Rogers, E. W., Major

THIRTEENTH BATTALION, Texas Cavalry

First Commander: Lieutenant Colonel Edward Waller, Jr.

Boone, Hannibal H., Major

THIRTEENTH REGIMENT, Texas Cavalry (dismounted)

First Colonel: John H. Burnett

Beaty, Charles Roambrose, Major

Crawford, Anderson F., Lieutenant Colonel

Seale, Elias T., Major

FOURTEENTH REGIMENT, Texas Cavalry (dismounted)

First Colonel: Middleton T. Johnson

Camp, John L., Colonel

Camp, Thompson, Major

Ector, Matthew Duncan, Colonel, later Brigadier General

Garrison, Fleming H., Major

Harris, Abram, Lieutenant Colonel

Mains, Samuel F., Lieutenant Colonel

Purdy, Lem, Major

FIFTEENTH REGIMENT, Texas Cavalry

First Colonel: George W. Sweet

Cathey, William H., Major

Masten, William K., Lieutenant Colonel

Pickett, George B., Major, later Lieutenant Colonel

Sanders, Valerius P., Major

SIXTEENTH REGIMENT, Texas Cavalry (dismounted)

First Colonel: William Fitzhugh

Diamond, William W., Major, later Lieutenant Colonel

Gregg, Edward Pearsall, Lieutenant Colonel, later Colonel

SEVENTEENTH REGIMENT, Texas Cavalry

First Colonel: George F. Moore

Hendricks, Sterling B., Lieutenant Colonel

McClarty, John, Major, later Lieutenant Colonel

Noble, Sebron M., Major, later Lieutenant Colonel

Tucker, Thomas F., Colonel

175

Taylor, James R., Colonel

EIGHTEENTH REGIMENT, Texas Cavalry (dismounted)
First Colonel: Nicholas H. Darnell
Coit, John T., Lieutenant Colonel
Morgan, Charles C., Major
Ryan, William A., Major

NINETEENTH REGIMENT, Texas Cavalry
First Colonel: Nathaniel M. Burford
Daves, Joel T., Major
Watson, Benjamin W., Lieutenant Colonel

TWENTIETH REGIMENT, Texas Cavalry
First Colonel: Thomas Coke Bass
Broughton, Dempsey W., Major
Fowler, Andrew J., Lieutenant Colonel
Johnson, John R., Major
Taliaferro, T. D., Lieutenant Colonel

TWENTY-FIRST REGIMENT, Texas Cavalry (also called First Lancers)
First Colonel: George Washington Carter
Ghenoweth, Benjamin D., Major
Giddings, DeWitt Clinton, Lieutenant Colonel
Neyland, Robert, Lieutenant Colonel

TWENTY-SECOND REGIMENT, Texas Cavalry (also called First Indian-Texas Regiment; dismounted)
First Colonel: Robert H. Taylor
Buck, John A., Major, later Lieutenant Colonel
Johnson, William H., Lieutenant Colonel
Lewelling, Thomas, Lieutenant Colonel
Merrick, George D., Major, later Lieutenant Colonel
Stevens, James G., Major, later Lieutenant Colonel
Stone, Robert D., Major, later Lieutenant Colonel

TWENTY-THIRD REGIMENT, Texas Cavalry
First Colonel: Nicholas C. Gould
Caton, William R., Major
Corley, John A., Major, later Lieutenant Colonel
Grant, Issac A., Lieutenant Colonel

TWENTY-FOURTH REGIMENT, Texas Cavalry (dismounted)
First Colonel: Franklin Collett Wilkes
Neyland, Robert Reese, Lieutenant Colonel
Swearingen, Patrick H., Major, later Lieutenant Colonel
Taylor, William A., Major, later Colonel

TWENTY-FIFTH REGIMENT, Texas Cavalry (dismounted)
First Colonel: Clayton Crawford Gillespie
Boggs, Francis J., Lieutenant Colonel
Dark, Joseph N., Major
Neyland, William Madison, Lieutenant Colonel
Pickett, Edward Bradford, Major

TWENTY-SIXTH REGIMENT, Texas Cavalry (formed from Seventh Battalion)
First Colonel: Xavier Blanchard De Bray
Menard, Medard, Major
Myers, John J., Lieutenant Colonel
Owens, George W., Major

TWENTY-SEVENTH REGIMENT, Texas Cavalry (Whitfield's Legion, formed from Fourth Battalion)
First Colonel: John W. Whitfield
Broocks, John H., Major, later Lieutenant Colonel
Hawkins, Edwin R., Lieutenant Colonel, later Colonel
Holman, Cyrus K., Major
Whitfield, John T., Major

TWENTY-EIGHTH REGIMENT, Texas Cavalry (dismounted)
First Colonel: Horace Randal
Baxter, Eli H., Lieutenant Colonel
Hall, Henry G., Major, later Lieutenant Colonel
Henry, Patrick, Major

TWENTY-NINTH REGIMENT, Texas Cavalry
First Colonel: Charles DeMorse
Carroll, Joseph A., Major
Welch, Otis G., Lieutenant Colonel

THIRTIETH REGIMENT, Texas Cavalry (also called First Texas Partisan Rangers)
First Colonel: Edward Jeremiah Gurley
Battle, Nicholas W., Lieutenant Colonel
Davenport, John H., Major
Nicholas, William B., Lieutenant Colonel

THIRTY-FIRST REGIMENT, Texas Cavalry (dismounted)
First Colonel: Trezevant C. Hawpe
Guess, George W., Lieutenant Colonel
Looscan, Michael, Major
Malone, Frederick J., Major
Peak, William W., Major

THIRTY-SECOND REGIMENT, Texas Cavalry (also called Fifteenth Regiment, formed from First Battalion)
First Colonel: Julius A. Andrews
Estes, William E., Major
Weaver, James A., Lieutenant Colonel

THIRTY-THIRD REGIMENT, Texas Cavalry (formed from Fourteenth Battalion)
First Colonel: James Duff
Benavides, Santos, Major
Brackenridge, John T., Major
Robinson, John H., Major
Sweet, James R., Colonel

THIRTY-FOURTH REGIMENT, Texas Cavalry (Alexander's Regiment)
First Colonel: Almerine M. Alexander
Bush, William M., Major, later Lieutenant Colonel
Caudle, John H., Lieutenant Colonel, later Colonel
Davenport, M. W., Major
Dove, Thomas, Major
Russell, John R., Major, later Lieutenant Colonel
Tackett, Sevier, Major
Wooten, George H., Lieutenant Colonel

THIRTY-FIFTH REGIMENT, Texas Cavalry (Brown's Regiment, formed from Rountree's Battalion and Twelfth Battalion)
First Colonel: Reuben R. Brown
Perkins, Samuel W., Lieutenant Colonel
Rountree, Lee C., Major

THIRTY-FIFTH REGIMENT, Texas Cavalry (Likens' Regiment, formed from Likens' Battalion and Burns' Battalion)
First Colonel: James B. Likens
Burns, James Randolph, Lieutenant Colonel
Worthan, William A., Major

THIRTY-SIXTH REGIMENT, Texas Cavalry (also called Woods' Regiment and Thirty-Second Regiment)
First Colonel: Peter C. Woods
Benton, Nathaniel, Lieutenant Colonel
Holmes, Stokely M., Major
Hutchison, William O., Major, later Lieutenant Colonel

FORTY-SIXTH REGIMENT, Texas Cavalry (Frontier Regiment)
First Colonel: James M. Norris
Alexander, W. J., Major
Barry, James B., Lieutenant Colonel

McCord, James Ebenezer, Major, later Colonel

Obenchain, Alfred T., Lieutenant Colonel

ANDERSON'S REGIMENT, Texas Cavalry (formed from Fulcrod's Battalion and Border's Battalion)
First Colonel: Thomas Scott Anderson
Border, John P., Lieutenant Colonel
Egbert, Daniel, Major
Fulcrod, Philip, Lieutenant Colonel
Randle, James A., Major

BOURLAND'S REGIMENT, Texas Cavalry (Border Regiment)
First Colonel: James Bourland
Diamond, John R., Lieutenant Colonel
Roff, Charles L., Major

BRADFORD'S REGIMENT, Texas Cavalry
First Colonel: Charles M. Bradford
Hoxey, Thomas R., Major
Mann, Walter L., Colonel
Oliver, John E., Major
Upton, William F., Lieutenant Colonel

CATER'S BATTALION, Texas Cavalry
First Commander: Major Thomas C. Cater

DALY'S BATTALION, Texas Cavalry
First Commander: Lieutenant Colonel Andrew Daly
Ragsdale, Samuel G., Major, later Lieutenant Colonel

GANO'S BATTALION, Texas Cavalry (merged into Seventh Regiment, Kentucky Cavalry, September, 1862)
First Commander: Lieutenant Colonel Richard M. Gano

GIDDINGS' BATTALION, Texas Cavalry
First Commander: Lieutenant Colonel George H. Giddings

HERBERT'S BATTALION, Arizona Brigade

First Commander: Lieutenant Colonel P. T. Herbert
Frazer, George M., Major

MORGAN'S BATTALION, Texas Cavalry (recruited to a regiment in 1865 but never recognized as regiment by War Department)
First Commander: Major C. L. Morgan
McKie, B. D., Major

RAGSDALE'S BATTALION, Texas Cavalry
First Commander: Major Samuel G. Ragsdale

SAUFLEY'S SCOUTING BATTALION, Texas Cavalry
First Commander: Major William P. Saufley

TERRELL'S REGIMENT, Texas Cavalry (formed from Terrell's Battalion; dismounted)
First Colonel: Alexander W. Terrell
Morgan, Hiram S., Major
Owens, George W., Major
Robertson, John C., Lieutenant Colonel

TERRY'S REGIMENT, Texas Cavalry
First Colonel: David Smith Terry (brother to Benjamin Franklin Terry of Eighth Regiment, Texas Cavalry)
Brooks, S. H., Lieutenant Colonel
Evans, J. M., Major

WAUL'S LEGION, Texas Cavalry (one battalion infantry, one battalion cavalry)
First Colonel: Thomas N. Waul
Bolling, E. S., Major
Cameron, Allen, Major
Nathusius, Otto, Major
Parker, H. S., Major
Smith, John R., Major
Steele, Oliver, Lieutenant Colonel
Timmons, Barnard, Lieutenant Colonel

178

Weeks, Benjamin F., Major

Willis, Leonidas M., Lieutenant Colonel

Wrigley, James, Lieutenant Colonel

WELLS' REGIMENT, Texas Cavalry (also called Thirty-Fourth Regiment)

First Colonel: John W. Wells

Good, Chaplin, Lieutenant Colonel

Gillett, L. E., Major

WILLIS' BATTALION, Texas Cavalry

First Commander: Lieutenant Colonel Leonidas M. Willis

Parker, H. S., Major

Smith, John R., Major

Weeks, Benjamin F., Major

TOTALS: Regiments 57
Battalions 15

APPENDIX B

TOTAL STRENGTH OF CAVALRY UNITS RAISED
IN THE TRANS-MISSISSIPPI

To estimate the total number of Confederate cavalrymen recruited west of the River during the war, it is necessary first to determine the average numerical strength of regiments and battalions, and then to multiply these averages by the total numbers of regiments and battalions listed in Appendix A. The totals reached by this method are imperfect at best. After 1863 most recruits and conscripts were assigned to existing outfits to keep them up to strength. Since it is virtually impossible to estimate the number of these additional troops, no effort is made to include them here. Their exclusion is, however, presumed to be offset in great measure by the fact that many men who transferred from old regiments and battalions to new ones have been counted twice in the present computations. It should be noted that the totals are not the number of troops at any given time; they are cumulations for the entire period of the war.

Unfortunately, the *Official Records* are of limited help in ascertaining the average size of cavalry regiments and battalions. They do not include an official roll of cavalry outfits in the Confederate Army nor show the strength of organizations when mustered in, and even the periodic returns of Trans-Mississippi mounted units with total numbers present and absent are incomplete and sometimes even inaccurate. Nevertheless, these returns for 1861 and early 1862, before regiments and battalions either lost heavily in campaigning or gained new recruits, were helpful in computing the initial strength of units in Table I, Chapter 1, and in the lists in Chapter 2. Using the figures given there, the average initial strength of regiments and battalions raised by December, 1862, may be estimated as follows:

180

Area	Number of Units Reg.	Bns.	Average Initial Strength
Texas	39		947
		10	440
Indian Territory	5		917
		2	400
Arkansas	8		779
		6	275
Louisiana	4		832
		2	388
Missouri	11		635

These figures do not include the units raised from January, 1863, to the end of the War: in Texas, eighteen regiments and five battalions; in the Indian Territory, six regiments and six battalions; in Arkansas, seven regiments and nine battalions; in Louisiana, seven regiments and three battalions; and in Missouri, nine regiments and four battalions. Since little is known of the initial strength of these outfits, averages cannot be ascertained by the method employed above. It is likely, however, that the number in a company fell between sixty and one hundred, as Confederate law required. If eighty be used as the average size of cavalry companies, the average strength of a cavalry regiment (ten companies) at organization was 800, of a battalion (usually five companies), 400. These figures will be used as the averages for regiments and battalions raised after 1862. With these averages, plus those above, the number of cavalrymen from each state and the total raised in the Trans-Mississippi may be computed as follows:

| | 1861–1862 | | | | | 1863–1865 | | | | | 1861–1865 |
| | Regs. | | Bns. | | | Regs. | | Bns. | | | |
Area	No.	Av. Size	No.	Av. Size	Total Strength	No.	Av. Size	No.	Av. Size	Total Strength	Total Strength
Texas	39	947	10	440	41,333	18	800	5	400	16,400	57,733
Indian Territory	5	917	2	400	5,385	6	800	6	400	7,200	12,585
Arkansas	8	779	6	275	7,882	7	800	9	400	9,200	17,082
Louisiana	4	832	2	388	4,104	7	800	3	400	6,800	10,904
Missouri	11	635			6,985	9	800	4	400	8,800	15,785
Total Cavalrymen Raised in the Trans-Mississippi											114,089

APPENDIX C

ORGANIZATION OF PRICE'S CAVALRY CORPS[1]

FAGAN'S DIVISION

Major General JAMES F. FAGAN

Cabell's Brigade — Brigadier General William L. Cabell
  Monroe's Regiment, Arkansas Cavalry — Colonel James C. Monroe
  Gordon's Regiment, Arkansas Cavalry — Colonel Anderson Gordon
  Second Regiment, Arkansas Cavalry — Colonel Thomas J. Morgan
  Seventh Regiment, Arkansas Cavalry — Colonel John F. Hill
  Gunter's Battalion, Arkansas Cavalry — Lieutenant Colonel Thomas M. Gunter
  Harrell's Battalion, Arkansas Cavalry — Lieutenant Colonel John M. Harrell
  Thirteenth Battalion, Arkansas Cavalry — Major J. L. Witherspoon
  Hughey's Arkansas Battery — Captain W. M. Hughey

Slemons' Brigade — Colonel W. F. Slemons (first commander)
Colonel William A. Crawford (second commander
  Second Regiment, Arkansas Cavalry — Colonel W. F. Slemons
  Crawford's Regiment, Arkansas Cavalry — Colonel William A. Crawford
  Carlton's Regiment, Arkansas Cavalry — Colonel Charles H. Carlton
  Wright's Regiment, Arkansas Cavalry — Colonel John C. Wright

Dobbin's Brigade — Colonel Archibald S. Dobbin
  Dobbin's Regiment, Arkansas Cavalry — Colonel Archibald S. Dobbin
  McGhee's Regiment, Arkansas Infantry (mounted) — Colonel James McGhee
  Tenth Regiment, Arkansas Infantry (mounted) — Colonel A. R. Witt
  Blocher's Arkansas Battery (one section) — Lieutenant J. V. Zimmerman

McCray's Brigade — Colonel Thomas H. McCray
  Baber's Regiment, Arkansas Cavalry — Colonel Milton D. Baber
  Forty-Seventh Regiment, Arkansas Infantry (mounted) — Colonel Lee Crandall
  Reves' Battalion, Missouri Cavalry — Colonel Timothy Reves

[1] *Official Records*, ser. I, vol. XLI, pt. I, 641–642.

Unattached
Twenty-Third Regiment,
    Arkansas Infantry (mounted)   Colonel Oliver P. Lyles
Thirtieth Regiment, Arkansas Infantry
            (mounted)   Colonel James W. Rogan
Anderson's Battalion,
    Arkansas Infantry (mounted)   Captain W. L. Anderson

MARMADUKE'S DIVISION

Major General JOHN S. MARMADUKE
(first commander)

Brigadier General JOHN B. CLARK, JR.
(second commander)

Marmaduke's Brigade	Brigadier General John B. Clark, Jr.
	(first commander)
	Colonel Colton Greene
	(second commander)
Third Regiment, Missouri Cavalry	Colonel Colton Greene
Fourth Regiment, Missouri Cavalry	Colonel John Q. Burbridge
Seventh Regiment, Missouri Cavalry	Colonel Solomon G. Kitchen
Eighth Regiment, Missouri Cavalry	Colonel William L. Jeffers
Tenth Regiment, Missouri Cavalry	Colonel Robert R. Lawther
Fourteenth Battalion, Missouri Cavalry	Lieutenant Colonel Robert C. Wood
Davies' Battalion, Missouri Cavalry	Lieutenant Colonel J. F. Davies
Hynson's Texas Battery	Captain H. C. Hynson
Harris' Missouri Battery	Captain S. S. Harris
Engineer Company	Captain James T. Hogan
Freeman's Brigade	Colonel Thomas R. Freeman
Freeman's Regiment, Missouri Cavalry	Colonel Thomas R. Freeman
Fristoe's Regiment, Missouri Cavalry	Colonel Edward T. Fristoe
Ford's Battalion, Arkansas Cavalry	Lieutenant Colonel Barney Ford

SHELBY'S DIVISION

Brigadier General JOSEPH O. SHELBY

Shelby's Iron Brigade	Colonel David Shanks
	(first commander)
	Brigadier General M. Jeff. Thompson
	(second commander)
Fifth Regiment, Missouri Cavalry	Colonel B. Frank Gordon
Eleventh Regiment, Missouri Cavalry	Colonel Moses Smith
Twelfth Regiment, Missouri Cavalry	Colonel David Shanks
First Regiment, Missouri Cavalry	Colonel Benjamin F. Elliott
Slayback's Battalion, Missouri Cavalry	Lieutenant Colonel A. W. Slayback
Collins' Missouri Battery	Captain Richard A. Collins

CONFEDERATE CAVALRY WEST OF THE RIVER

Jackman's Brigade	Colonel Sidney D. Jackman
Jackman's Regiment, Missouri Infantry (mounted)	Lieutenant Colonel C. H. Nichols
Hunter's Regiment, Missouri Cavalry	Colonel DeWitt C. Hunter
Williams' Battalion, Missouri Cavalry	Lieutenant Colonel D. A. Williams
Schnable's Battalion, Missouri Cavalry	Lieutenant Colonel J. A. Schnable
Collins' Missouri Battery (one section)	Lieutenant J. D. Connor
Unattached	
Forty-Sixth Regiment, Arkansas Infantry (mounted)	Colonel W. O. Coleman
Tyler's Brigade	Colonel Charles H. Tyler
Perkins' Regiment, Missouri Cavalry	Colonel Caleb Perkins
Coffee's Regiment, Missouri Cavalry	Colonel John T. Coffee
Searcy's Regiment, Missouri Cavalry	Colonel James T. Searcy

BIBLIOGRAPHY

PRIMARY SOURCES

Manuscripts

(Unless otherwise noted all manuscripts are in the Archives Collection of the Library of the University of Texas.)

Robert Franklin Bunting Papers. These contain much valuable information on the affairs of Terry's Texas Rangers after they left the Trans-Mississippi. The papers consist of the Diary of Frank Bunting, 1862–1863, and the Letters of Robert Franklin Bunting, November 9, 1861, to 1865. The latter is a typescript copy of Bunting's war correspondence to the Houston *Daily Telegraph* and the San Antonio *Herald*. Bunting was chaplain of the Rangers.

M. W. Bowers Papers. Only Package VI is relevant here. The dates on this package (1870–1877) are misleading, for it contains loose copies of General Orders No. 45, September 16, 1863; No. 91, November 4, 1863; and the Galveston *Tri-Weekly News*, January 11, 1865 (this issue may also be found in the Newspaper Collection of the Library of the University of Texas).

Claiborne, Jno. M., comp., Muster Rolls of Terry's Texas Rangers, Reunion in Galveston, February 20, 1882.

John Salmon Ford Memoirs. Of the seven typescript volumes, the last three are concerned with Ford's activities as a Confederate cavalry colonel in Texas. These reminiscences constitute a meaty source of information about Texas in the Civil War period.

Letters of Governor Francis R. Lubbock and Governor Pendleton Murrah, Executive Correspondence, in the Archives Division of the Texas State Library, Austin. This collection contains a valuable letter pertaining to the illegal impressment practices of cavalry units stationed in Texas.

185

John W. Hill Letters, 1861–1865. Hill was a member of Terry's Texas Rangers. Most of his letters are concerned with the activities of the regiment after it departed from the Trans-Mississippi.

Thomas C. Reynolds Papers, Library of Congress, Washington, D.C., microfilm copies in the Library of the University of Texas, Ramsdell Microfilms, Rolls 145C–146A. Among these valuable papers are several letters dealing with Price's Missouri Expedition of 1864.

Oran M. Roberts Papers. Roberts commanded the Eleventh Texas Infantry during the war and later became governor of Texas. His papers include some information on cavalry affairs in the state. Roberts wrote the Texas section in Clement Evans' monumental *Confederate Military History*. See below, under Printed Sources.

B. Warren Stone's Texas Battalion (later the Sixth Texas Cavalry Regiment), Photostatic Copy of the Record Book of Company F, December, 1863, to April, 1865. This book comprises morning reports and monthly returns.

General and Special Orders of Major General J. Bankhead Magruder for the District of Texas, New Mexico, and Arizona.

Newspapers

Arkansas Gazette. Little Rock, Arkansas. June 20, 1863 (incomplete).

Civilian. Galveston, Texas. February 1, 1861, to December 31, 1862.

Countryman. Bellville, Texas. May 29, 1861, to May 30, 1865.

Daily Arkansas Patriot. Little Rock, Arkansas. October 27, 1906.

Daily Crescent. New Orleans, Louisiana. September 6, 1861, to March 5, 1862.

Daily Picayune. New Orleans, Louisiana. March 1, 1861, to December 31, 1862.

Daily State Journal. Little Rock, Arkansas. November 2, 1861, to February 7, 1862.

Daily Times and Herald. Fort Smith, Arkansas. April 5, 1861, to October 9, 1861.

Democrat. Belton, Texas. March 8 to September 27, 1861.

Express. San Antonio, Texas. October 10, 1890.

Gazette. Plaquemine, Louisiana. November 2, 1861.

Herald. Dallas, Texas. June 5, 1861, to May 18, 1865.

Herald. San Antonio, Texas. February 23, 1861, to March 11, 1865.

News Messenger. Marshall, Texas. August 23, 1936.

Patriot. Little Rock, Arkansas. October 1, 1862, to September 11, 1863.

Press. Van Buren, Arkansas. January 5, 1861, to January 30, 1862.

Standard. Clarksville, Texas. May 11, 1861, to November 23, 1861.

Southern Intelligencer. Austin, Texas. January 23, 1861, to July 24, 1861.

Telegraph. Houston, Texas. July 27, 1861, to July 6, 1865.

Texas Almanac—Extra. Austin, Texas. September 18, 1862, to June 6, 1863.

Texas State Gazette. Austin, Texas. January 5, 1861, to May 10, 1865.

Tri-Weekly News. Galveston, Texas. April 8, 1862, to May 15, 1865.

Tri-Weekly Telegraph. Houston, Texas. November 2, 1861, to January 31, 1865.

True Delta. New Orleans, Louisiana. May 19, 1863, to May 19, 1865.

True Democrat. Little Rock, Arkansas. June 19, 1862, to April 22, 1863.

Other Printed Sources

Abney, James A. *An Abridged Autobiography of Some of the Many Incidents and Experiences of James A. Abney, M.D., Confederate Veteran.* Brownwood, Texas: [n. pub.], 1928.

Anderson, Ephraim M. *Memoirs: Historical and Personal; Including the Campaigns of the First Missouri Confederate Brigade.* St. Louis: Times Printing Co., 1868. This contains useful information on the First, Second, and Third Missouri Cavalry Regiments.

Barron, Samuel B. *The Lone Star Defenders: A Chronicle of the Third Texas Cavalry, Ross' Brigade.* New York and Washington: The Neale Publishing Company, 1908. Barron, a lieutenant in Company A, writes a reliable history of the regiment.

Barry, James B. *A Texas Ranger and Frontiersman: The Days of Buck Barry in Texas, 1845–1906.* Edited by James K. Greer. Dallas: The Southwest Press, 1932. Barry, a member of Henry E. McCulloch's First Texas Mounted Rifles in 1861 and later an officer in the Frontier Regiment of Texas Cavalry, tells about the hardships of life on a cavalry outpost.

[Bartlett, Napier]. *A Soldier's Story of the War: Including the Marches and Battles of the Washington Artillery, and of Other Louisiana Troops.* New Orleans: Clark & Hofeline, 1874. Bartlett's book includes reports by the Louisiana Adjutant General, M. Grivot, for 1860, 1861, and 1862.

Baxter, William. *Pea Ridge and Prairie Grove: or, Scenes and Incidents of the War in Arkansas.* Cincinnati: Poe & Hitchcock, 1864. Despite what the title might indicate, there is little in this work about the Prairie Grove campaign.

Bevier, R. S. *History of the First and Second Missouri Confederate Brigades, 1861–1865.* St. Louis: Bryan, Brand & Co., 1879. Bevier has some interesting details about the First, Second, and Third Missouri Cavalry Regiments.

187

Blackburn, J. K. P., "Reminiscences of the Terry Rangers," *Southwestern Historical Quarterly*, XXII (July, October, 1918), 38–78, 143–179. This is not as reliable as Giles' work on the celebrated regiment. See Giles, Leonidas B.

Blessington, Joseph P. *The Campaigns of Walker's Texas Division*. New York: Lang, Little and Co., 1875.

Booth, Andrew B., comp. *Records of Louisiana Confederate Soldiers and Louisiana Confederate Commands*. 3 books in 4 vols. New Orleans: [n. pub.], 1920. Arranged alphabetically by name, this useful compilation gives the date of enrollment, the rank (or ranks), and the outfit of each soldier.

Britton, Wiley. *The Civil War on the Border*. 2 vols. New York: G. P. Putnam's Sons, 1890. Though it emphasizes the Union side, this work presents a well-balanced account of military events in Arkansas and Missouri. Britton was a member of the Sixth Kansas Cavalry (Union).

Burch, John P. *Charles W. Quantrell: A True History of His Guerilla Warfare on the Missouri and Kansas Border during the Civil War of 1861–1865*. As told by Captain Harrison Trow, one who followed Quantrell through his whole course. Vega, Texas: [n. pub.], 1923.

Confederate States Army. Trans-Mississippi Department. *General Orders, Headquarters, Trans-Mississippi Department, from March 6, 1863, to January 1, 1865*. Houston: E. H. Cushing & Company, 1865.

Confederate States Army. Trans-Mississippi Department. *Report of Major General Hindman of His Operations in the Trans-Mississippi District*. Published by order of Congress. Richmond: R. M. Smith, 1864.

Confederate States War Department. *General Orders from the Adjutant and Inspector-General's Office, Confederate Army from January 1 to June 30, 1864*. Prepared by R. C. Gilchrist. Columbia, South Carolina: Evans & Cogswell, 1864. Only a few orders in this set bear directly on cavalry affairs.

Confederate States War Department. *Official Reports of Battles*. Richmond: Enquirer Book and Job Press, 1862.

Confederate States War Department. *Official Reports of Battles*. 2 vols. Richmond: R. M. Smith, 1864.

Confederate States War Department. *The Ordnance Manual for the Use of Officers of the Confederate States Army, 1862*. Prepared under the direction of Colonel Josiah Gorgas, Chief of Ordnance, and approved by the Secretary of War. Charleston, South Carolina: Evans & Cogswell, 1863.

188

Confederate States War Department. *Regulations for the Army of the Confederate States, and for the Quartermaster's and Pay Departments, 1861.* New Orleans: Bloomfield & Steel, 1861.

Confederate States War Department. *Regulations of the Army of the Confederate States, 1862: Containing a Complete Set of Forms.* Austin, Texas: Printed at State Gazette Office, 1862.

Confederate States War Department. *Southern History of the War: Official Records of Battles as Published by Order of the Confederate Congress at Richmond.* New York: C. B. Richardson, 1863.

Confederate States War Department. *Uniform and Dress of the Army of the Confederate States.* . . . Richmond: C. H. Wynne, 1861.

Connelley, William E. *Quantrill and the Border Wars.* Cedar Rapids, Iowa: The Torch Press, 1910.

Cook, Colonel V. Y., "List of General and Field Officers, Arkansas Troops, C.S.A., and State Troops," in *Publications of the Arkansas Historical Association,* I (1906), 411–422. This list may also be found in the (Little Rock) *Daily Arkansas Patriot,* October 27, 1906.

Cooke, Phillip St. George. *Cavalry Tactics: or, Regulations for the Instruction, Formations and Movements of the Cavalry of the United States.* Houston: Texas Printing House, 1863.

Crowninshield, Brevet Colonel Benjamin W., "Cavalry in Virginia during the War of the Rebellion," in *Civil and Mexican Wars, 1861, 1846.* Volume XIII of *Publications of the Military Historical Society of Massachusetts.* Boston, 1913.

Curry, John P. *Volunteers' Camp and Field Book: Containing Useful and General Information on the Art and Science of War, for the Leisure Moments of the Soldier.* Richmond: West & Johnston, 1862.

Dacus, Robert H. *Reminiscences of Company "H," First Arkansas Mounted Rifles.* Dardanelle, Arkansas: Post Dispatch Press, 1897.

Dale, Edward Everett, and Gaston Litton, eds. *Cherokee Cavaliers: Forty Years of Cherokee History as Told in the Correspondence of the Ridge-Watie-Boudinot Family.* Norman: University of Oklahoma Press, 1940.

Dalton, Captain Kit. *Under the Black Flag: A Guerilla Captain under Quantrill and a Border Outlaw for Seventeen Years.* Memphis, Tennessee: Lockard Publishing Company, 1914.

Darrow, Caroline B., "Recollections of the Twiggs Surrender," in Volume I of *Battles and Leaders of the Civil War,* edited by Robert V. Johnson and Clarence C. Buel.

Davis, Colonel James Lucius, comp. *The Trooper's Manual: or, Tactics for Light Dragoons and Mounted Riflemen.* 3rd edition. Richmond: A. Morris, 1862.

Davis, Jefferson. *The Rise and Fall of the Confederate Government.* 2 vols. New York: D. Appleton and Company, 1881.

De Bray, Xavier B. *A Sketch of the History of De Bray's Twenty-Sixth Regiment of Texas Cavalry.* Austin, Texas: E. Von Boeckman, 1884. Also printed in the *Southern Historical Society Papers,* XIII (1885), 153–165.

Dodd, Ephraim S. *Diary of Ephraim Shelby Dodd, December 4, 1862, to January 1, 1864.* Austin, Texas: Press of E. L. Steck, 1914. Dodd was a member of Company D of Terry's Texas Rangers.

Dodge, Colonel Richard Irving. *Our Wild Indians: Thirty-Three Years' Personal Experience among the Red Men of the Great West.* Hartford, Connecticut: A. D. Worthington and Company, 1883.

Edwards, John N. *Shelby and His Men: or, The War in the West.* Cincinnati: Miama Printing and Publishing Co., 1867. Edwards was adjutant of the Fifth Missouri Cavalry and wrote most of Shelby's battle reports. His book is valuable, but must be used with care since it displays a strong Southern bias and contains many exaggerations and errors.

Evans, Clement A., ed. *Confederate Military History.* 12 vols. Atlanta: Confederate Publishing Company, 1899. Contains volumes on "Missouri" (Volume IX by John C. Moore), "Arkansas" (Volume X by John M. Harrell), and "Texas" (Volume XI by Oran M. Roberts).

Fay, Edwin H. *This Infernal War: The Confederate Letters of Sgt. Edwin H. Fay.* Edited by Bell I. Wiley. Austin: University of Texas Press, 1958. The Louisiana cavalry company to which Fay belonged spent the greater part of the war east of the Mississippi.

Fremantle, James Arthur Lyon. *The Fremantle Diary: Being the Journal of Lieutenant Colonel James Arthur Lyon Fremantle, Coldstream Guards, on His Three Months in the Southern States.* Edited by Walter Lord. Boston: Little, Brown, 1954. This contains an interesting description of the "uniforms" of Texas cavalrymen.

Giles, Leonidas B. *Terry's Texas Rangers.* Austin, Texas: Von Boeckman-Jones Company, 1911. This is the best work on the history of the regiment.

Gilham, William, *Manual of Instruction for the Volunteers and Militia of the Confederate States.* Richmond: West and Johnston, 1862.

Gorgas, Josiah, "Extracts from My Notes Written Chiefly after the Close of the War," in *The Confederate Soldier in the Civil War, 1861–1865* ... edited by Ben La Bree.

Grivot, M., "Report to the Louisiana Legislature Upon State Troops, for the Years 1860, '61 and '62," in [Napier Bartlett], *A Soldier's Story of the War.*

Grover, Captain George S., "The Price Campaign of 1864," *Missouri Historical Review,* VI (July, 1912), 167–181. A captain in Foster's Cavalry Battalion, Missouri Volunteers, Grover tells fairly accurately the Yankee side of the invasion.

————., "The Shelby Raid, 1863," *Missouri Historical Review,* VI (April, 1912), 107–126. Again, Grover emphasizes the Federal side of the operation.

Harding, George C. *Miscellaneous Writings.* Indianapolis, Indiana: Carlon & Hollenbeck, 1882.

Harrell, John M., "Arkansas," in Volume X of *Confederate Military History,* edited by Clement A. Evans. Harrell was a staff officer in Monroe's Arkansas Cavalry Regiment, then was commander of a battalion of Arkansas cavalry until 1864, when he took charge of Cabell's Arkansas Brigade. His account is useful for the campaigns in Arkansas.

Heartsill, William W. *Fourteen Hundred and Ninety-One Days in the Confederate Army: or, Camp Life, Day by Day, of the W. P. Lane Rangers from April 19, 1861 to May 20, 1865.* First publication, 1876; facsimile reprint, edited by Bell I. Wiley. Jackson, Tennessee: Mc-Cowat-Mercer Press, 1954. This diary is by far the richest available source of information on the daily life of a cavalryman in the Trans-Mississippi.

[Hinton, Richard J.]. *Rebel Invasion of Missouri and Kansas, and the Campaign of the Army of the Border.* . . . 2nd edition. Chicago: Church & Goodman, 1865.

Holmes, Sarah Katherine (Stone). *Brokenburn: The Journal of Kate Stone, 1861–1868.* Edited by John Q. Anderson. Baton Rouge: Louisiana State University Press, 1955.

Johnson, Robert V., and Clarence C. Buel, eds. *Battles and Leaders of the Civil War.* . . . First publication, 1887–1888. Facsimile reprint, 4 vols.; New York: Thomas Yoseloff, Inc., 1956. This monumental narrative contains several articles by Confederate officers and civilians on military operations in the Trans-Mississippi. Among the topics are Twigg's surrender of San Antonio, 1861 (Caroline B. Darrow), Sib-

191

ley's expedition into New Mexico (Captain George H. Pettis), and the conquest of Arkansas (Thomas L. Snead).

La Bree, Ben. ed. *The Confederate Soldier in the Civil War, 1861– 1865.* . . . Louisville, Kentucky: The Courier-Journal Job Printing Company, 1895.

Lane, Walter P. *The Adventures and Recollections of General Walter P. Lane.* . . . First publication, 1887; second publication, Marshall, Texas: News Messenger Publishing Company, 1928.

Lee, Robert E. *Lee's Dispatches . . . to Jefferson Davis and the War Department of the C.S.A., 1862–1865.* Edited by Douglas Southall Freeman. New York: G. P. Putnam's Sons, 1915.

Lothrop, Charles H. *A History of the First Regiment Iowa Cavalry.* . . . Lyons, Iowa: Beers & Eaton, 1890.

Lubbock, Francis R. *Six Decades in Texas.* . . . Austin: Ben C. Jones and Co., 1900.

Mallet, Lieutenant Colonel J. W., "Work of the Ordnance Bureau," *Southern Historical Society Papers,* XXXVII (January, 1909), 1–20.

Matthews, James M., ed. *The Statutes at Large of the Provisional Government of the Confederate States of America.* . . . Richmond: R. M. Smith, 1864.

McCorkle, John. *Three Years with Quantrill: A True Story.* Armstrong, Missouri: Armstrong Herald Print, 1914.

McDougal, Henry Clay. *Recollections, 1844–1909.* Kansas City, Missouri: Franklin Hudson Publishers, 1910.

Moore, John C., "Missouri," in Volume IX of *Confederate Military History,* edited by Clement A. Evans. Moore was chief of staff for both Marmaduke and Shelby during the war. Though dealing only briefly with the various cavalry raids, his book is an informative study of the war in Missouri.

Moore, Frank, ed. *The Rebellion Record: A Diary of American Events.* . . . 12 vols. New York: D. Van Nostrand, 1862–1871. Volume VI affords lively accounts (mostly by Union newspapermen) of the action at Cane Hill, the battle of Prairie Grove, and the several cavalry expeditions into Missouri.

Mosby, John S. *Mosby's War Experiences and Stuart's Cavalry Campaigns.* First publication, 1887; reprint, New York: Pageant Book Company, 1958.

Noel, Theo. *A Campaign from Santa Fe to the Mississippi: Being a History of the Old Sibley Brigade from Its First Organization to the Pres-*

ent Time; Its Campaigns in New Mexico, Arizona, Texas, Louisiana and Arkansas, in the Years 1861–2–3–4. Shreveport, Louisiana: Shreveport News Printing Establishment, 1865. This is a superb contemporary account.

North, Thomas. *Five Years in Texas: or, What You Did Not Hear during the War from January 1861 to January 1866.* Cincinnati: Elm Street Printing Company, 1871. This is a rare collection of anecdotes with an accurate discussion of military events in the state.

Pearce, N. Bart, "Price's Campaigns of 1861," in *Publications of the Arkansas Historical Association,* IV (1917), 332–351.

Pettis, Captain George H., U.S.V., "The Confederate Invasion of New Mexico and Arizona," in Volume II of *Battles and Leaders of the Civil War,* edited by Robert V. Johnson and Clarence C. Buel.

Roberts, Oran M., "Texas," in Volume XI of *Confederate Military History,* edited by Clement A. Evans. Roberts' account is useful for the recruiting of Texas cavalry regiments.

Rose, Victor M. *Ross' Texas Brigade.* Louisville, Kentucky: The Courier-Journal Job Printing Company, 1881. Rose, who was a member of Greer's Texas Cavalry, gives an interesting and reliable history of his regiment and brigade.

Scott, Joe M. *Four Years' Service in the Southern Army.* Mulberry, Arkansas: Leader Office Print, 1897. During the course of the war, Scott served in Captain Ruff's Company, Arkansas cavalry; the Sixth Texas Cavalry; and Colonel Brooks' Texas Cavalry. His book is, in the main, a personal narrative.

Snead, Colonel Thomas L., "The Conquest of Arkansas," in Volume III of *Battles and Leaders of the Civil War,* edited by Robert V. Johnson and Clarence C. Buel.

———. *The Fight for Missouri.* . . . New York: Charles Scribner's Sons, 1886.

Taylor, Richard. *Destruction and Reconstruction: Personal Experiences of the Late War.* New York: D. Appleton and Company, 1879. This is an accurate and well-balanced story of the fighting in Louisiana.

Terrell, Alexander Watkins. *From Texas to Mexico and the Court of Maximilian in 1865.* Dallas: The Book Club of Texas, 1933. Terrell commanded a regiment of Texas cavalry which followed Shelby, Hindman, and Kirby Smith into Mexico after the War.

Texas Adjutant General. *Report, November, 1861.* Austin, Texas, 1861.

Texas Almanac, 1861–1865. Galveston: D. Richardson & Co., 1861–1865.

Texas Governor, March 16—November 7, 1861 (Edward Clark). *Governor's Message: Executive Office, Austin, March 29, 1861*. [Austin: John Marshall & Company, 1861.]

Texas Governor, March 16—November 7, 1861 (Edward Clark). *Governor's Message to the Senators and Representatives of the Ninth Legislature of the State of Texas, November 1, 1861*. Austin: John Marshall & Company, 1861.

United States Congress. *Journals of the Congress of the Confederate States of America, 1861–1865*. Senate Executive Documents (58th Congress, 2nd Session, 1903–1904), vols. XXV–XXXI, no. 234. 7 vols. Washington, D.C.: Government Printing Office, 1904–1905.

United States Eighth Census, 1860. Volume I, *Population*. Washington, D.C.: Government Printing Office, 1864.

United States Eighth Census, 1860. Volume III, *Agriculture*. Washington, D.C.: Government Printing Office, 1864.

United States Record and Pension Office. *Organization and Status of Missouri Troops, Union and Confederate, during the Civil War*. Washington, D.C.: Government Printing Office, 1902.

United States War Department. *List of Field Officers, Regiments and Battalions in the Confederate Army, 1861–1865*. [Washington, D.C.: Government Printing Office, 189 ?] This compilation is quite useful.

United States War Department. *The War of the Rebellion: A Compilation of the Official Records of the Union and Confederate Armies*. 70 vols. in 128. Washington, D.C.: Government Printing Office, 1880–1901. These records were, of course, the principal reliance in the preparation of this work.

Vaught, Elsa, ed. *The Diary of an Unknown Soldier, September 5, 1862 to December 7, 1862*. Van Buren, Arkansas: Press-Argus Printing Company, 1951. This was written by a member of the Nineteenth Iowa Infantry Regiment.

Walker, Charles W., "Battle of Prairie Grove," in *Publications of the Arkansas Historical Association*, II (1908), 354–361. This contains a helpful list of the Confederate outfits involved.

Wheeler, Joseph. *A Revised System of Cavalry Tactics for Use of the Cavalry and Mounted Infantry, C.S.A.* Mobile, Alabama: Goetzel, 1863. This manual is indispensable to an understanding of the organization and tactics of the Confederate cavalry.

Wilson, Major General James H., "The Cavalry of the Army of the Potomac," in *Civil and Mexican Wars, 1861, 1846*. Volume XII of *Publi-*

cations of the Military Historical Society of Massachusetts. Boston, 1913.

Woodruff, William E. *With the Light Guns in '61–'65: Reminiscences of Eleven Arkansas, Missouri, and Texas Light Batteries in the Civil War. . . .* Little Rock, Arkansas: Central Printing Company, 1903.

Wood, William D., comp. *A Partial Roster of the Officers and Men Raised in Leon County, Texas, for the Service of the Confederate States . . .* [San Marcos, Texas: n. pub.], 1899. This contains a short history of Colonel Robert S. Gould's Sixth Texas Battalion.

Yeary, Mamie, comp. *Reminiscences of the Boys in Gray, 1861–1865.* Dallas: Smith & Lamar, M. E. Church, South, 1912.

SECONDARY SOURCES
Unpublished Material

Barksdale, Ethelbert C. "Semi-Regular and Irregular Warfare in the Civil War." Unpublished Ph.D. dissertation. University of Texas, Austin, 1941.

Brown, Walter Lee. "Albert Pike, 1809–1891." Unpublished Ph.D. dissertation. University of Texas, Austin, 1955.

Ellsworth, Lois Council. "San Antonio during the Civil War." Unpublished master's thesis. University of Texas, Austin, 1938.

Felgar, Robert P. "Texas in the War for Southern Independence, 1861–1865." Unpublished Ph.D. dissertation. University of Texas, Austin, 1935.

Goodlet, Margaret N. "The Enforcement of the Confederate Conscription Acts in the Trans-Mississippi Department." Unpublished master's thesis. University of Texas, Austin, 1914.

Gunn, Jack Winton. "Life of Ben McCulloch." Unpublished master's thesis. University of Texas, Austin, 1947.

Kroh, Robert F. "Tom Green: Shield and Buckler." Unpublished master's thesis. University of Texas, Austin, 1951.

Megee, Jonnie M. "The Confederate Impressment Acts of the Trans-Mississippi States." Unpublished master's thesis. University of Texas, Austin, 1915.

Morrow, Norman Potter. "Price's Missouri Expedition, 1864." Unpublished master's thesis. University of Texas, Austin, 1949. This competent and scholarly study was written by a retired colonel of the United States Army.

Nichols, James Lynn. "Confederate Quartermaster Operations in the Trans-Mississippi Department." Unpublished master's thesis. University of Texas, Austin, 1947.

Printed Sources

Abel, Annie H. *The American Indian as Slaveholder and Secessionist.* Volume I of *The Slaveholding Indians.* 3 vols. Cleveland: The Arthur H. Clark Company, 1915–1925.

———. *The American Indian as a Participant in the Civil War.* Volume II of *The Slaveholding Indians.* 3 vols. Cleveland: The Arthur H. Clark Company, 1915–1925.

———., "The Indians in the Civil War," *American Historical Review,* XV (January, 1910), 281–296.

Albaugh, William A., and Edward N. Simmons. *Confederate Arms.* Harrisburg, Pennsylvania: The Stackpole Co., 1957.

Allen, Albert H. *Arkansas Imprints, 1821–1876.* New York: R. R. Bowker Co., 1947.

Anderson, John Q. *A Texas Surgeon in the C.S.A.* (Confederate Centennial Series, No. 6.) Tuscaloosa, Alabama: Confederate Publishing Company, 1957.

Anderson, Mabel W. *Life of General Stand Watie: The Only Indian Brigadier General of the Confederate Army and the Last General To Surrender.* Prior, Oklahoma: Mayes County Republican, 1915.

Bancroft, Hubert Howe. *History of the North Mexican States and Texas.* 2 vols. San Francisco: The History Company, 1886–1889.

Bankston, Mary L. *Camp-Fire Stories of the Mississippi Valley Campaign.* New Orleans: L. Graham & Co., 1914.

Bartlett, Napier. *Military Record of Louisiana: Including Biographical and Historical Papers Relating to the Military Organizations of the State....* New Orleans: L. Graham & Co., 1875.

Berglund, Ernest, Jr. *History of Marshall* [Texas]. Austin, Texas: Steck Co., 1948.

Borland, William P., "General Jo Shelby," *Missouri Historical Review,* VII (October, 1912), 10–19.

Bowser, O. P., "Granbury's Brigade," in Volume II of *A Comprehensive History of Texas,* edited by Dudley G. Wooten.

Bragg, Jefferson Davis. *Louisiana in the Confederacy.* Baton Rouge: Louisiana State University Press, 1941.

Brackett, Albert G. *History of the United States Cavalry, from the Formation of the Federal Government to the First of June, 1863....* New York: Harper & Bros., 1865.

196

Brown, John Henry. *History of Texas from 1685 to 1892*. 2 vols. St. Louis: L. E. Daniell, 1893.

Brownlee, Richard S. *Gray Ghosts of the Confederacy: Guerrilla Warfare in the West, 1861–1865*. Baton Rouge: Louisiana State University Press, 1958.

Byers, S. H. M. *Iowa in War Times*. Des Moines, Iowa: W. D. Condit & Co., 1888.

Carter, Major General William Harding, U.S.A., "The Story of the Horse: the Development of Man's Companion in War, Camp, on Farm, in the Marts of Trade, and in the Field of Sports," *National Geographic Magazine*, XLIV (November, 1923).

Castel, Albert E. *A Frontier State at War: Kansas, 1861–1865*. Ithaca, New York: Cornell University Press, 1958.

Colton, Ray C. *The Civil War in the Western Territories*. Norman: University of Oklahoma Press, 1959. This includes a fairly reliable account of Sibley's New Mexico expedition.

Conrad, Howard L., ed. *Encyclopedia of the History of Missouri*. 6 vols. New York: The Southern History Company, 1881.

Coulter, E. Merton. *The Confederate States of America, 1861–1865*. Volume VII of *A History of the South*. Baton Rouge: Louisiana State University Press, 1950.

Cunningham, Frank. *General Stand Watie's Confederate Indians*. San Antonio, Texas: The Naylor Company, 1959. This does not compete seriously with Abel's monumental work on the Confederate Indians. See Abel, Annie H.

Dale, Edward Everett, "The Cherokees in the Confederacy," *Journal of Southern History*, XIII (May, 1947), 160–185.

Demby, James William. *The War in Arkansas: or, A Treatise on the Great Rebellion of 1861*... Little Rock, Arkansas: Egis Print, 1864.

Denison, George T. *A History of Cavalry from the Earliest Times*. 2nd edition. London: Macmillan and Co., 1913.

Diamond, William, "Imports of the Confederate Government from Europe and Mexico," *Journal of Southern History*, VI (November, 1940), 470–503.

Dobie, J. Frank. *The Mustangs*. Boston: Little, Brown, [1952].

Dyer, J. P., "Some Aspects of Cavalry Operations in the Army of Tennessee," *Journal of Southern History*, VIII (May, 1942), 210–225.

Eaton, Clement. *A History of the Southern Confederacy*. New York: The Macmillan Company, 1954.

Edwards, John N. *Noted Guerrillas*. St. Louis: H. W. Brand & Company, 1879.

Fay, Major E. S. *Guns and Cavalry: Their Performances in the Past and Their Prospects in the Future*. Boston: Little, Brown & Company, 1896.

Fitzhugh, Lester N. *Terry's Texas Rangers, 8th Texas Cavalry, C.S.A.: An Address . . . before the Houston Civil War Round Table, March 21, 1958*. Houston: [n. pub.], 1958.

————., comp. *Texas Batteries, Battalions, Regiments, Commanders and Field Officers Confederate States Army, 1861–1865*. Midlothian, Texas: Mirror Press, 1959. Accurate and detailed, this is the best compilation of Texas outfits that fought the war.

Fletcher, William A. *Rebel Private Front and Rear*. First publication, 1908; facsimile reprint, Austin: University of Texas Press, 1954.

Fox, William F. *Regimental Losses in the American Civil War, 1861–1865*. Albany, New York: Albany Publishing Co., 1889.

Fuller, Claude E., and Richard D. Steuart. *Firearms of the Confederacy: The Shoulder Arms, Pistols and Revolvers of the Confederate Soldier, Including the Regular United States Models, the Imported Arms, and Those Manufactured Within the Confederacy*. Huntington, West Virginia: Standard Publications, Inc., 1944.

Fuller, Major General J. F. C. *The Generalship of Ulysses S. Grant*. New York: Dodd, Mead and Company, 1929.

————. *Grant & Lee: A Study in Personality and Generalship*. First publication, 1932; facsimile reprint, Bloomington: Indiana University Press, 1957.

Gilbey, Sir Walter. *Small Horses in Warfare*. London: Vinton & Co., Ltd., 1900.

Gleaves, First Lieutenant S. R., "The Strategic Use of Cavalry," *Journal of the U.S. Cavalry Association*, XVIII (July, 1907), 9–25.

Graves, H. A. *Andrew Jackson Potter: The Fighting Parson of the Texas Frontier. . . .* Nashville, Tennessee: Southern Methodist Publishing House, 1882.

Gray, Captain Alonzo. *Cavalry Tactics as Illustrated by the War of the Rebellion. . . .* Fort Leavenworth, Kansas: U.S. Cavalry Association, 1910. This is an excellent study of cavalry tactics in the war.

The Gray Jackets: And How They Lived, Fought, and Died, For Dixie, with Incidents and Sketches of Life in the Confederacy. Richmond, 1867.

Hall, Martin H., "The Formation of Sibley's Brigade and the March to New Mexico," *Southwestern Historical Quarterly*, LXI (January, 1958), 383–405.

———. *Sibley's New Mexico Campaign*. Austin: University of Texas Press, 1960. This is the most able study of the enterprise.

Hempstead, Fay. *Historical Review of Arkansas*. 3 vols. Chicago: The Lewis Publishing Company, 1911.

———. *A Pictorial History of Arkansas from Earliest Times to the Year 1890*. St. Louis and New York: N. D. Thompson Publishing Company, 1890. This contains a helpful, though not too accurate, list of Arkansas cavalry units.

Henderson, G. F. R. *The Civil War: A Soldier's View*. Edited by Jay Luvaas. Chicago: University of Chicago Press, 1958.

Henderson, Harry M. *Texas in the Confederacy*. San Antonio, Texas: The Naylor Company, 1955. Henderson's little volume contains a list of Texas outfits which seems to have been copied from the list in Dudley G. Wooten, ed., *A Comprehensive History of Texas*.

Henry, Robert S. *The Story of the Confederacy*. New York: Grosset & Dunlap, 1936.

Herr, Major John K., and Edward S. Wallace. *The Story of the United States Cavalry, 1775–1942*. Boston: Little, Brown, 1953.

Holladay, Florence E., "The Powers of the Commander of the Confederate Trans-Mississippi Department," *Southwestern Historical Quarterly*, XXI (January, April, 1918), 279–298, 333–359.

Hollister, Wilfred R., and Harry Norman. *Five Famous Missourians*. Kansas City, Missouri: Hudson-Kimberly Publishing Co., 1900.

Ingersoll, Lurton Dunham. *Iowa and the Rebellion: A History of the Troops Furnished by the State of Iowa to the Volunteer Armies of the Union....* Philadelphia: J. B. Lippincott and Co., 1866.

Jenkins, Paul B. *The Battle of Westport*. Kansas City, Missouri: F. Hudson Publishing Co., 1906.

Johnson, Allen, and Dumas Malone, eds. *Dictionary of American Biography*. 20 vols. New York: Charles Scribner's Sons, 1928–1936.

Johnson, Francis W. *A History of Texas and Texans*. Edited by Eugene C. Barker. 5 vols. Chicago and New York: American Historical Society, 1914.

Johnson, Ludwell H. *Red River Campaign: Politics and Cotton in the Civil War*. Baltimore, Maryland: The Johns Hopkins Press, 1958. This is by far the best study of the campaign.

Johnson, Sidney Smith. *Texans Who Wore the Gray*. [Tyler, Texas: n. pub. 1907.]

Kerby, Robert Lee. *The Confederate Invasion of New Mexico and Arizona*. Los Angeles: Westernlore Press, 1958. Originally a master's thesis, this is not too reliable.

La Bree, Ben, ed. *Camp Fires of the Confederacy*. . . . Louisville, Kentucky: Courier-Journal Job Printing Company, 1898.

Lamb, John, "The Confederate Cavalry: Its Wants, Trials, and Heroism," *Southern Historical Society Papers*, XXVI (December, 1898), 359–364.

Livermore, Thomas L. *Numbers and Losses in the Civil War in America, 1861–1865*. Boston and New York: Houghton, Mifflin and Company, 1901.

Logan, Robert R., "The Battle of Prairie Grove," *Arkansas Historical Quarterly*, XVI (Autumn, 1957), 258–267.

Lonn, Ella, *Foreigners in the Confederacy*. Chapel Hill: University of North Carolina Press, 1940.

Lossing, Benson John. *Pictorial History of the Civil War in the United States of America*. 3 vols. Philadelphia: G. W. Childs, 1866–1868.

Louisiana Adjutant General. *Annual Report, 1891*. New Orleans, 1892. This report contains a list of cavalry and infantry outfits raised in Louisiana for the Confederacy.

Luvaas, Jay. *The Military Legacy of the Civil War: The European Inheritance*. Chicago: University of Chicago Press, 1959.

Mahan, Alfred T. *The Influence of Sea Power Upon History, 1660–1783*. First edition, 1890; 25th edition, Boston: Little, Brown & Company, 1918.

McLeary, J. H., "History of Green's Brigade," in Volume II of *A Comprehensive History of Texas*, edited by Dudley G. Wooten.

McNutt, Walter Scott. *A History of Arkansas from the Earliest Times to the Present*. Little Rock, Arkansas: Democrat Printing and Lithographing Company, 1933.

Miller, Francis T., ed. *Photographic History of the Civil War*. 10 vols. New York: The Review of Reviews Co., 1911. Volume IV, of which Theodore H. Rodenbough was chief editor, is concerned with the cavalry of the Civil War and is composed of articles contributed by military authorities. See Rodenbough, Theodore H.

Missouri Historical Company. *History of Lafayette County, Missouri*. St. Louis: Missouri Historical Company, 1881.

Monaghan, Jay. *Civil War on the Western Border, 1854–1865*. Boston: Little, Brown, 1955. Though provocative, this study is inaccurate in many details.

Monks, William. *A History of Southern Missouri and Northern Arkansas*. West Plains, Missouri: West Plains Journal Co., 1907.

Nolan, Captain Lewis E. *Cavalry: Its History and Tactics*. 1st American from the London edition. Columbia, South Carolina: Evans and Cogswell, 1864.

O'Flaherty, Daniel. *General Jo Shelby: Undefeated Rebel*. Chapel Hill: University of North Carolina Press, 1954. This is based on John N. Edwards, *Shelby and His Men*.

Parks, Joseph H. *General Edmund Kirby Smith, C.S.A.* Baton Rouge: Louisiana State University Press, 1954.

Peterson, Cyrus A., and Joseph M. Hanson. *Pilot Knob: The Thermopylae of the West*. New York: The Neale Publishing Company, 1914.

Ramsdell, Charles W., "General Robert E. Lee's Horse Supply, 1862–1865," *American Historical Review*, XXXV (July, 1930), 758–777.

———., "The Texas State Military Board, 1862–1865," *Southwestern Historical Quarterly*, XXVII (April, 1924), 253–275.

Rees, P. S. Hugh. *Cavalry in Action*. London: Macmillan & Co., Ltd., 1905.

Rodenbough, Brigadier General Theodore H., U.S.A. (retired), ed. *The Cavalry*. Volume IV of *Photographic History of the Civil War*, edited by Francis T. Miller.

Rose, Victor M. *The Life and Services of Gen. Ben McCulloch*. Philadelphia: Pictorial Bureau of the Press, 1888.

Rywell, Martin. *Confederate Guns and Their Current Prices*. Harriman, Tennessee: Pioneer Press, 1952.

Sheffy, L. F. *The Spanish Horse on the Great Plains*. [n.p., n. pub.], 1933.

Shoemaker, Floyd Calvin. *Missouri and Missourians*. 5 vols. Chicago: The Lewis Publishing Company, 1943.

Smith, Charles H. *Bill Arp, So Called*. New York: Metropolitan Record Office, 1866.

Smith, Edward C. *The Borderland in the Civil War*. New York: The Macmillan Company, 1927.

Steuart, Richard D., "How Johnny Got His Gun," *Confederate Veteran Magazine*, XXXII (May, 1924), 166–169.

Stevens, Walter B. *Missouri the Center State, 1821–1915*. 3 vols. Chicago: The S. J. Clark Publishing Company, 1915.

Terrell, Mrs. Kate Scurry, "Terry's Texas Rangers," in Volume II of *A Comprehensive History of Texas*, edited by Dudley G. Wooten.

Thomas, David Y. *Arkansas in War and Reconstruction, 1861–1874*. Little Rock: Arkansas Division, United Daughters of the Confederacy, 1926.

Turner, Gordon B., ed. *A History of Military Affairs Since the Eighteenth Century*. Revised edition. New York: Harcourt, Brace and Company, 1956.

United States War Department Library. *Bibliography of State Participation in the Civil War*. Washington, D.C.: Government Printing Office, 1913.

Vandiver, Frank E., ed., "A Collection of Louisiana Confederate Letters," *Louisiana Historical Quarterly*, XXVI (October, 1943), 937–974.

Vandiver, Frank E. *Ploughshares into Swords: Josiah Gorgas and Confederate Ordnance*. Austin: University of Texas Press, 1952.

———. *Rebel Brass: The Confederate Command System*. Baton Rouge: Louisiana State University Press, 1956.

Wagner, Captain Arthur L., ed. *Cavalry Studies from Two Great Wars*. (International Series No. 2.) Kansas City, Missouri: Hudson-Kimberly Publishing Company, 1896. This consists of Lieutenant Colonel Bowie, "The French Cavalry in 1870"; Major Kaehler, "The German Cavalry in the Battle of Vionville—Mars-La-Tour"; and Lieutenant Colonel George B. Davis, "The Operations of the Cavalry in the Gettysburg Campaign."

Warner, Ezra J. *Generals in Gray: Lives of the Confederate Commanders*. Baton Rouge: Louisiana State University Press, 1959.

Webb, Walter Prescott. *The Great Plains*. New York: Grosset & Dunlap, 1931.

Webb, W. L. *Battles and Biographies of Missourians: or, The Civil War Period of Our State*. Kansas City, Missouri: Hudson-Kimberely Publishing Co., 1900.

Wooten, Dudley G., ed. *A Comprehensive History of Texas*. 2 vols. Dallas: William G. Scarff, 1898. In Volume II, pt. V ("Texas and Texans in the Civil War, 1861–1865"), Chapter I is an essay on military operations in Texas, 1861–1865, and Chapter II is a list of all Texas outfits that served in the Confederate Army. Chapters III through VI are essays on four famous Texas organizations: "Hood's Texas Brigade," by Mrs. A. V. Winkler; "Terry's Texas Rangers," by Mrs. Kate Scurry Terrell; "Green's Brigade," by J. H. McLeary; and "Granbury's Brigade," by O. P. Bowser.

Young, Bennett H. *Confederate Wizards of the Saddle: Being Reminiscences and Observations of One Who Rode with Morgan.* First publication, 1914; facsimile reprint, Kennesaw, Georgia: Continental Book Co., 1958.

INDEX

Adair, William P.: 168
Adams, J. L.: 166
Alamo: capture of, 3–4
Alexander, Almerine M.: 44, 49, 50, 177
Alexander, W. J.: 177
Alligator [a Seminole Indian]: 33
Amacker, P. O.: 169
ammunition: scarcity of, 73, 74
Anderson, Bill: as leader of partisan cavalry, 43
Anderson, Thomas Scott: 178
Anderson, W. L.: as commander of Anderson's Battalion, 183
Andrews, Julius A.: 177
Arizona: cavalry campaign in, 20
Arkadelphia, Arkansas: Sterling Price at, 131, 132
Arkansas: Ben McCulloch in 11, 12; secession of, 12; Army of, 14 n; Confederate withdrawal to, 17; strength of units of, in Confederate service, 25; recruiting in, 34; Union forces in, 36, 87, 88–89, 112, 131, 147; cavalry and infantry in, 37; delegation of, in Confederate Congress, 38; Texas cavalry stationed in, 44; cavalry organized in, 46, 75; Texas infantry brigade in, 46, 47; food of Confederate Army in, 53; citizens of, send clothing to cavalry, 57; gets no War Department arms, 64; blacksmiths make weapons in, 69; home manufacture of ammunition in, 73; ratio of horses to military population of, 75; skirmishing in, 78; illegal impressments in, 81; endangering of, 89; military activity in, 114; Federal objectives in, 123; district of, under command of Sterling Price, 140; Sterling Price retreats to, 151; raiders return to, 152

Arkansas Cavalry Battalion: commanded by Chrisman, 49
—, Brooks': strength of, 37
—, Wright's: merging of, 49
Arkansas Cavalry Brigade: formation of, 47; joins Marmaduke's division, 51; loses few horses, 78
Arkansas Cavalry Regiment, First: at Camp Walker, 13; organization of, 29; reorganization of, 29 n; strength of, 37; merging of, 49; at Van Buren, 52
—, First [Mounted Rifles]: recruiting of, 14; strength of, 29
—, Second: transfer of, to Kentucky, 22; strength of, 29, 37; organization of, 47
—, Second [Mounted Rifles]: organization of, 14; strength of, 29; moves up the Verdigris, 32
—, Third: formation of, 34; strength of, 37; appeals for aid by, 59
—, Fifth: strength of, 29; disbanding of, 47; led by Newton, 124
—, Crawford's: 47; merging of, 49
—, Monroe's: strength of, 47; merging of, 49
Arkansas Infantry, First [Federal]: defeated by Thorp, 132
—, Third: under John Gratiot, 12
—, Fourth: under J. D. Walker, 12
—, Fifth: under Tom P. Dockery, 12

205

McClellan bridles: 76

McClellan saddles: 76

McCord, James Ebenezer: 178

McCown, Jerome B.: recruiting by, in Hempstead-Bellville area, 20, 21; bivouacked at Bellville, Texas, 52

McCoy, Arthur: at Boston Mountains, Arkansas, 95

McCrae, Dandridge: at Prairie Grove, Arkansas, 105, 109

McCray, Thomas H.: 152, 182

McCulloch, Benjamin: capture of San Antonio by, 3–4; raises first Confederate army in Trans-Mississippi, 11; Arkansas troops under the command of, 13, 14, 15, 34; in command of Confederate troops in Missouri, 16, 17; actions of, against the Indians, 18, 33; at Fort Smith, 30; death of, at Elkhorn, 36; place of, taken by Hindman, 49; receives donations, 58; gets arms for Indian Territory, 63, 64; joins Sterling Price, 65

McCulloch, Henry Eustace: 173; recruiting by, for the Army of Texas, 5; as commander of First Regiment Texas Mounted Rifles, 8, 28; in command of division in Arkansas, 49; as commander of three infantry brigades, 88

McCulloch, Robert, Jr.: 171: as commander of Second Missouri Cavalry Regiment, 36, 37

McCullough, Frisby H.: 171

McCurtain, Jackson: 168

McDaniels, W.: 171

McGhee, Charley: of Terry's Texas Rangers, 23

McGhee, James: as commander of McGhee's Regiment, 182

McHenry, James: 169

McIntosh, Chilly: 169; as commander of First Creek Cavalry Battalion, 20, 29

McIntosh, Daniel N.: 169; as commander of First Creek Cavalry Regiment, 19, 29

McIntosh, James: 166; as commander of First Arkansas Mounted Rifles, 12; as commander of Second Arkansas Mounted Rifles, 14, 29; at Wilson's Creek, 17; as commander of brigade in McCulloch's army, 30; as temporary commander of Confederate forces, 32; returns to Fort Smith, Arkansas, 33; death of, 36; regiment of, receives clothing from Arkansas, 57

McIntosh, William R.: 169

McKie, R. D.: 178

McKissick's Springs, Arkansas: Shelby's men at, 41; Hunter joins Shelby at, 134

McKowen, John C.: 170

McLean, James B.: 173

McLennan County, Texas: recruiting in, for Terry's Texas Rangers, 24

McLeod, Hugh: in command of Brazos de Santiago, 8

McMurtrey, E. L.: 167

McNeil, A. J.: 169

McNeil, John: in command of Federals at Bloomfield, Missouri, 124–125; in command at Cape Girardeau, Missouri, 126, 127; takes offensive, 127–129; avoids capture, 131

McNeill, Henry C.: 174

McPhail, Hugh A.: 174

McSmith, J.: as commander of Creek cavalry company, 20, 29

McWaters, J.: 169

Menard, Medard: 176

Meramec River: railroad bridge destroyed on, 146

Merrick, George D.: 176

Messick, Otis M.: 175

Mexican War: 3; W. P. Lane in, 9

Mexico: efforts to bring ammunition from, 73; flight of Confederate leaders to, 161

Meyer, Benjamin W.: 167

Miles Legion Contingent, Louisiana Cavalry: 46

Miller, Crill: 173

Millican, Texas: resolution of "W. P. Lane Rangers" at, 159

Mingo Swamps, Missouri: Carter bogs down in, 126, 131